NOT FOR TOURISTS
ILLUSTRATED GUIDE TO
CHICAGO

D1004525

GET MORE ON
WWW.NOTFORTOURISTS.COM

STAY CONNECTED WITH:

TWITTER: @NOTFORTOURISTS
FACEBOOK: NOTFORTOURISTS
IPHONE APPS: AVAILABLE ON ITUNES

SKYHORSE PUBLISHING

Aug 2015

DESIGNED BY:

NOT FOR TOURISTS, INC
NFT™ — NOT FOR TOURISTS™ GUIDE TO NEW YORK CITY
WWW.NOTFORTOURISTS.COM

PUBLISHER

SKYHORSE PUBLISHING

CREATIVE DIRECTION & INFORMATION DESIGN

JANE PIRONE

DIRECTOR

STUART FARR

MANAGING EDITORS

SCOTT SENDROW
ROB TALLIA

CITY EDITORS

ANNE KASDORF
BENJAMIN KELNER

GRAPHIC DESIGN & PRODUCTION MANAGER

JOHN BERGDAHL

ILLUSTRATORS

LUISITO NAZARIO
ELLEN LINDNER

INFORMATION SYSTEMS MANAGER

JUAN MOLINARI

PRINTED IN CHINA

PRINT ISBN: 978-1-63450-116-3 $12.99

EBOOK ISBN: 978-1-63450-117-0

ISSN 2376-6794

COPYRIGHT ©2015 BY NOT FOR TOURISTS, INC.

1ST EDITION

EVERY EFFORT HAS BEEN MADE TO ENSURE THAT THE INFORMATION IN THIS BOOK IS AS UP-TO-DATE AS POSSIBLE AT PRESS TIME. HOWEVER, MANY DETAILS ARE LIABLE TO CHANGE—AS WE HAVE LEARNED. NOT FOR TOURISTS CANNOT ACCEPT RESPONSIBILITY FOR ANY CONSEQUENCES ARISING FROM THE USE OF THIS BOOK.

NOT FOR TOURISTS DOES NOT SOLICIT INDIVIDUALS, ORGANIZATIONS, OR BUSINESSES FOR LISTINGS INCLUSION IN OUR GUIDES, NOR DO WE ACCEPT PAYMENT FOR INCLUSION INTO THE EDITORIAL PORTION OF OUR BOOK; THE ADVERTISING SECTIONS, HOWEVER, ARE EXEMPT FROM THIS POLICY. WE ALWAYS WELCOME COMMUNICATIONS FROM ANYONE REGARDING ANYTHING HAVING TO DO WITH OUR BOOKS; PLEASE VISIT US ON OUR WEBSITE AT WWW.NOTFORTOURISTS.COM FOR APPROPRIATE CONTACT INFORMATION.

DEAR NFT USER:

THERE ARE CERTAIN THINGS CHICAGOANS KNOW: THE BEST STORIES HAPPEN ON THE RED LINE LATE AT NIGHT, THE CUBBIES ARE GOING TO WIN THE WORLD SERIES (...NEXT YEAR); THE SWEAR JAR IN RAHM'S OFFICE IS OVERFLOWING WITH COINS; YOUR OUT-OF-TOWN RELATIVES ARE GOING TO ASK YOU ABOUT AL CAPONE; THERE'S A 50/50 CHANCE YOUR ALDERMAN IS GOING TO BE INDICTED THIS YEAR; THE WINTERS MAKE YOU STRONGER AND THE SUMMERS MAKE YOU LAZIER; AND EVERY NEW YORKER YOU KNOW WILL TELL YOU HOW SHOCKED THEY ARE THAT THERE AREN'T COWS AND CORN FILLING UP YOUR DOWNTOWN ("WOW, THIS ACTU-ALLY IS AN AMAZING CITY!").

IF YOU'RE FAMILIAR WITH NOT FOR TOURISTS, YOU'LL NOTICE THAT THIS BRAND NEW GUIDE IS A BOLD REDESIGN OF NFT CLASSIC. IN ADDITION TO BEAUTIFUL CITY PHOTOS, SCHMANCY ORIGINAL ILLUSTRATIONS, AND A GENERAL STYLISH APPEAL (IF WE DO SAY SO OURSELVES), YOU'LL ALSO NOTICE THAT EACH NEIGHBORHOOD IS PARED DOWN TO ITS ESSENTIAL HIGH-LIGHTS. INDUSTRY FOLKS LIKE TO CALL THIS "CAREFULLY CURATED." WE JUST WANT TO POINT OUT SOME OF OUR FAVORITE SPOTS.

HAVE SOME FEEDBACK? PLEASE, DON'T BE SHY, BECAUSE WE CERTAINLY ARE NOT. SEND US A NOTE AT WWW.NOTFORTOURISTS.COM OR ON TWITTER @NOTFORTOURISTS, BECAUSE IN THE END, NFT IS A FAMILY, AND WE WOULDN'T BE WHO WE ARE WITHOUT YOU. SO IF YOU'RE NEW TO US AND THE CITY, WELCOME! AND IF YOU'VE BEEN WITH NFT FOR THE LONG HAUL, THANKS FOR PICKING UP OUR NEWEST ADVENTURE IN CITY GUIDES.

—JANE, ROB, SCOTT, BEN, ANNE, ET AL.

TABLE OF CONTENTS

NEIGHBORHOODS

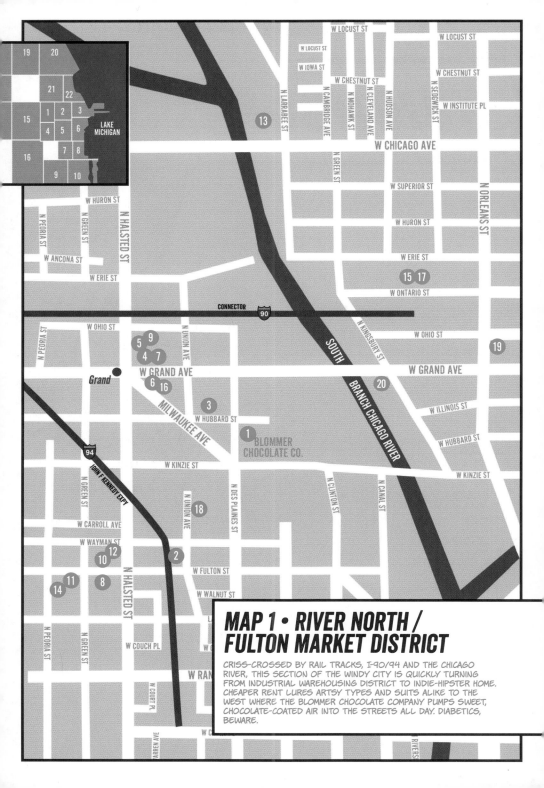

MAP 1 • RIVER NORTH / FULTON MARKET DISTRICT

CRISS-CROSSED BY RAIL TRACKS, I-90/94 AND THE CHICAGO RIVER, THIS SECTION OF THE WINDY CITY IS QUICKLY TURNING FROM INDUSTRIAL WAREHOUSING DISTRICT TO INDIE-HIPSTER HOME. CHEAPER RENT LURES ARTSY TYPES AND SUITS ALIKE TO THE WEST WHERE THE BLOMMER CHOCOLATE COMPANY PUMPS SWEET, CHOCOLATE-COATED AIR INTO THE STREETS ALL DAY. DIABETICS, BEWARE.

1 BLOMMER CHOCOLATE CO.
W KINZIE ST
OPENED IN 1939. EVENTUALLY BECAME THE LARGEST COMMERCIAL CHOCOLATE MANUFACTURER IN THE US.

2 CARNIVALE
702 W FULTON ST
AUTHENTIC, SOULFUL LATIN FUSION CUISINE.

3 CITY POOL HALL
640 W HUBBARD ST
SHOOT POOL ALL NIGHT LONG.

4 THE DAWSON
730 W GRAND AVE
FULTON MARKET'S NEWEST HOT SPOT FROM BILLY LAWLESS.

5 DOOLIN'S
511 N HALSTED ST
PARTY DECORATIONS FOR EVERY OCCASION.

6 EMMIT'S IRISH PUB
495 N MILWAUKEE AVE
AN OLD-SCHOOL CHICAGO ESTABLISHMENT.

7 FUNKY BUDDHA LOUNGE
728 W GRAND AVE
SEE AND BE SEEN AT THIS TRENDY LIVE MUSIC LOUNGE.

8 GLAZED & INFUSED
813 W FULTON MARKET
DOUGHNUTS ARE THE NEW CUPCAKES.

9 IGUANA CAFÉ
N HALSTED ST
INTERNET CAFÉ WITH BAGELS AND SUCH.

10 ISSACSON & STEIN FISH COMPANY
800 W FULTON MARKET
FISH GUTTERS! QUICK AND FRESH!

11 LUMEN
839 FULTON ST
COOL, EXPENSIVE DÉCOR AND COOL, EXPENSIVE DRINKS.

12 THE MID
306 N HALSTED ST
DANCE YOUR HEART OUT TO THE BIGGEST DJ SUPERSTARS.

13 THE MOTEL BAR
600 W CHICAGO AVE
MOTEL BAR WITHOUT THE HOURLY RATES!

14 PUBLICAN
837 W FULTON MARKET
MUCH BUZZED KAHAN JOINT IS MEAT AND BEER LOVER'S NIRVANA.

15 REZA'S
432 W ONTARIO ST
HUGE PORTIONS OF PERSIAN FARE.

16 RICHARD'S BAR
491 N MILWAUKEE AVE
OLD MAN BAR THAT BLATANTLY DISREGARDS CHICAGO'S SMOKING LAW.

17 ROBUST COFFEE LOUNGE
416 W ONTARIO ST
SECOND LOCATION FOR THE SOUTH SIDE COFFEEHOUSE.

18 SALVATION ARMY OUTLET STORE
509 N UNION AVE
GET YOUR THRIFT ON.

19 TRUNK CLUB
325 W OHIO ST
HIGH-END MENSWEAR LOFT WITH ATTENTIVE STYLISTS.

20 VERUCA SALT
520 N KINGSBURY ST
FLIRTY LADIES FASHIONS.

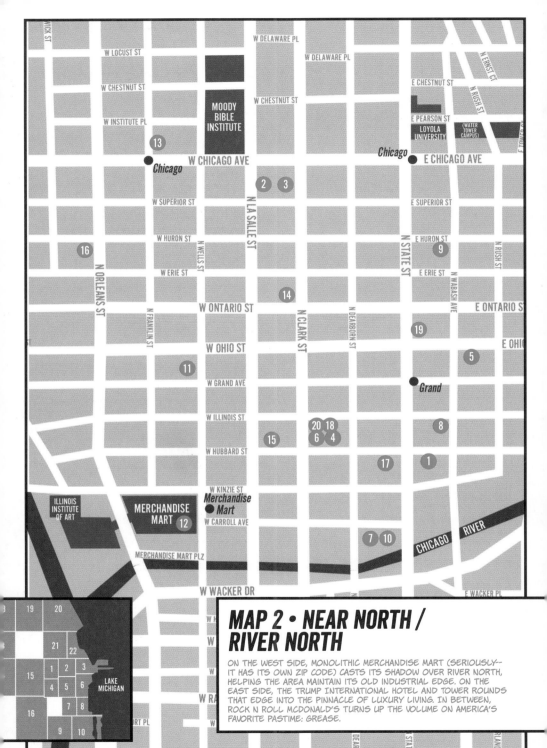

MAP 2 • NEAR NORTH / RIVER NORTH

ON THE WEST SIDE, MONOLITHIC MERCHANDISE MART (SERIOUSLY—
IT HAS ITS OWN ZIP CODE) CASTS ITS SHADOW OVER RIVER NORTH,
HELPING THE AREA MAINTAIN ITS OLD INDUSTRIAL EDGE. ON THE
EAST SIDE, THE TRUMP INTERNATIONAL HOTEL AND TOWER ROUNDS
THAT EDGE INTO THE PINNACLE OF LUXURY LIVING. IN BETWEEN,
ROCK N ROLL MCDONALD'S TURNS UP THE VOLUME ON AMERICA'S
FAVORITE PASTIME: GREASE.

1 ANDY'S JAZZ CLUB
11 E HUBBARD ST
OLD SCHOOL JAZZ...A CHICAGO LEGEND.

2 CAFÉ IBERICO
737 N LASALLE ST
SHOULDER-TO-SHOULDER TAPAS JOINT.

3 CLARK STREET ALE HOUSE
742 N CLARK ST
NO PRETENSE, JUST BEER – AND LOTS OF IT.

4 COURTHOUSE PLACE
54 W HUBBARD ST
THIS ROMANESQUE-STYLE FORMER COURTHOUSE HAS WITNESSED MANY LEGENDARY TRIALS.

5 EATALY
43 W OHIO ST
HIGH-END ITALIAN FOODS AT THIS NEW BUT ALREADY BELOVED EMPORIUM.

6 FIRECAKES DONUTS
68 W HUBBARD ST
OLD STANDBYS (CHOCOLATE ICED) AND NEW FAVORITES (LEMON VERBENA MERINGUE).

7 HOUSE OF BLUES
329 N DEARBORN ST
BRANCH LOCATION OF THE WELL-KNOWN CHAIN O' BLUES CLUBS. FEAST ON LIVE MUSIC AND CAJUN COOKING AT THE GOSPEL BRUNCH.

8 JAZZ RECORD MART
27 E ILLINOIS ST
JAZZ LOVER'S EMPORIUM.

9 JONATHAN ADLER
676 N WABASH AVE
HIP AND HAPPY HOME FURNISHINGS.

10 MARINA TOWERS
300 N STATE ST
BERTRAND GOLDBERG'S RIVERSIDE MASTERWORK. LOVE THE PARKING.

11 MELI CAFE & JUICE BAR
540 N WELLS ST
FRESH, INVITING; FAVORS HEALTHY SELECTIONS AND EARLY RISERS.

12 MERCHANDISE MART
222 MERCHANDISE MART PLZ
HOUSES FURNITURE SHOWROOMS AND A SMALL MALL.

13 PAPER SOURCE
232 W CHICAGO AVE
GREAT PAPER AND INVITATIONS.

14 PORTILLO'S
100 W ONTARIO ST
CLASSIC CHICAGO-STYLE DOGS.

15 SLURPING TURTLE
116 W HUBBARD ST
CELEBRITY CHEF TAKASHI YAGIHASHI'S RAMEN, LIBATIONS AND OTHER TREATS.

16 THE GREEN DOOR TAVERN
678 N ORLEANS ST
A CHICAGO LANDMARK; OLD-SCHOOL CLASSIC.

17 THEORY
9 W HUBBARD ST
LAIDBACK SPORTS LOUNGE.

18 THREE DOTS AND A DASH
435 N CLARK ST
DOWNTOWN TIKI BAR.

19 WATERSHED
601 N STATE ST
DRINKING IS EASIER WITHOUT WINDOWS IN THIS BASEMENT BAR.

20 XOCO
449 N CLARK ST
MEXICAN FOOD GURU RICK BAYLESS' MOST AFFORDABLE CANTINA.

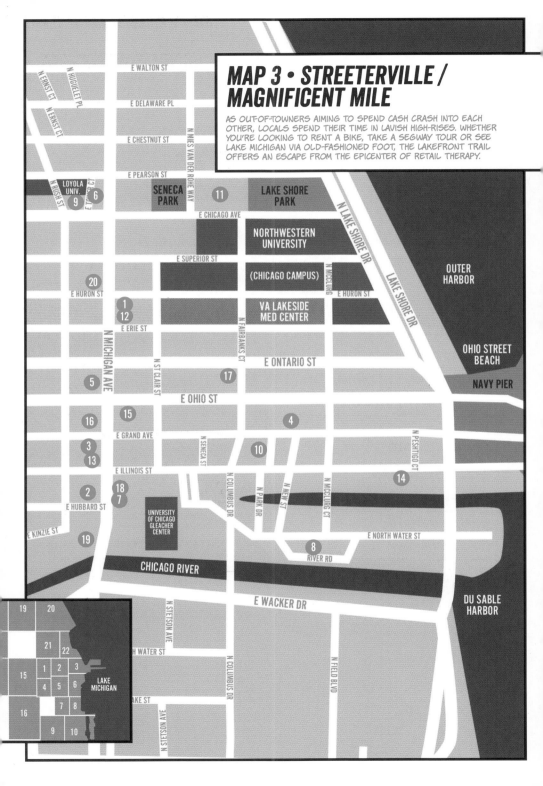

MAP 3 • STREETERVILLE / MAGNIFICENT MILE

AS OUT-OF-TOWNERS AIMING TO SPEND CASH CRASH INTO EACH OTHER, LOCALS SPEND THEIR TIME IN LAVISH HIGH-RISES. WHETHER YOU'RE LOOKING TO RENT A BIKE, TAKE A SEGWAY TOUR OR SEE LAKE MICHIGAN VIA OLD-FASHIONED FOOT, THE LAKEFRONT TRAIL OFFERS AN ESCAPE FROM THE EPICENTER OF RETAIL THERAPY.

1 APPLE STORE
679 N MICHIGAN AVE
GEEK HEAVEN.

2 BILLY GOAT TAVERN
430 N MICHIGAN AVE
CHEEZEBOIGA; NO FRIES, CHIPS; PEPSI, NO COKE.

3 CANDYALITY
520 N MICHIGAN AVE
RETRO CANDY TO SATISFY YOUR SWEETTOOTH.

4 D4 IRISH PUB & CAFÉ
345 E OHIO ST
UPSCALE IRISH PUB WITH A COPY OF THE BOOK OF KELLS.

5 HEAVEN ON SEVEN
600 N MICHIGAN AVE
CAJUN GRUB AND COCKTAILS.

6 HISTORIC WATER TOWER
806 N MICHIGAN AVE
ONE OF A FEW BUILDINGS TO SURVIVE THE GREAT CHICAGO FIRE OF 1871 NOW CONTAINS A FREE ART GALLERY.

7 HOWELLS & HOOD
435 N MICHIGAN AVE
ECLECTIC DINING AND CRAFT BEER IN THE ICONIC TRIBUNE TOWER.

8 LIZZIE MCNEILL'S IRISH PUB
400 N MCCLURG CT
IRISH PUB DOWN BY THE RIVER.

9 LOYOLA UNIVERSITY MUSEUM OF ART
820 N MICHIGAN AVE
LOW-COST AND SURPRISINGLY COMPREHENSIVE UNI-VERSITY MUSEUM.

10 LUCKY STRIKE
322 E ILLINOIS ST
THROW BACK SOME BEERS AND STRIKE DOWN SOME BOWLING PINS.

11 MUSEUM OF CONTEMPORARY ART
220 E CHICAGO AVE
MIND-BLOWING, CUTTING-EDGE EXHIBITS AND PERFORMANCES.

12 NIKETOWN
669 N MICHIGAN AVE
PARADISE FOR THE SPORTS ENTHUSIAST.

13 THE PURPLE PIG
500 N MICHIGAN AVE
SMALL PLATE HEAVEN.

14 QUAY ATRIUM LOUNGE
465 E ILLINOIS ST
APPS, BEER AND BUBBLY ON A BOAT SLIP.

15 SECOND STORY BAR
157 E OHIO ST
SUPER DIVEY GAY BAR WHEN YOU'RE LOOKING TO ESCAPE THE COIFFED GENTS OF BOYSTOWN.

16 THE SHOPS AT NORTH BRIDGE
520 N MICHIGAN AVE
NORDSTROM-ANCHORED MALL ON THE MAG MILE.

17 TIMOTHY O'TOOLE'S PUB
622 N FAIRBANKS CT
IRISH SPORTS BAR WITH TONS OF TV SPACE.

18 TRIBUNE TOWER
435 N MICHIGAN AVE
CHECK OUT THE STONES FROM FAMOUS BUILDINGS AROUND THE WORLD, INCLUDING A REAL-LIFE ROCK FROM THE MOON!

19 WRIGLEY BUILDING
401 N MICHIGAN AVE
MONUMENT TO CHEWING GUM.

20 ZARA
700 N MICHIGAN AVE
THE SPANISH RETAILER'S CHICAGO FLAGSHIP.

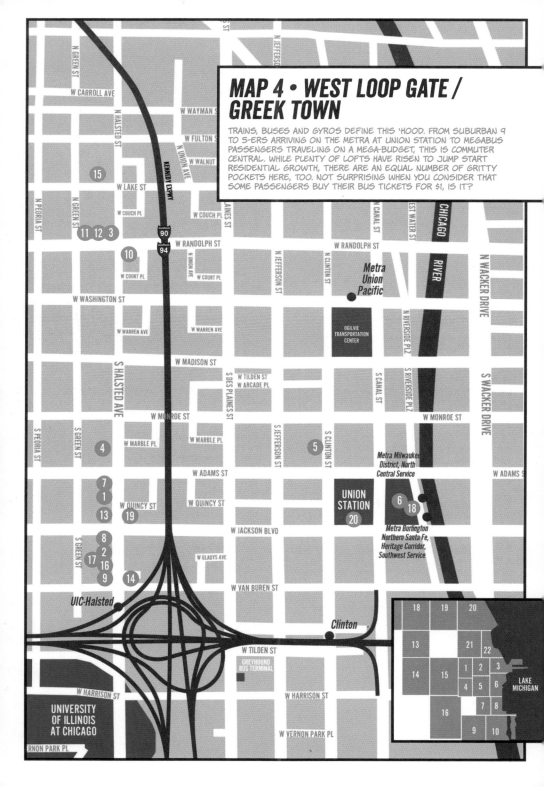

MAP 4 • WEST LOOP GATE / GREEK TOWN

TRAINS, BUSES AND GYROS DEFINE THIS 'HOOD. FROM SUBURBAN 9 TO 5-ERS ARRIVING ON THE METRA AT UNION STATION TO MEGABUS PASSENGERS TRAVELING ON A MEGA-BUDGET, THIS IS COMMUTER CENTRAL. WHILE PLENTY OF LOFTS HAVE RISEN TO JUMP START RESIDENTIAL GROWTH, THERE ARE AN EQUAL NUMBER OF GRITTY POCKETS HERE, TOO. NOT SURPRISING WHEN YOU CONSIDER THAT SOME PASSENGERS BUY THEIR BUS TICKETS FOR $1, IS IT?

1 ATHENA
212 S HALSTED
GODDESS ATHENA-INSPIRED OUTDOOR AND INDOOR.

2 ATHENIAN CANDLE CO.
300 S HALSTED ST
CANDLES, CURSE-BREAKERS, GREEK TRINKETS AND MUCH MORE.

3 AU CHEVAL
800 W RANDOLPH ST
5-STAR FLAVOR PAIRINGS IN AN AFFORDABLE DINER VIBE.

4 DUGAN'S ON HALSTED
128 S HALSTED ST
SPORTS BAR IN GREEKTOWN. FANTASTIC BEER GARDEN AND FAVORITE COP HANGOUT.

5 DYLAN'S TAVERN & GRILL
118 S CLINTON ST
UNPRETENTIOUS WEST LOOPER WITH GRUB.

6 GOLD COAST DOGS
225 S CANAL ST
GOTTA HAVE THE DOGS.

7 GREEK ISLANDS
200 S HALSTED ST
NOISY, FUN CROWD-PLEASING SPECTACLE.

8 GREEKTOWN MUSIC
304 S HALSTED ST
MUSIC, T-SHIRTS, HATS—EVERYTHING GREEK!

9 GREEKTOWN PERISTYLE
CORNER OF HALSTED ST AND VAN BUREN ST
WELCOME GATEWAY SCULPTURE INTO HELLENIC HEAVEN.

10 HAYMARKET PUB AND BREWERY
737 W RANDOLPH ST
LESSER-KNOWN MEMBER OF CHICAGO'S BEER SCENE WITH LATE-NIGHT EATS.

11 LITTLE GOAT
820 W RANDOLPH ST
COMFY LITTLE SIB TO FAMED GIRL AND THE GOAT.

12 LONE WOLF
806 W RANDOLPH ST
THEMATIC DRINK SUGGESTIONS MATCH YOUR DINNER RESERVATIONS DOWN THE STREET.

13 MR. GREEK GYROS
234 S HALSTED ST
THE BEST LATE NIGHT GYRO SPOT IN THE CITY, HANDS DOWN.

14 NATIONAL HELLENIC MUSEUM
333 S HALSTED ST
THE ONLY MUSEUM IN THE U.S. THAT INTERPRETS THE AMERICAN EXPERIENCE THROUGH THE HISTORY OF GREEK IMMIGRANTS.

15 NORTHWESTERN CUTLERY
810 W LAKE ST
THE SELF-DESCRIBED "CANDY STORE FOR COOKS."

16 PAN HELLENIC PASTRY SHOP
322 S HALSTED ST
GREEK SWEETS IN GREEKTOWN.

17 THE PARTHENON
314 S HALSTED ST
CREATORS OF FLAMING SAGANAKI!

18 SNUGGERY
222 S RIVERSIDE PLAZA
COMMUTER BAR INSIDE UNION STATION.

19 SPECTRUM BAR & GRILL
233 S HALSTED ST
SPORTS BAR WITH MEDITERRANEAN FLAIR.

20 UNION STATION
210 S CANAL ST
BUILT IN 1925, THE ARCHITECTURE IS NOT TO BE MISSED.

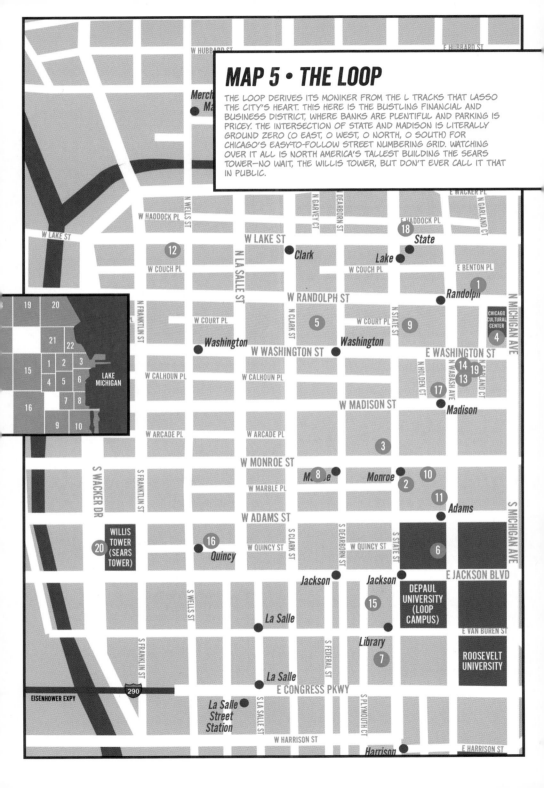

MAP 5 · THE LOOP

THE LOOP DERIVES ITS MONIKER FROM THE L TRACKS THAT LASSO THE CITY'S HEART. THIS HERE IS THE BUSTLING FINANCIAL AND BUSINESS DISTRICT, WHERE BANKS ARE PLENTIFUL AND PARKING IS PRICEY. THE INTERSECTION OF STATE AND MADISON IS LITERALLY GROUND ZERO (0 EAST, 0 WEST, 0 NORTH, 0 SOUTH) FOR CHICAGO'S EASY-TO-FOLLOW STREET NUMBERING GRID. WATCHING OVER IT ALL IS NORTH AMERICA'S TALLEST BUILDING THE SEARS TOWER—NO WAIT, THE WILLIS TOWER, BUT DON'T EVER CALL IT THAT IN PUBLIC.

1 AFTER SCHOOL MATTERS RETAIL STORE
66 E RANDOLPH ST
SPECIALTY GIFTS AND ART MADE BY LOCAL TEENS.

2 THE BAR BELOW
127 S STATE ST
LOOP BASEMENT HIDEAWAY TO HIDE FROM YOUR BOSS ON LUNCH BREAK.

3 BLICK ART MATERIALS
42 S STATE ST
GET CREATIVE HERE.

4 CHICAGO CULTURAL CENTER
78 E WASHINGTON ST
THE SPOT FOR FREE CONCERTS, EXHIBITS, MOVIES AND LECTURES.

5 DALEY PLAZA
50 WASHINGTON ST
HOME OF THE FAMOUS PICASSO SCULPTURE, FARMER'S MARKET, CHRISTMAS TREE AND YEAR-LONG PROGRAMMING.

6 EXCHEQUER
226 S WABASH AVE
LOOP LOCATION FOR THE WORKING CLASS.

7 HAROLD WASHINGTON LIBRARY CENTER
400 S STATE ST
THE WORLD'S LARGEST PUBLIC LIBRARY BUILDING WITH NEARLY 100 WORKS OF ART ON EVERY FLOOR.

8 THE ITALIAN VILLAGE
71 W MONROE ST
OLD SCHOOL ITALIAN. ONE OF CHICAGO'S OLDEST ITALIAN RESTAURANTS—HAS LOOKED THE SAME SINCE IT OPENED IN 1927.

9 MACY'S
111 N STATE ST
THE FORMER HOME OF CHICAGO ESTABLISHMENT MARSHALL FIELD'S. COME FOR THE SALES, STAY FOR THE ARCHITECTURE.

10 MERZ APOTHECARY
17 E MONROE ST
LOOP LOCATION OF THE LINCOLN SQUARE STALWART.

11 MILLER'S PUB
134 S WABASH AVE
A LOOP TRADITION. DOWN-TO-EARTH GRUB IN A PUB.

12 MONK'S PUB
205 W LAKE ST
PEANUT SHELLS ON THE GROUND, BEER IN YOUR BELLY.

13 OASIS CAFÉ
21 N WABASH AVE
MIDDLE EASTERN HIDEOUT INSIDE OF A JEWELRY STORE.

14 PITTSFIELD CAFÉ
55 E WASHINGTON ST
DOWNTOWN-STYLE DINER FOOD.

15 PLYMOUTH RESTAURANT
327 S PLYMOUTH CT
BAR AND GRILL MAINSTAY.

16 QUINCY L STATION
220 S WELLS ST
THE CTA'S COOLEST L STATION, RESTORED TO ITS ORIGINAL GLORY.

17 RECKLESS RECORDS
26 E MADISON ST
INSTANT SATISFACTION FOR THE VINYLHUNGRY MASSES.

18 ROOF ON THE WIT
201 N STATE ST
A ROOFTOP PLAYGROUND FOR THOSE WHO WANT TO BE SEEN.

19 TONI PATISSERIE & CAFÉ
65 E WASHINGTON ST
FIN-DE-SIECLE AMBIANCE, FRENCH PASTRIES AND LIGHT FARE.

20 WILLIS TOWER (SEARS TOWER)
233 S WACKER DR
UNTIL RECENTLY THE TALLEST BUILDING IN THE US, WITH A COOL SKYDECK.

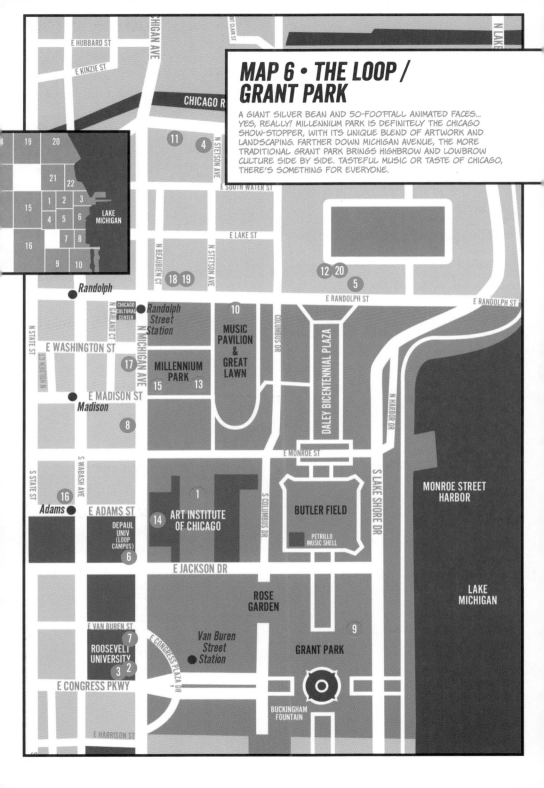

MAP 6 · THE LOOP / GRANT PARK

A GIANT SILVER BEAN AND 50-FOOT-TALL ANIMATED FACES... YES, REALLY! MILLENNIUM PARK IS DEFINITELY THE CHICAGO SHOW-STOPPER, WITH ITS UNIQUE BLEND OF ARTWORK AND LANDSCAPING. FARTHER DOWN MICHIGAN AVENUE, THE MORE TRADITIONAL GRANT PARK BRINGS HIGHBROW AND LOWBROW CULTURE SIDE BY SIDE. TASTEFUL MUSIC OR TASTE OF CHICAGO, THERE'S SOMETHING FOR EVERYONE.

1 ART INSTITUTE OF CHICAGO
111 S MICHIGAN AVE
WORLD CLASS ART MUSEUM.

2 ARTISTS CAFÉ
412 S MICHIGAN AVE
LONG-STANDING DINER FARE.

3 AUDITORIUM BUILDING
430 S MICHIGAN AVE
DESIGNED BY LOUIS SULLIVAN; ON NATIONAL REGISTER OF HISTORIC PLACES.

4 BIG BAR
151 E UPPER WACKER DR
MASSIVE HYATT HOTEL BAR.

5 BROWN BAG SEAFOOD CO
340 E RANDOLPH ST
CHEAP AND DELICIOUS SEAFOOD.

6 CHICAGO ARCHITECTURE FOUNDATION
224 S MICHIGAN AVE
ONE OF THE BEST GIFT SHOPS IN CHICAGO; PLUS EXHIBITS AND TOURS.

7 FINE ARTS BUILDING
410 S MICHIGAN AVE
THE COUNTRY'S FIRST ARTISTS' COLONY, CONVERTED FROM A STUDEBAKER CARRIAGE PLANT IN 1898.

8 THE GAGE
24 S MICHIGAN AVE
CLASSY BREWS, BURGERS AND MEAT.

9 GRANT PARK
331 E RANDOLPH ST
WHERE MARATHON, MUSIC AND TASTE ALL BEGIN AND END.

10 HARRIS THEATER
205 E RANDOLPH ST
VENUE WITH BOTH TRADITIONAL AND CUTTING EDGE MUSIC, THEATER AND DANCE PERFORMANCES.

11 HOULIHAN'S
111 E WACKER DR
TRENDY, SEMI-OBNOXIOUS SPORTS BAR.

12 MARIANO'S
333 E BENTON PL
FULL SERVICE GOURMET GROCERY, BUTCHER AND DELI.

13 MILLENNIUM PARK
201 E RANDOLPH ST
ONE OF THE BEST PUBLIC SPACES ON THE PLANET.

14 MUSEUM SHOP OF THE ART INSTITUTE
111 S MICHIGAN AVE
MUST-STOP SHOPPING FOR EVERY ART ENTHUSIAST.

15 PARK GRILL
11 N MICHIGAN AVE
CONTEMPORARY AMERICAN COOKING IN MILLENNIUM PARK.

16 POSTER PLUS
30 E ADAMS ST
VINTAGE POSTERS AND CUSTOM FRAMING.

17 PRECIOUS POSSESSIONS
28 N MICHIGAN AVE
MINERAL AND STONES SHOP.

18 THE TREE HOUSE AT TAVERN AT THE PARK
130 E RANDOLPH ST
ROOFTOP VIEWS OF MILLENNIUM PARK.

19 WILDBERRY PANCAKES AND CAFÉ
130 E RANDOLPH ST
BREAKFAST AND BRUNCH YOUR HEART OUT.

20 YUM CHA DIM SUM PARLOR
333 E RANDOLPH ST
DIM SUM DOWNTOWN.

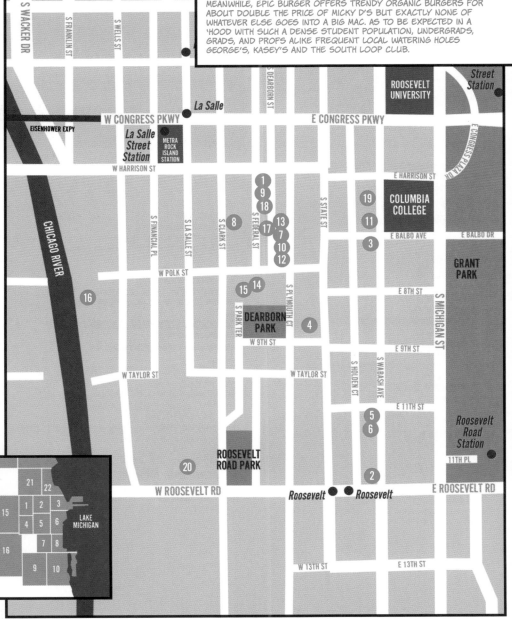

MAP 7 • SOUTH LOOP / PRINTERS ROW / DEARBORN PARK

WITH ALL THE STUDENT-FRIENDLY DINING NEAR THE COLUMBIA COLLEGE CAMPUS, THE UPSCALE MERCAT A LA PLANXA IS A WELCOME ADDITION, OFFERING ELEGANT TAPAS AND LOVELY WINES. MEANWHILE, EPIC BURGER OFFERS TRENDY ORGANIC BURGERS FOR ABOUT DOUBLE THE PRICE OF MICKY D'S BUT EXACTLY NONE OF WHATEVER ELSE GOES INTO A BIG MAC. AS TO BE EXPECTED IN A 'HOOD WITH SUCH A DENSE STUDENT POPULATION, UNDERGRADS, GRADS, AND PROFS ALIKE FREQUENT LOCAL WATERING HOLES GEORGE'S, KASEY'S AND THE SOUTH LOOP CLUB.

1 AMARIT THAI
600 S DEARBORN ST
PRETTY GOOD THAI.

2 BONGO ROOM
1152 S WABASH
SOUTH LOOP'S BEST BRUNCH. FAIR WARNING:
NO BOOZE.

3 BUDDY GUY'S LEGENDS
700 S WABASH AVE
ONE OF THE OLDEST BLUES CLUBS IN CHICAGO.

4 CHICAGO CURRY HOUSE
899 S PLYMOUTH CT
INDIAN-NEPALESE DINING WITH A SERIOUS LUNCH
BUFFET.

5 COLUMBIA COLLEGE CENTER FOR BOOK & PAPER ARTS
1104 S. WABASH
TWO GALLERIES FEATURE CHANGING EXHIBITS OF
HANDMADE BOOKS, PAPER, LETTERPRESS, AND OTHER
RELATED OBJECTS.

6 ELEVEN CITY DINER
1112 S WABASH AVE
TRADITIONAL JEWISH DELI AND BREAKFAST ALL DAY.

7 FLACO'S TACOS
725 S DEARBORN
FRESH, ECO-FRIENDLY TAQUERIA CHAIN.

8 FIRST DRAFT
649 S CLARK ST
BREW PUB BOASTING OVER 60 BEERS ON TAP.

9 FORMER ELLIOT NESS BUILDING
600 S DEARBORN ST
IF HE SENDS ONE OF YOURS TO THE HOSPITAL, YOU
SEND ONE OF HIS TO THE MORGUE...

10 GENTILE'S WINE SHOP
719 S DEARBORN ST
UNPRETENTIOUS STAFF AND A HUGE SELECTION OF
WINES AND CRAFT BEERS.

11 GEORGE'S COCKTAIL LOUNGE
646 S WABASH AVE
COLUMBIA STUDENTS AND FACULTY QUAFF IN THIS
DIVE BETWEEN CLASSES.

12 HACKNEY'S
733 S DEARBORN ST
PREPARE FOR THE MAMMOTH HACKNEY BURGER WITH
AN ONION LOAF.

13 KASEY'S TAVERN
701 S DEARBORN ST
108-YEAR-OLD NEIGHBORHOOD OASIS.

14 LOOPY YARNS
47 W POLK ST
FOR ALL YOUR KNITTING NEEDS. CLASSES, TOO.

15 OLD DEARBORN TRAIN STATION
47 W POLK ST
TURN-OF-THE-CENTURY TRAIN STATION WITH A LIGHTED
CLOCKTOWER VISIBLE FOR SEVERAL BLOCKS.

16 RIVER CITY
800 S WELLS ST
A FLUID CEMENT DESIGN EXPERIMENT BUILD BY
ARCHITECT BERTRAND GOLDBERG IN THE 80S.

17 SANDMEYER'S BOOKSTORE
714 S DEARBORN ST
INDEPENDENT, FAMILY-OWNED SHOP.

18 SRO
610 S DEARBORN ST
BOASTING CHICAGO'S #1 TURKEY BURGER.

19 TAMARIND
614 S WABASH AVE
SUSHI AND PAN ASIAN; SAKE-BASED "FRUITINIS."

20 THE SHOPS AT ROOSEVELT COLLECTION
150 W ROOSEVELT
OPEN AIR RETAIL RIVALING LINCOLN PARK'S NORTH &
CLYBOURN.

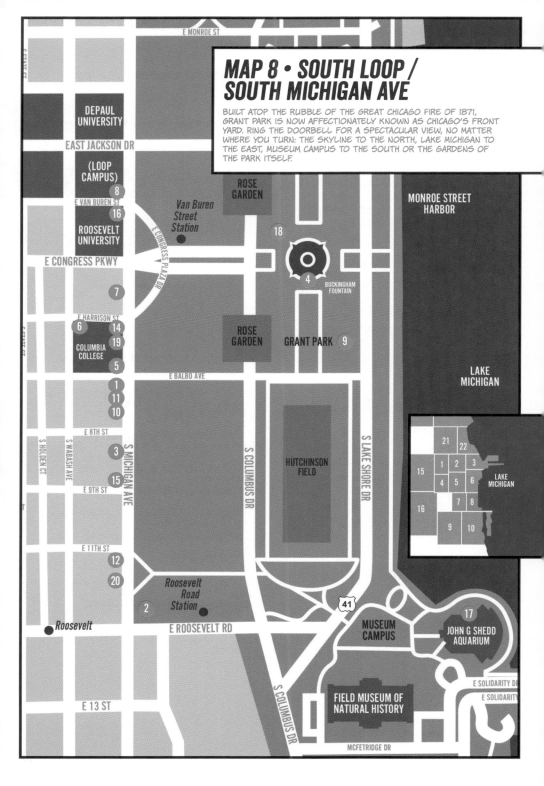

MAP 8 • SOUTH LOOP / SOUTH MICHIGAN AVE

BUILT ATOP THE RUBBLE OF THE GREAT CHICAGO FIRE OF 1871, GRANT PARK IS NOW AFFECTIONATELY KNOWN AS CHICAGO'S FRONT YARD. RING THE DOORBELL FOR A SPECTACULAR VIEW, NO MATTER WHERE YOU TURN: THE SKYLINE TO THE NORTH, LAKE MICHIGAN TO THE EAST, MUSEUM CAMPUS TO THE SOUTH OR THE GARDENS OF THE PARK ITSELF.

E MONROE ST

DEPAUL UNIVERSITY

EAST JACKSON DR

(LOOP CAMPUS)

E VAN BUREN ST

ROOSEVELT UNIVERSITY

E CONGRESS PKWY

E CONGRESS PLAZA DR

Van Buren Street Station

ROSE GARDEN

MONROE STREET HARBOR

18

4

BUCKINGHAM FOUNTAIN

7

E HARRISON ST

6   14

19

COLUMBIA COLLEGE

5

1

11

10

E BALBO AVE

ROSE GARDEN

GRANT PARK   9

LAKE MICHIGAN

E 8TH ST

3

S HOLDEN CT

S WABASH AVE

S MICHIGAN AVE

15

E 9TH ST

HUTCHINSON FIELD

S COLUMBUS DR

S LAKE SHORE DR

21   22

15   1   2   3

4   5   6

LAKE MICHIGAN

E 11TH ST

12

20

2

Roosevelt Road Station

16   7   8

9   10

E ROOSEVELT RD

Roosevelt

41

MUSEUM CAMPUS

17

JOHN G SHEDD AQUARIUM

E SOLIDARITY DR

E SOLIDARITY

E 13 ST

S COLUMBUS DR

FIELD MUSEUM OF NATURAL HISTORY

MCFETRIDGE DR

1 720 SOUTH BAR AND GRILL
720 S MICHIGAN AVE
UPSCALE BAR FOOD AT THE HILTON.

2 AGORA
S MICHIGAN AVE & E ROOSEVELT RD
PUBLIC ART FEATURING 106 HEADLESS METAL FIGURES.

3 BRASSERIE BY LM
800 S MICHIGAN AVE
WALLETFRIENDLY FRENCH BISTRO.

4 BUCKINGHAM FOUNTAIN
500 S COLUMBUS DR
BUILT OF PINK MARBLE; INSPIRED BY VERSAILLES.

5 COLUMBIA BOOKSTORE
624 S MICHIGAN AVE
COLLEGE GEAR AND TEXTS.

6 COLUMBIA COLLEGE
600 S MICHIGAN AVE
PRIVATE ART SCHOOL KNOWN FOR ITS FILM, TV AND FICTION PROGRAMS.

7 CONGRESS PLAZA HOTEL
520 S MICHIGAN AVE
THE 100+ YEAR OLD HOTEL IS SUPPOSEDLY HAUNTED.

8 FONTANO'S SUBS
332 S MICHIGAN AVE
CLASSIC ITALIAN SUBS.

9 GRANT PARK
337 E RANDOLPH ST
CHICAGO'S ICONIC 300+ ACRE PUBLIC PARK.

10 HILTON CHICAGO
720 S MICHIGAN AVE
CHECK OUT THE FRESCOS IN THE LOBBY.

11 KITTY O'SHEA'S
720 S MICHIGAN AVE
IRISH FARE & LIVE MUSIC IN THE HILTON.

12 MEI'S KITCHEN
1108 S MICHIGAN AVE
NO-WAIT BRUNCH SPOT.

13 MERCAT A LA PLANXA
638 S MICHIGAN AVE
PRECIOUS CATALAN TAPAS OR A WHOLE SUCKLING PIG (WITH 48 HOURS NOTICE).

14 MUSEUM OF CONTEMPORARY PHOTOGRAPHY
600 S MICHIGAN AVE
COLLECTIONS FROM EMERGING AND MID-CAREER ARTISTS HOUSED AT COLUMBIA COLLEGE.

15 NIU B
888 S MICHIGAN AVE
ASIAN FUSION SMALL PLATES, SUSHI AND RAMEN.

16 OSAKA EXPRESS
400 S MICHIGAN AVE
SUSHI IN A FLASH.

17 SHEDD AQUARIUM
1200 S LAKE SHORE DR
MARINE AND FRESHWATER CREATURES FROM AROUND THE WORLD ON VIEW IN THIS 1929 CLASSICAL GREEK-INSPIRED BEAUX ARTS STRUCTURE.

18 SPIRIT OF MUSIC GARDEN
601 S MICHIGAN AVE
WHERE THE CITY STRUTS DURING CHICAGO SUMMERDANCE.

19 THE SPERTUS SHOP
610 S MICHIGAN AVE
UNIQUE HANUKKAH GIFTS INCLUDE YIDDISHWEAR AND THE MOSES ACTION FIGURE.

20 YOLK
1120 S MICHIGAN
BRIGHT BRUNCH SPOT WITH EGGS O' PLENTY.

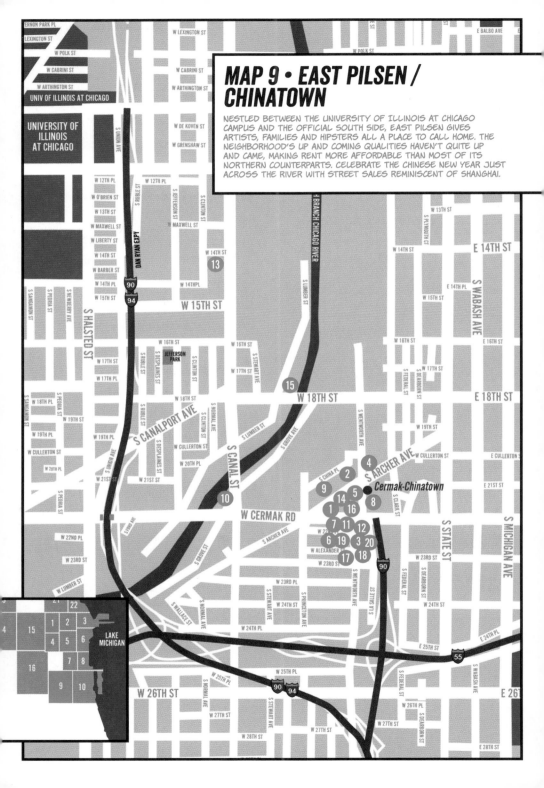

1 AHJOOMAH'S APRON
218 W CERMAK RD
LONE TASTE OF KOREAN AMONGST DIM SUM AND DUCK SAUCE.

2 AJI ICHIBAN
2117A S CHINA PLACE
KALEIDOSCOPIC ARRAY OF ASIAN CANDIES AND SNACKS.

3 CHINATOWN BAZAAR
2221 S WENTWORTH AVE
PART CLOTHING STORE, PART KNOCK KNACK STORE.

4 CHINATOWN GATE
S WENTWORTH AVE & W CERMAK RD
BUILT IN 1976. THE CHARACTERS ON THE GATE READ, "THE WORLD BELONGS TO THE PEOPLE."

5 DOUBLE LI
228 W CERMAK AVE
SWEAT-INDUCING SPICY SZECHUAN DISHES.

6 FEIDA BAKERY
2228 S WENTWORTH AVE
TASTY CHINESE BAKED GOODS.

7 GIFTLAND
2212 S WENTWORTH AVE
WITH A PREMIUM ON HELLO KITTY AND OTHER SORTS OF "ASIAN ADORABLENESS."

8 HILLIARD APARTMENTS
2111 S CLARK ST
ANOTHER BERTRAND GOLBERG GEM GOING FROM SUBSIDIZED SENIOR HOUSING TO MIXED-INCOME RESIDENTIAL.

9 LAO SHANGHAI
2163 S CHINA AVE
FRESH, AUTHENTIC CHINESE DISHES.

10 LAWRENCE'S FISH AND SHRIMP
2120 S CANAL ST
DESTINATION FOR FRIED SHRIMP.

11 ON LEUNG MERCHANTS ASSOCIATION BUILDING
2216 S WENTWORTH AVE
1926 BUILDING INSPIRED BY ARCHITECTURE OF THE KWANGTUNG DISTRICT OF CHINA. NOW THE HOME OF THE PUI TAK CENTER.

12 PACIFIC FURNITURE
2200 S WENTWORTH AVE
MOSTLY HOME FURNISHINGS.

13 PACIFIC GARDEN MISSION
1458 S CANAL ST
AMERICA'S OLDEST CONTINUOUSLY-OPERATING RESCUE MISSION WITH FREE SHOWINGS OF LONG RUNNING RADIO DRAMA UNSHACKLED!

14 PHOENIX
2131 S ARCHER AVE
THE BEST CHINESE BREAKFAST IN TOWN.

15 PING TOM PARK
300 W 19TH ST
PARK WITH CHINESE LANDSCAPE ELEMENTS.

16 SAKURA KARAOKE LOUNGE
234 W CERMAK RD
PRIVATE ROOM KARAOKE.

17 SUN SUN TONG CO
2260 S WENTWORTH AVE
STOCK UP ON HERBS AND CHINESE TEAS.

18 TEN REN TEA
2247 S WENTWORTH AVE
THE ONLY PLACE TO BUY GINSENG.

19 WOKS 'N THINGS
2243 S WENTWORTH AVE
STIR-FRY UTENSILS AND COOKWARE.

20 WON KOW
2237 S WENTWORTH AVE
CHEAP, TASTY DIM SUM.

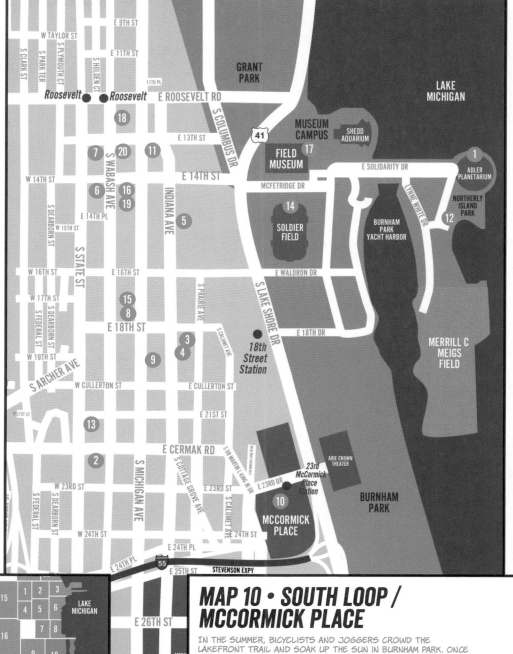

MAP 10 • SOUTH LOOP / MCCORMICK PLACE

IN THE SUMMER, BICYCLISTS AND JOGGERS CROWD THE LAKEFRONT TRAIL AND SOAK UP THE SUN IN BURNHAM PARK. ONCE TEMPERATURES REACH A FRIENDLY SUB-ZERO READING IN DECEMBER, BEARS FANS TURN PARKING LOTS INTO 6:30 A.M. SUNDAY FUNDAY SPOTS. THROUGHOUT THE YEAR, MCCORMICK PLACE LOOMS OVER THE NEIGHBORHOOD TO WELCOME MEETINGS, TRADE SHOWS AND BUSINESS GATHERINGS OF ALL KINDS.

① ADLER PLANETARIUM
1300 S LAKE SHORE DR
FOUNDED IN 1930 TO EXHIBIT MAX ADLER'S COLLECTION OF ASTRONOMICAL INSTRUMENTS, THE MUSEUM INCLUDES AN OBSERVATORY, AN INTERACTIVE THEATER AND A NOTED RESEARCH COLLECTION.

② CHEF LUCIANO
49 E CERMAK RD
WALK-IN RESTAURANT WITH ITALIAN/AFRICAN/CAJUN INFLUENCES.

③ CHICAGO WOMEN'S PARK AND GARDENS
1800 S PRAIRIE AVE
A GARDEN FROM A FORMER FIRST LADY.

④ CLARKE HOUSE MUSEUM
1827 S INDIANA AVE
BUILT IN 1836 BY AN UNKNOWN ARCHITECT, THIS GREEK REVIVAL-STYLE HOME HAS BEEN RELOCATED TWICE AND IS NOW AN OFFICIAL CHICAGO LANDMARK.

⑤ CYCLE BIKE SHOP
1465 S MICHIGAN AVE
FOR WHEN YOU'RE READY TO UPGRADE FROM YOUR DIVVY RENTAL.

⑥ FLO & SANTOS
1310 S WABASH AVE
CASUAL SPOT SERVING UP ITALIAN AND POLISH CLASSICS.

⑦ GIOCO
1312 S WABASH AVE
OLD WORLD ITALIAN DINING HOUSED IN A TURN-OF-THE-CENTURY GANGSTER DEN.

⑧ KROLL'S
1736 S MICHIGAN AVE
CHICAGO OUTPOST OF GREEN BAY GRILL. PACKER BACKERS BETTER WATCH THEIR BACKS.

⑨ LA CANTINA GRILL
1911 S MICHIGAN AVE
COMFY MEXICAN WITH NO SURPRISES.

⑩ MCCORMICK PLACE
2301 S LAKE SHORE DR
HARD TO MISS.

⑪ NEPAL HOUSE
1301 S MICHIGAN AVE
NEPALESE AND HIMALAYAN CUISINE.

⑫ NORTHERLY ISLAND
1400 S LINN WHITE DR
GREENSPACE NOW ENCOMPASSING FORMER SITE OF MEIGS FIELD AIRPORT.

⑬ REGGIE'S
2105 S STATE ST
RECORD STORE, ALL-AGE MUSIC VENUE AND SPORTS BAR IN ONE.

⑭ SOLDIER FIELD
1410 MUSEUM CAMPUS DR
ONCE ON THE NATIONAL REGISTER OF HISTORIC PLACES, THIS RENOVATED MONSTERS IS HOME TO DA BEARS.

⑮ SOUTH LOOP MARKET
1720 S MICHIGAN AVE
LOCAL BIG-BOX ALTERNATIVE.

⑯ SQUARE 1
1400 S MICHIGAN AVE
CRAFT BREWS, COCKTAILS AND...WAIT FOR IT... SELF-SERVICE WINE DISPENSERS.

⑰ THE FIELD MUSEUM
1400 S LAKE SHORE DR
PERMANENT AND ROTATING EXHIBITS ON SCIENCE, ENVIRONMENT AND CULTURE IN A 1893 WORLD'S FAIR BUILDING.

⑱ WABASH TAP
1233 S WABASH AVE
SOUTH LOOP'S NO TIES, RELAX-AFTER-WORK JOINT.

⑲ WAFFLES
1400 S MICHIGAN AVE
YOUR MORNING MADE BETTER WITH SYRUP.

⑳ ZAPATISTA
1307 S WABASH AVE
FANCIFIED MEXICAN FOOD IN BIG, LOUD ENVIRONMENT.

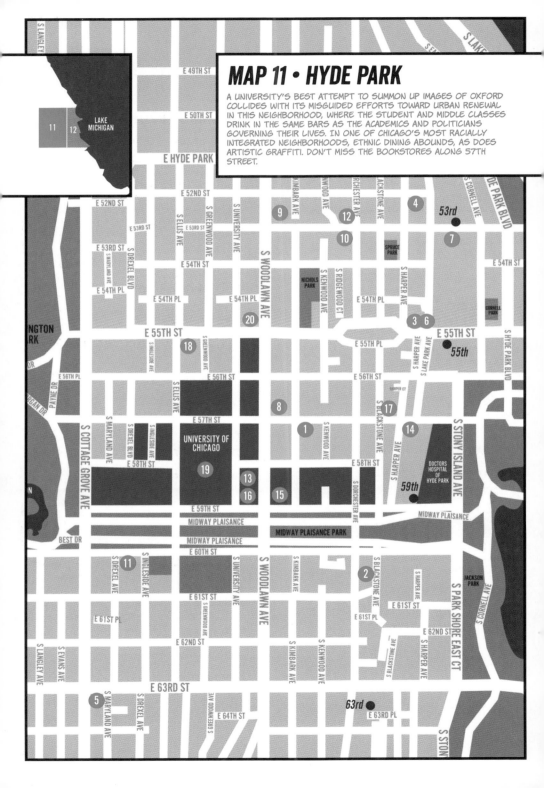

MAP 11 • HYDE PARK

A UNIVERSITY'S BEST ATTEMPT TO SUMMON UP IMAGES OF OXFORD COLLIDES WITH ITS MISGUIDED EFFORTS TOWARD URBAN RENEWAL IN THIS NEIGHBORHOOD, WHERE THE STUDENT AND MIDDLE CLASSES DRINK IN THE SAME BARS AS THE ACADEMICS AND POLITICIANS GOVERNING THEIR LIVES. IN ONE OF CHICAGO'S MOST RACIALLY INTEGRATED NEIGHBORHOODS, ETHNIC DINING ABOUNDS, AS DOES ARTISTIC GRAFFITI. DON'T MISS THE BOOKSTORES ALONG 57TH STREET.

1 57TH STREET BOOKS
1301 E 57TH ST
BRAINY, INDEPENDENT BOOKSTORE.

2 BLACKSTONE BICYCLE WORKS
6100 S BLACKSTONE AVE
SUPER FRIENDLY AND WELCOMING WOODLAWN BIKE SHOP.

3 BONJOUR CAFÉ BAKERY
1550 E 55TH ST
HAVE A PASTRY AND BE SEEN.

4 CHECKERBOARD LOUNGE
5201 S HARPER AVE
THIS LEGENDARY BLUES AND JAZZ CLUB IS BACK.

5 DALEY'S RESTAURANT
809 E63RD ST
CENTURY OLD RESTAURANT SERVING COMFORT FOOD.

6 DJ'S BIKE DOCTOR
1500 E 55TH ST
TRUSTWORTHY, FRIENDLY SERVICE AND PARTS FOR YOUR BIKE.

7 FALCON INN
1601 E 53RD ST
CHEAP DIVE OF REGULARS WHERE YOU CAN HIDE OUT.

8 FREDERICK C ROBIE HOUSE
5757 S WOODLAWN AVE
DESIGNED BY FRANK LLOYD WRIGHT.

9 HAROLD'S CHICKEN
1208 E 53RD ST
BUCKETS AND BUCKETS OF CRISPY, CRUMBLING CHICKEN.

10 HYDE PARK RECORDS
1377 E 53RD ST
BUY/SELL VINTAGE LPS.

11 LOGAN CENTER FOR THE ARTS
915 E 60TH ST
U OF C MULTIDISCIPLINARY ARTS HUB.

12 NATHAN'S CHICAGO STYLE
1372 E 53RD ST
A TASTE OF JAMAICA.

13 THE ORIENTAL INSTITUTE
1155 E 58TH ST
EDUCATE YOURSELF ON THE ANCIENT NEAR EAST.

14 POWELL'S BOOKSTORE
1501 E 57TH ST
FAMOUS BOOK PURVEYOR.

15 THE PUB
1212 E 59TH ST
A BASEMENT STUDENT BAR REDEEMED BY THE PEOPLE-WATCHING AND WOOD PANELS.

16 ROCKEFELLER MEMORIAL CHAPEL
5850 S WOODLAWN AVE
BUILT IN 1928, THIS ENGLISH GOTHIC STYLED CATHEDRAL CONTAINS ONE OF THE WORLD'S LARGEST CARILLONS.

17 SALONICA
1440 E 57TH ST
WHERE TO GO THE MORNING AFTER.

18 SEVEN TEN LANES
1055 E 55TH ST
1920S DÉCOR IN HYDE PARK HAVEN.

19 UNIVERSITY OF CHICAGO
S UNIVERSITY AVE & E 57TH ST
A PRETTY SPOT FOR WANDERING ON THE SOUTH SIDE.

20 WOODLAWN TAP
1172 E 55TH ST
U OF CHICAGO LEGEND.

MAP 12 • EAST HYDE PARK / JACKSON PARK

WELCOME TO THE RITZIER SIDE OF HYDE PARK. HERE, VICTORIAN HOUSES SPAN KENWOOD TO THE NORTH DOWN TO THE MUSEUM OF SCIENCE AND INDUSTRY, ITSELF A DECADENT VESTIGE OF THE 1893 WORLD'S COLUMBIAN EXPOSITION. CHECK OUT THE MODERN INTERPRETATIONS ON THIS ARCHITECTURAL THEME ON HARPER AND DORCHESTER AVENUES, CLIMB THE MODEL TRACTOR AT THE MUSEUM, AND DON'T FORGET THE JAPANESE GARDEN IN JACKSON PARK.

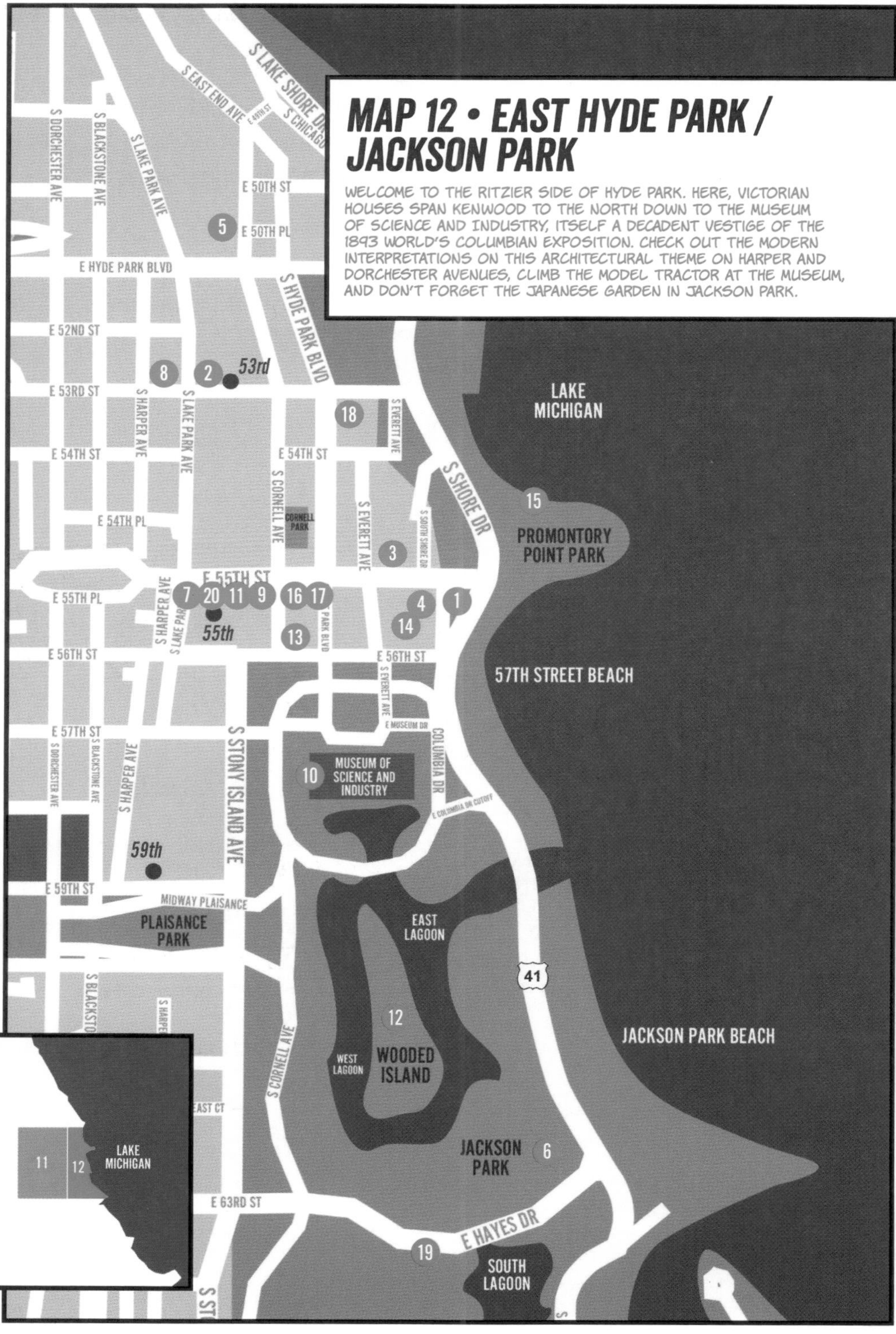

1 BAR LOUIE
5500 S SOUTH SHORE DR
CORPORATE CHAIN MARTINI BAR.

2 BIKE AND ROLL CHICAGO
1558 E 53RD ST
BIKE RENTALS.

3 THE COVE LOUNGE
1750 E 55TH ST
DOWN-AND-OUTERS MEET LIFE-OF-THE-MINDERS.

4 FLAMINGO-ON-THE-LAKE APARTMENTS
5500 S SHORE DR
1927 BUILDING ON THE NATIONAL REGISTER OF HISTORIC PLACES.

5 HYDE PARK ART CENTER
5020 S CORNELL AVE
HAS PLENTY OF VISUAL ARTS ACTIVITIES FOR THE SHORTIES AND GROWN FOLK.

6 JACKSON PARK
6401 S STONY ISLAND AVE
543-ACRE PARK, SITE OF THE 1893 COLUMBIAN EXPOSITION.

7 KIKUYA
1601 E 55TH ST
BEST SUSHI IN HYDE PARK.

8 MELLOW YELLOW RESTAURANT
1508 E 53RD ST
FEEDING HYDE PARK FOR FOUR DECADES.

9 MORRY'S DELI
5500 S CORNELL AVE
GOOD ON THE GO.

10 MUSEUM OF SCIENCE AND INDUSTRY
5700 S LAKE SHORE DR
GET YOUR GEEK ON.

11 THE NILE
1162 E 55TH ST
VARIED MIDDLE EASTERN.

12 OSAKA GARDEN/WOODED ISLAND
6401 S STONY ISLAND AVE
A JAPANESE GARDEN IN THE MIDDLE OF JACKSON PARK—WHY NOT?

13 PICCOLO MONDO
1642 E 56TH ST
BEST ITALIAN IN THE AREA.

14 PROMONTORY APARTMENTS
5530 S SHORE DR
MIES VAN DER ROHE'S FIRST EXPOSED SKELETON BUILDING.

15 PROMONTORY POINT
5491 S SHORE DR
PICNIC WITH A VIEW.

16 SIAM RESTAURANT
1639 E 55TH ST
MORE THAI IN HYDE PARK.

17 THE SNAIL THAI CHICAGO
1649 E 55TH ST
GREAT HYDE PARK THAI.

18 SOUTH SIDE SHRIMP
5319 S HYDE PARK BLVD
SHRIMP AND MORE SHRIMP.

19 STATUE OF THE REPUBLIC
E HAYES DR & S RICHARDS DR
25TH ANNIVERSARY COMMEMORATIVE STATUE OF THE 1893 COLUMBIAN EXPOSITION.

20 THAI 55 RESTAURANT
1607 E 55TH ST
GOOD AMERICANIZED THAI.

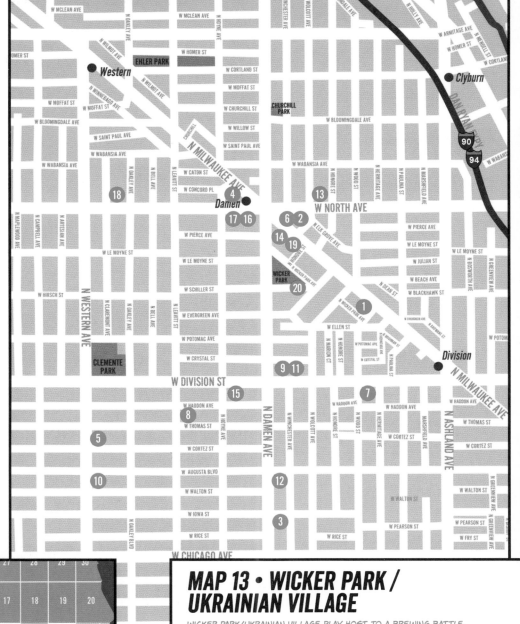

MAP 13 • WICKER PARK / UKRAINIAN VILLAGE

WICKER PARK/UKRAINIAN VILLAGE PLAY HOST TO A BREWING BATTLE BETWEEN SHINY GENTRIFIED DISTRICT AND GRITTY ARTS ENCLAVE. MAMMOTH VICTORIAN HOMES AND ANGULAR NEW CONSTRUCTIONS LINE THE LEAFY AND HISTORIC STREETS. STROLLER-WIELDERS AND TATTOOED-CYCLISTS SHARE MILWAUKEE AVENUE: EACH EQUALLY COMFORTABLE SIPPING METROPOLIS COFFEE NEXT TO THE FULLSIZE REPLICA OF A DELOREAN TIME MACHINE AT WORMHOLE. WHO WILL ULTIMATELY CLAIM THE TERRITORY AS THEIR OWN? JUST ASK BUCKTOWN.

1 ANTIQUE TACO
1360 N MILWAUKEE AVE
SHABBY CHIC TAQUERIA.

2 ASRAI GARDEN
1935 W NORTH AVE
UNIQUE GIFTS AND GARDEN DOODADS.

3 BLACK DOG GELATO
859 N DAMEN AVE
BELOVED SPOT FOR THE FROZEN ITALIAN DELICACY.

4 COYOTE BUILDING
1600 N MILWAUKEE AVE
THIS 12-STORY ART DECO BUILDING AND FORMER BANK
NOW HOUSES A SLEEK, EXPANSIVE WALGREENS ON
ITS GROUND FLOOR.

5 EMPTY BOTTLE
1035 N WESTERN AVE
AVANT GARDE JAZZ AND INDIE ROCK.

6 FLAT IRON ARTS BUILDING
1579 N MILWAUKEE AVE
A PART OF THE CHICAGO COALITION OF
COMMUNITY CULTURAL CENTERS, THE DISTINCT
TRIANGULAR-SHAPED BUILDING HOUSES ARTIST
STUDIOS.

7 GOLD STAR BAR
1755 W DIVISION
HEAR THE CARS AND CASH IN UNDER AND HOUR.

8 HOLY TRINITY CATHEDRAL AND RECTORY
1121 N. LEAVITT ST
DESIGNED BY LOUIS SULLIVAN TO LOOK LIKE A
RUSSIAN CATHEDRAL.

9 JERRY'S WICKER PARK
1938 W DIVISION ST
JERRY'S KNOWS GOOD SANDWICHES AND ISN'T
AFRAID TO...MAKE THEM.

10 LEGHORN CHICKEN
959 N WESTERN AVE
I SAY I SAY: THE FRIED CHICKEN TREND CONTINUES.

11 MILK & HONEY
1920 W DIVISION
HEAVEN FOR BREAKFAST.

12 OLA'S LIQUOR
947 N DAMEN AVE
POLISH-UKRAINIAN LIQUOR STORE-BAR (OLD STYLE,
LITERALLY AND FIGURATIVELY).

13 QUIMBY'S
1854 W NORTH AVE
EDGY, COUNTER-CULTURE BOOKSHOP.

14 RECKLESS RECORDS
1532 N MILWAUKEE AVE
INSTANT SATISFACTION FOR THE VINYL HUNGRY
MASSES.

15 SMALL BAR
2049 W DIVISION ST
SMALL IS THE NEW BIG AT THIS HIPSTER-COOL, COZY
HANG.

16 SUBTERRANEAN
2011 W NORTH AVE
SEMI-COOL MUSIC SPOT.

17 SULTAN'S MARKET
2057 W NORTH AVE
CHEAP MIDDLE EASTERN, GROCERIES.

18 THAI LAGOON
2322 W NORTH AVE
GREAT THAI, FUNKY ATMOSPHERE.

19 UNA MAE'S
1528 N MILWAUKEE AVE
A WICKER PARK STAPLE—VINTAGE AND NEW CLOTHING.

20 WICKER PARK
W SCHILLER & N DAMEN AVE
HOMES IN THIS DISTRICT REFLECT THE STYLE OF OLD
CHICAGO.

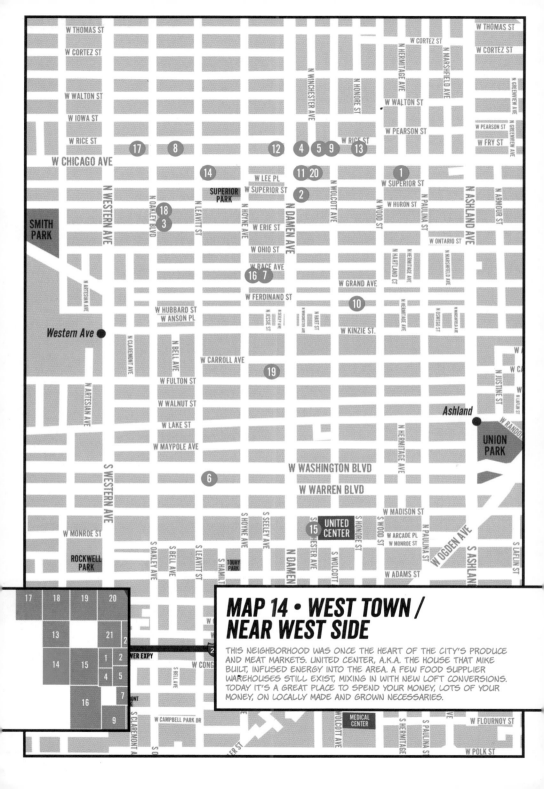

MAP 14 • WEST TOWN / NEAR WEST SIDE

THIS NEIGHBORHOOD WAS ONCE THE HEART OF THE CITY'S PRODUCE AND MEAT MARKETS. UNITED CENTER, A.K.A. THE HOUSE THAT MIKE BUILT, INFUSED ENERGY INTO THE AREA. A FEW FOOD SUPPLIER WAREHOUSES STILL EXIST, MIXING IN WITH NEW LOFT CONVERSIONS. TODAY IT'S A GREAT PLACE TO SPEND YOUR MONEY, LOTS OF YOUR MONEY, ON LOCALLY MADE AND GROWN NECESSARIES.

1 ALCALA'S WESTERN WEAR
1733 W CHICAGO AVE

WESTERN-WEAR EMPORIUM SELLS BOOTS, JEANS AND COWBOY HATS.

2 BAR DEVILLE
701 N DAMEN

A LOCAL SCENE FOR THOSE WHO LOVE A PROPER DRINK AND A RESPECTABLE ATMOSPHERE.

3 FIORE'S DELICATESSEN
2258 W ERIE ST

HOMESTYLE ITALIAN DELI.

4 HIGH DIVE
1938 W CHICAGO AVE

BEATING THE PANTS OFF EVERYDAY BAR FOOD. MAKE THIS YOUR RELIABLE FAVORITE.

5 HOMESTEAD
1924 W CHICAGO AVE

ROOFTOP GARDEN PROVIDES THE SHORTEST FARM-TO-TABLE DISTANCE AROUND.

6 METROPOLITAN MISSIONARY BAPTIST CHURCH
2151 W WASHINGTON BLVD

AN ATTEMPT TO FIND AN APPROPRIATE DESIGN FOR THEN-NEW CHRISTIAN SCIENCE RELIGION. SOLD TO BAPTISTS IN 1947.

7 MODERN TIMES
2100 W GRAND AVE

VINTAGE MID-CENTURY MODERN FURNISHINGS.

8 OLD LVIV
2228 W CHICAGO AVE

EASTERN EUROPEAN BUFFET.

9 PERMANENT RECORDS
1914 W CHICAGO AVE

THE PLACE TO HEAD FOR VINYL.

10 SALVAGE ONE
1840 W HUBBARD ST

WAREHOUSE OF ANTIQUE, VINTAGE, AND SALVAGED ARCHITECTURAL PIECES FOR HOME/LOFT RESTORATION.

11 SPROUT HOME
745 N DAMEN AVE

PLANTS AND GARDENING SUPPLIES MEET MODERNISM.

12 SUNRISE CAFE
2012 W CHICAGO AVE

GOOD COFFEE, GOOD BREAKFAST PUTS A SMILE ON THE FACE.

13 TECALITIAN RESTAURANT
1814 W CHICAGO AVE

POPULAR FAMILY-STYLE MEXICAN RESTAURANT.

14 TUMAN'S TAP AND GRILL
2159 W CHICAGO AVE

UKRAINIAN VILLAGE COZY BAR. RESPECTABLE WEEKEND DANCE FLOOR.

15 UNITED CENTER
1901 W MADISON ST

STATUE OF HIS AIRNESS STILL DRAWS TOURISTS.

16 UPTON'S BREAKROOM
2054 W GRAND AVE

TINY CAFÉ ATTACHED TO THE SEITAN-PRODUCING FACTORY.

17 UKRAINIAN INSTITUTE OF MODERN ART
2320 W CHICAGO AVE

PERMANENT COLLECTION OF UKRAINIAN WORKS AND ROTATING LOCAL ARTIST EXHIBITS.

18 UKRAINIAN NATIONAL MUSEUM
2249 W SUPERIOR ST

MUSEUM, LIBRARY, AND ARCHIVES DETAIL THE HERITAGE, CULTURE, AND PEOPLE OF UKRAINE.

19 UNISON
2000 W FULTON ST

MODERN HOME DESIGN STUDIO OFFERING LOCALLY-MANUFACTURED TEXTILES.

20 VERY BEST VINTAGE
1919 W CHICAGO AVE

HUGE SELECTION OF VINTAGE THREADS, SHOES AND ACCESSORIES.

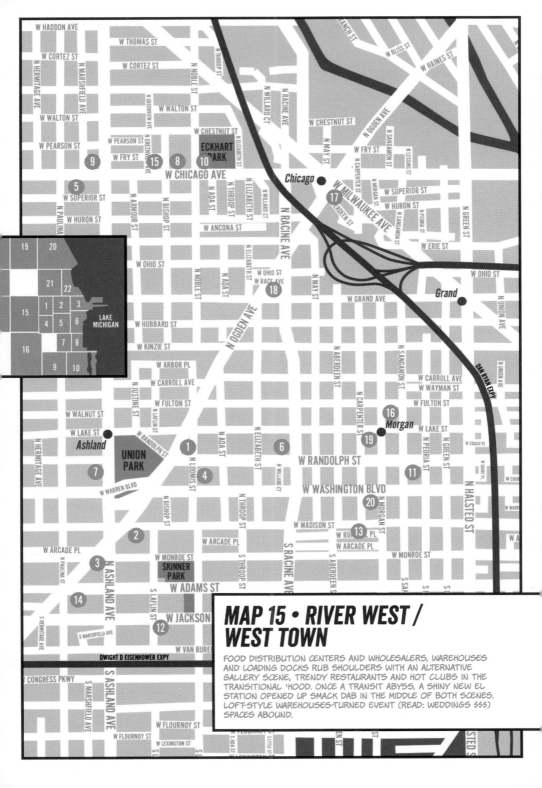

MAP 15 • RIVER WEST / WEST TOWN

FOOD DISTRIBUTION CENTERS AND WHOLESALERS, WAREHOUSES AND LOADING DOCKS RUB SHOULDERS WITH AN ALTERNATIVE GALLERY SCENE, TRENDY RESTAURANTS AND HOT CLUBS IN THE TRANSITIONAL 'HOOD. ONCE A TRANSIT ABYSS, A SHINY NEW EL STATION OPENED UP SMACK DAB IN THE MIDDLE OF BOTH SCENES. LOFT-STYLE WAREHOUSES-TURNED EVENT (READ: WEDDINGS $$$) SPACES ABOUND.

1 BELLY Q
1400 W RANDOLPH ST
NEW, YET BELOVED ASIAN BBQ.

2 BILLY GOAT TAVERN
1535 W MADISON ST
CHEEZBOIGA CHAIN.

3 BOMBON CAFÉ
36 S ASHLAND AVE
UPSCALE TORTAS IN A BRIGHT, SUNNY SETTING!

4 CHICAGO ANTIQUE MARKET
1340 W RANDOLPH ST
LEASES SPACE TO A VARIETY OF VENDORS.

5 CHICAGO AVENUE DISCOUNT
1637 W CHICAGO AVE
SHOES FOR $1.93.

6 CITY WINERY
1200 W RANDOLPH ST
RED, WHITE AND EVERYTHING IN BETWEEN MADE IN-HOUSE.

7 FIRST BAPTIST CONGREGATIONAL CHURCH
1613 W WASHINGTON BLVD
CAN SEAT 2000 PEOPLE AND HOUSES ONE OF THE LARGEST TOTALLY ENCLOSED ORGANS IN THE COUNTRY.

8 FIVE STAR BAR
1424 W CHICAGO AVE
THIRTY BOURBONS, UPSCALE BAR MENU, POOL AND A STRIPPER POLE.

9 HOOSIER MAMA PIE COMPANY
1618 W CHICAGO AVE
"KEEP YOUR FORK, THERE'S PIE!"

10 IDA CROWN NATATORIUM
1330 W CHICAGO AVE
ONE OF TWO SWIMMING POOLS IN THE AREA.

11 J.P. GRAZIANO GROCERY CO.
901 W RANDOLPH ST
SPICES, PASTA AND DRIED BEANS IN BULK.

12 JACKSON BOULEVARD HISTORIC DISTRICT
W JACKSON BLVD AND S LAFLIN ST
AMAZINGLY, THIS CLUSTER OF PRESERVED LATE-NINETEENTH CENTURY MANSIONS SURVIVES IN THIS DECLINING AREA.

13 OLD FIFTH
1027 W MADISON ST
WHISKEY-DRIVEN SPORTS BAR.

14 PARK TAVERN
1645 W JACKSON BLVD
PRE-BULLS/HAWKS GAME STOP FOR CRAFT BEERS.

15 SEEK VINTAGE
1432 W CHICAGO AVE
RETRO CLOTHING AND HOUSEWARES FOR THE "MAD MED" ERA.

16 THE AVIARY
955 W FULTON MARKET
RESERVATIONS BY EMAIL ONLY AT THIS UPSCALE COCKTAIL CREATION DESTINATION.

17 THE MATCHBOX
770 N MILWAUKEE AVE
CHICAGO'S SMALLEST BAR...BAR NONE.

18 TWISTED SPOKE
501 N OGDEN AVE
FAMOUS FOR SERVING SMUT MOVIES AND EGGS SIMULTANEOUSLY.

19 VERA
1023 W LAKE ST
DELECTABLE SMALL PLATES AND AN EXTENSIVE WINE LIST.

20 WISHBONE
1001 W WASHINGTON BLVD
COMFORT FOOD. COMFORT FOLKS.

MAP 16 • UNIVERSITY VILLAGE / LITTLE ITALY / PILSEN

JANE ADDAMS WOULDN'T RECOGNIZE HER OLD 'HOOD TODAY, BUT IT RETAINS HER FEISTY SPIRIT. UIC DEFINITELY HOLDS SWAY AROUND HERE; THE AREA BUSTLES WITH THE TEXTBOOK-TOTING SET FROM SUNUP TO SUNDOWN. FURTHER SOUTH, A PROUD MEXICAN COMMUNITY RUBS SHOULDERS WITH WORKING CREATIVES AROUND THE 18TH AND HALSTED ARTISTIC EPICENTER OF PILSEN.

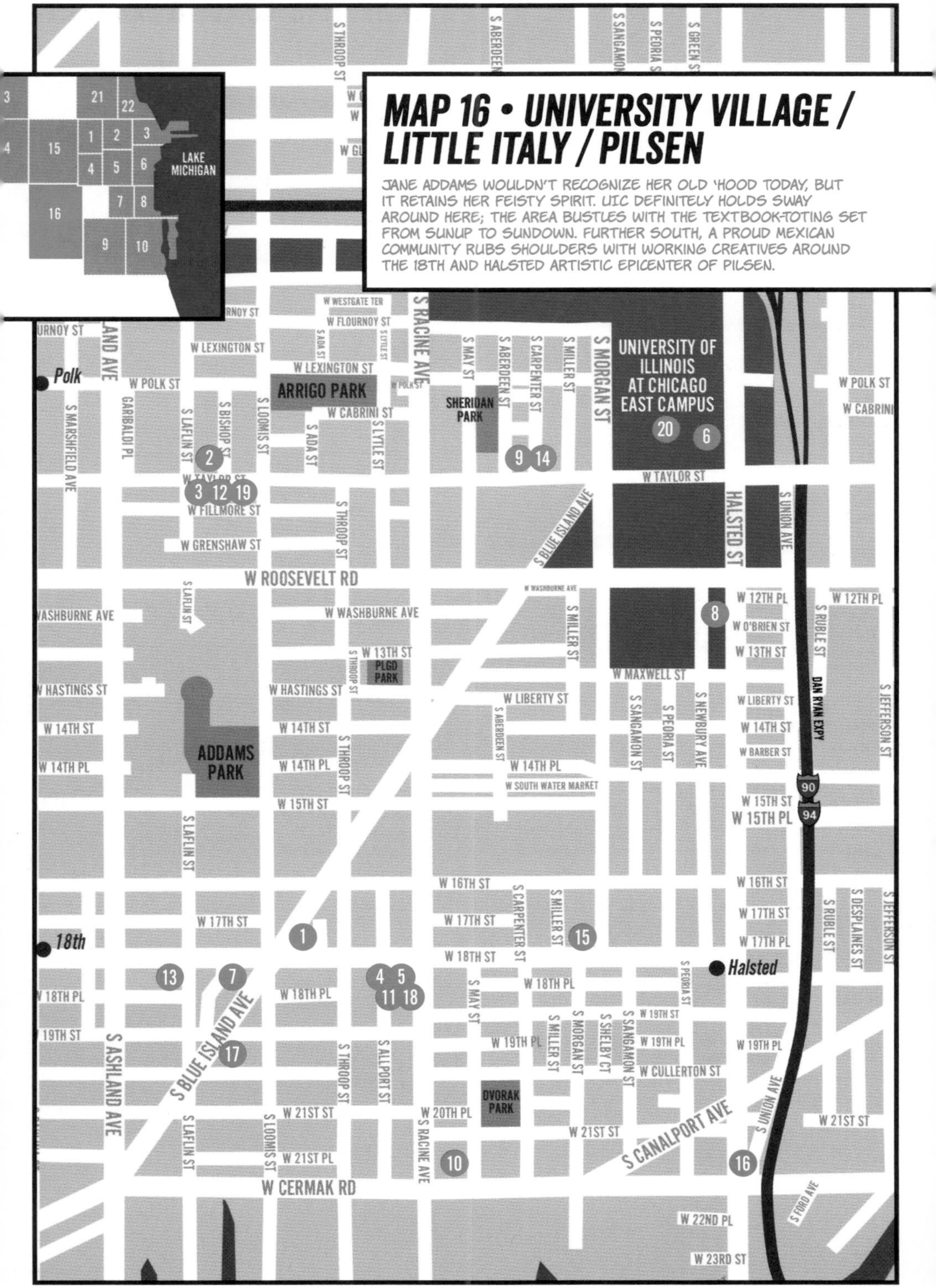

1 BIRRERIA REYES DE OCOTLAN
1322 W 18TH ST
LOCAL NO-FRILLS MEXICAN FAVORED BY RICK BAYLESS.

2 CONTE DI SAVOIA
1438 W TAYLOR ST
EUROPEAN AND ITALIAN GROCERY.

3 COUSCOUS
1445 W TAYLOR ST
MIDDLE EASTERN AND MAGHREBIN CUISINE. UNIQUE FALAFEL.

4 DUSEK'S
1227 W 18TH ST
BEER-CENTRIC DINING IN THALIA HALL TRIFECTA.

5 HONKY TONK BBQ
1800 S RACINE AVE
HIP SALOON AT ITS BEST WITH LIVE MUSIC AND SMOKED BRISKET.

6 JANE ADDAMS HULL-HOUSE MUSEUM
800 S HALSTED
MEMORIAL TO THE BIRTHPLACE OF CHICAGO SOCIAL REFORM.

7 KNEE DEEP VINTAGE
1425 W 18TH ST
BEAUTIFUL VINTAGE. KINDHEARTED PROPRIETORS.

8 LUSH WINE & SPIRITS
1257 S HALSTED
WINE, MICROBREWS AND BOOZE.

9 MARIO'S ITALIAN LEMONADE
1068 W TAYLOR ST
THE BEST SUMMER TREAT IN THE CITY. PREPARE TO WAIT.

10 MAY STREET CAFÉ
1146 W CERMAK
INEXPENSIVE, SUPER CASUAL PAN-LATIN.

11 MODERN COOPERATIVE
818 W 18TH ST
HOME FURNISHINGS OLD AND NEW.

12 NATIONAL ITALIAN AMERICAN SPORTS HALL OF FAME
1431 W TAYLOR ST
HOW MANY ITALIAN AMERICAN SPORTS STARTS DO YOU KNOW? DIMAGGIO IS RIGHT OUT FRONT.

13 NUEVO LEON
1515 W 18TH ST
REAL-DEAL MEXICAN GRUB.

14 SAINT IGNATIUS COLLEGE PREP
1076 W ROOSEVELT RD
ONE OF FEW CITY BUILDINGS PRE-DATING THE CHICAGO FIRE OF 1871.

15 SIMONE'S
960 W 18TH ST
HIPSTER BAR MADE FROM FUNKY RECYCLED MATERIALS.

16 SKYLARK
2149 S HALSTED ST
CHEAP, GOOD BEER LIST.

17 TAQUERIA EL MILAGRO
1923 S BLUE ISLAND AVE
GOOD, CHEAP MEXICAN STANDBYS FROM THE TORTILLA GIANT.

18 THALIA HALL
1807 S ALLPORT ST
LIVE MUSIC AND COCKTAILS AND THE RESTORED PILSEN LANDMARK.

19 THE DRUM AND MONKEY
1435 W TAYLOR ST
IRISH PUB-STYLE STUDENT HANGOUT.

20 UNIVERSITY OF ILLINOIS AT CHICAGO
1200 W HARRISON ST
THE LARGEST UNIVERSITY IN THE CITY.

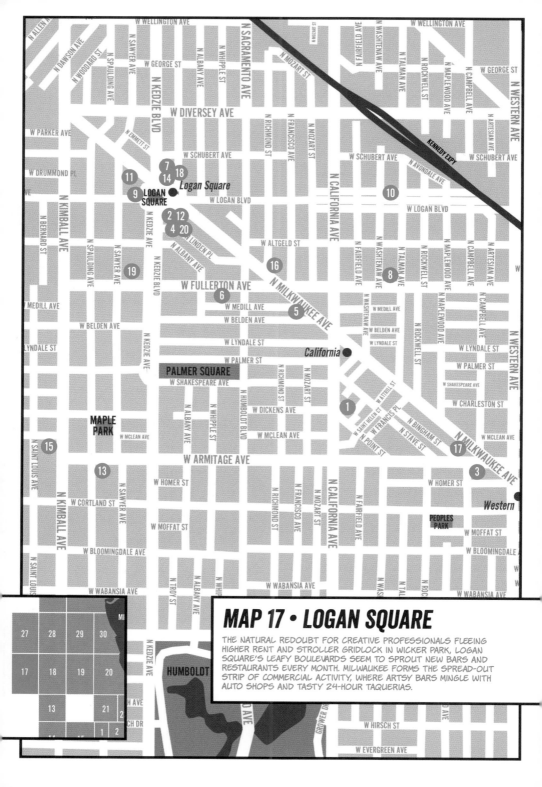

MAP 17 • LOGAN SQUARE

THE NATURAL REDOUBT FOR CREATIVE PROFESSIONALS FLEEING
HIGHER RENT AND STROLLER GRIDLOCK IN WICKER PARK, LOGAN
SQUARE'S LEAFY BOULEVARDS SEEM TO SPROUT NEW BARS AND
RESTAURANTS EVERY MONTH. MILWAUKEE FORMS THE SPREAD-OUT
STRIP OF COMMERCIAL ACTIVITY, WHERE ARTSY BARS MINGLE WITH
AUTO SHOPS AND TASTY 24-HOUR TAQUERIAS.

1 BANG BANG PIE SHOP
2051 N CALIFORNIA AVE
PIE, PIE, AND MORE HOMEMADE PIE.

2 BOULEVARD BIKES
2535 N KEDZIE BLVD
FRIENDLY NEIGHBORHOOD BIKE SHOP.

3 CHILAPAN
2466 W ARMITAGE AVE
AUTHENTIC AND TRADITIONAL MEXICAN DISHES.

4 CITY LIT BOOKS
2523 N KEDZIE BLVD
INDIE BOOKSTORE WITH EXTENSIVE CHILDREN'S AND
SPANISH SECTIONS.

5 COLE'S
2338 N MILWAUKEE AVE
FOR MUSIC BUFFS, FREE LIVE MUSIC NIGHTLY.

6 DILL PICKLE FOOD CO-OP
3039 W FULLERTON AVE
TINY AS AN ORGANIC KUMQUAT, BUT WITH A DENSE
FOOD SELECTION.

7 EL CID
2645 N KEDZIE BLVD
RELIABLE MEXICAN AND A FESTIVE PATIO.

8 FIRESIDE BOWL
2648 W FULLERTON AVE
FORMERLY AN ALGAES PUNK ROCK DIVE. AND I MEAN
DIVE.

9 ILLINOIS CENTENNIAL
3100 W LOGAN BLVD
EVERY CITY NEEDS AN OBELISK TO TWO...

10 LOGAN HOUSE
2656 W LOGAN BLVD
RENOWNED FOR OVER-THE-TOP HOLIDAY DÉCOR.

11 LOGAN THEATRE
2646 N MILWAUKEE AVE
HISTORIC, RECENTLY REFURBISHED MOVIE THEATER
WITH A FULL BAR.

12 LULA
2537 N KEDZIE BLVD
PAN-ETHNIC NOVEAU FOR HIPSTERS.

13 MARBLE
3281 W ARMITAGE AVE
MAKE YOUR WAY THROUGH THE LENGTHY BEER LIST ON
THE EQUALLY LARGE BACKYARD PATIO.

14 RENO
2607 N MILWAUKEE AVE
WOOD-FIRED BAGELS BY DAY, ARTISANAL PIZZAS BY
NIGHT.

15 ROSA'S LOUNGE
3420 W ARMITAGE AVE
NEIGHBORHOOD BLUES LOUNGE.

16 THE WHISTLER
2421 N MILWAUKEE AVE
CLASSIC COCKTAILS, LIVE MUSIC AND ART GALLERY
ALL IN ONE!

17 VILLAGE DISCOUNT OUTLET
2032 N MILWAUKEE AVE
TONS OF CLOTHES AND WEEKLY SPECIALS.

18 WEBSTER'S WINE BAR
2601 N MILWAUKEE AVE
WINE BAR WITH A FLAIR OF GASTROPUB.

19 WHIRLAWAY LOUNGE
3224 W FULLERTON AVE
OLD STYLE, OLD COUCHES, AND A TRULY ECLECTIC
JUKEBOX.

20 WOLFBAIT & B-GIRLS
3131 W LOGAN BLVD
TWO YOUNG DESIGNERS SHOWCASE FUNKY WARES BY
DOZENS OF LOCALS.

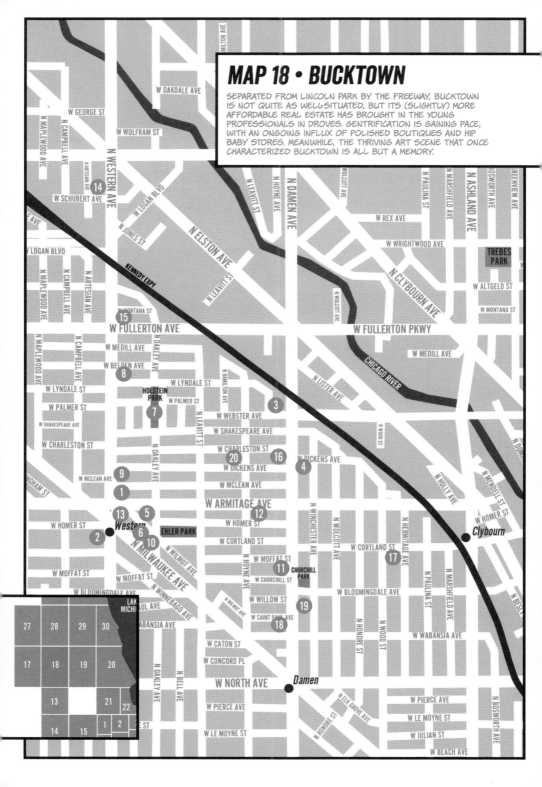

MAP 18 • BUCKTOWN

SEPARATED FROM LINCOLN PARK BY THE FREEWAY, BUCKTOWN IS NOT QUITE AS WELL-SITUATED, BUT ITS (SLIGHTLY) MORE AFFORDABLE REAL ESTATE HAS BROUGHT IN THE YOUNG PROFESSIONALS IN DROVES. GENTRIFICATION IS GAINING PACE, WITH AN ONGOING INFLUX OF POLISHED BOUTIQUES AND HIP BABY STORES. MEANWHILE, THE THRIVING ART SCENE THAT ONCE CHARACTERIZED BUCKTOWN IS ALL BUT A MEMORY.

1 ARTURO'S TACOS
2001 N WESTERN AVE
24-HOUR TAQUERIA BOASTS CHEAP EATS AND A BOISTEROUS CROWD.

2 BELLY SHACK
1912 N WESTERN AVE
LATIN/ASIAN/INCREDIBLE. DON'T SKIP THE BELLY DOG!

3 BURKE'S WEB PUB
2026 W WEBSTER AVE
DARTS AND PBR.

4 DANNY'S
1951 W DICKENS AVE
HIPSTER HOUSE BAR WITH CANDLELIT ALCOVES.

5 FLOYD'S
1944 N OAKLEY AVE
LAIDBACK SPOT WITH QUALITY BAR FOOD.

6 GORILLA TANGO THEATRE
1919 N MILWAUKEE
INDIE PERFORMANCE VENUE FEATURING CABARET AND COMEDY.

7 HOLSTEIN PARK FIELDHOUSE
2200 N OAKLEY AVE
100-YEAR-OLD PRAIRIE STYLE PARK DISTRICT BUILDING AND OLYMPIC-SIZE POOL.

8 HONEY 1 BBQ
2241 N WESTERN AVE
BBQ COOKED IN A BIG OLE SMOKER. YUM.

9 IPSENTO
2035 N WESTERN AVE
IN-HOUSE COFFEE ROASTING AND LITERARY-THEMED SANDWICHES.

10 IRAZU
1865 N MILWAUKEE AVE
HIPSTERS AND BIKERS GATHER 'ROUND FOR CENTRAL AMERICAL STAPLES.

11 LEMMING'S
1850 N DAMEN
LITE BRITE WORKS OF ART.

12 MAP ROOM
1949 N HOYNE AVE
CRAFT BREWS FROM ACROSS THE GLOBE.

13 MARGIE'S CANDIES
1960 N WESTERN AVE
THE BEATLES ATE HERE.

14 OWEN & ENGINE
2700 N WESTERN AVE
RUSTIC BRITISH MEALS SERVED WITH ARTISAN CRAFTED ALES.

15 QUENCHER'S SALOON
2401 N WESTERN AVE
CROWDED ON THE WEEKENDS, BUT ULTRA COMFY COUCHES AND FREE POPCORN.

16 ROBIN RICHMAN
2108 N DAMEN AVE
ARTY, INDIE BOUTIQUE.

17 SAINT MARY OF ANGELS
1850 N HERMITAGE AVE
ORNATE, HISTORIC CHURCH VISIBLE FROM ATOP THE NEIGHBORHOOD'S TREE-LINED GRID.

18 SILVER CLOUD
1700 N DAMEN AVE
A MAC & CHEESE AND MEATLOAF KIND OF PLACE.

19 T-SHIRT DELI
1739 N DAMEN AVE
PRICEY—BUT QUALITY—CUSTOM-MADE T-SHIRTS.

20 THE CHARLESTON
2076 N HOYNE AVE
YUPPY DIVE.

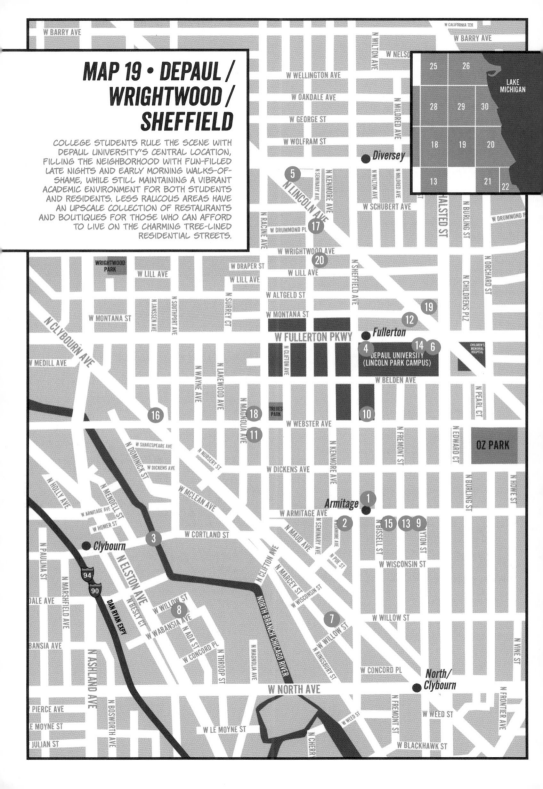

1 ART EFFECT
934 W ARMITAGE AVE
"A MODERN DAY GENERAL STORE" FOR EVERYTHING FABULOUS.

2 BUTCHER & THE BURGER
1021 W ARMITAGE AVE
DIY GOURMET BURGER JOINT.

3 CORTLAND STREET DRAWBRIDGE
1440 W CORTLAND ST
BUILT IN 1902 BY JOHN ERNST ERICKSON, THIS INNOVATIVE LEAF-LIFT BRIDGE CHANGED THE WAY THE WORLD BUILD BRIDGES.

4 DPAM
935 W FULLERTON AVE
DEPAUL'S ART MUSEUM.

5 DELILAH'S
2771 N LINCOLN AVE
PUNK ROCK DIVE SPECIALIZING IN WHISKY.

6 DEPAUL UNIVERSITY
2400 N SHEFFIELD AVE
THE COUNTRY'S LARGEST CATHOLIC UNIVERSITY.

7 GOOSE ISLAND
1800 N CLYBOURN AVE
PUB GRUB AT ITS BEST.

8 THE HIDEOUT
1354 W WABANSIA AVE
HAVEN FOR ALT-COUNTRY AND OTHER QUIRKY LIVE TUNE-AGE.

9 INTERMIX
841 W ARMITAGE AVE
THE NYC SHOPPER'S MECCA.

10 JAM 'N HONEY
958 W WEBSTER AVE
CREATIVE, CLASSIC BREAKFAST RESTAURANT ALSO SERVING LUNCH AND DINNER.

11 KAVERI
1211 W WEBSTER AVE
BOUTIQUE LINES BY DESIGNERS LIKE TROVATA AND ULLA JOHNSON.

12 LINCOLN HALL
2424 N LINCOLN AVE
ROCK CONCERT VENUE SERVING FOOD AND DRINK.

13 LUSH COSMETICS
859 W ARMITAGE AVE
HANDMADE SOAPS AND NATURAL COSMETICS.

14 MCCORMICK ROW HOUSE DISTRICT
830 W CHALMERS PL
QUAINT EXAMPLE OF LATE 19TH-CENTURTY URBAN PLANNING AND ARCHITECTURE.

15 PAPER SOURCE
919 W ARMITAGE AVE
NEED STATIONARY AND PRINTED INVITATIONS? GO TO THE SOURCE.

16 PEQUOD'S PIZZERIA
2207 N CLYBOURN AVE
SIGNATURE DEEP DISH WITH A CARAMELIZED CRUST.

17 ROSE'S LOUNGE
2656 N LINCOLN AVE
DEPAUL DIVE CHOCK FULL OF TCHOTCHKES AND BEER.

18 SWEET MANDY B'S
1208 W WEBSTER AVE
PICTURE-PERFECT SWEET SHOPPE.

19 VICTORY GARDENS BIOGRAPH THEATER
2433 N LINCOLN AVE
SITE OF GANGSTER JOHN DILLINGER'S INFAMOUS DEATH IN 1934.

20 WRIGHTWOOD TAP
1059 W WRIGHTWOOD AVE
NEIGHBORHOOD FEELGOOD SPOT.

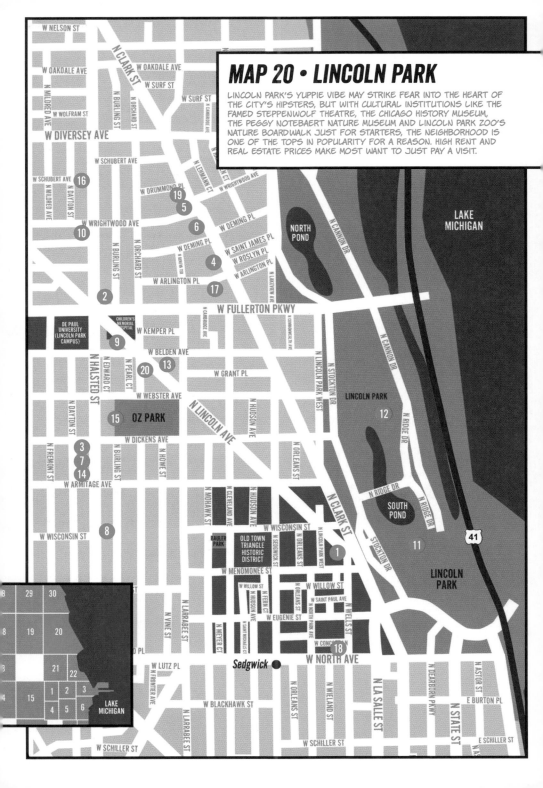

MAP 20 • LINCOLN PARK

LINCOLN PARK'S YUPPIE VIBE MAY STRIKE FEAR INTO THE HEART OF THE CITY'S HIPSTERS, BUT WITH CULTURAL INSTITUTIONS LIKE THE FAMED STEPPENWOLF THEATRE, THE CHICAGO HISTORY MUSEUM, THE PEGGY NOTEBAERT NATURE MUSEUM AND LINCOLN PARK ZOO'S NATURE BOARDWALK JUST FOR STARTERS, THE NEIGHBORHOOD IS ONE OF THE TOPS IN POPULARITY FOR A REASON. HIGH RENT AND REAL ESTATE PRICES MAKE MOST WANT TO JUST PAY A VISIT.

1 A NEW LEAF
1818 N WELLS ST
PERHAPS THE MOST ELEGANTLY DESIGNED FLOWER SHOP IN CHICAGO.

2 BOURGEOIS PIG CAFÉ
738 W FULLERTON AVE
LET THEM EAT CAKE (AND DRINK COFFEE).

3 CAFÉ BA-BA-REEBA
2604 N CLARK ST
NOISY, BUSTLING TAPAS JOINT.

4 CYCLE SMITHY
2468 N CLARK ST
BIKE PARTS & REPAIR OPTION.

5 DAVE'S RECORDS
2604 N CLARK ST
ALL LPS, FROM JANACEK TO JAY-Z.

6 FRANCES' DELI
2552 N HALSTED ST
NEIGHBORHOOD DELI SINCE 1938.

7 FRANCESCA'S COLLECTION
2012 N HALSTED ST
CURRENT WOMEN'S CLOTHING AND JEWELRY AND FOREVER 21 PRICES.

8 KARYN'S FRESH CORNER
1901 N HALSTED ST
THE QUEEN OF RAW FOOD.

9 KAUFMANN STORE AND FLATS
2312 N LINCOLN AVE
ONE OF THE OLDEST EXISTING BUILDINGS DESIGNED BY ADLER AND SULLIVAN.

10 KINGSTON MINES
2548 N HALSTED ST
CHICAGO BLUES BAR IN A NEIGHBORHOOD SAFE FOR TOURISTS.

11 LINCOLN PARK
N LAKE SHORE DR
1200-ACRE PARK ALONG THE LAKEFRONT BETWEEN STREETERVILLE AND EDGEWATER.

12 LINCOLN PARK ZOO
2001 N CLARK ST
OLDEST FREE ZOO IN THE U.S.

13 LION HEAD PUB
2251 N LINCOLN AVE
DEPAUL NIGHTSPOT.

14 LORI'S – THE SOLE OF CHICAGO
824 W ARMITAGE AVE
DESIGNER SHOES.

15 OZ PARK
2012 N BURLING ST
YOU'RE NOT IN KANSAS ANYMORE.

16 TANDOOR CHAR HOUSE
2652 N HALSTED ST
TRADITIONAL INDIAN AND PAKISTANI FARE.

17 SALVATORE'S RISTORANTE
525 W ARLINGTON PL
CUTE NEIGHBORHOOD ITALIAN.

18 THE SECOND CITY
1616 N WELLS ST
LEGENDARY CHICAGO IMPROV LAUNCHED MANY AND SNL'ER.

19 WIENER'S CIRCLE
2622 N CLARK ST
CLASSIC DOGS SERVED WITH A GENEROUS HELPING OF SASS.

20 WISE FOOLS PUB
2270 N LINCOLN AVE
VIBERS ARE HIGH FOR LIVE LOCAL LEGENDS AND JAM SESSIONS.

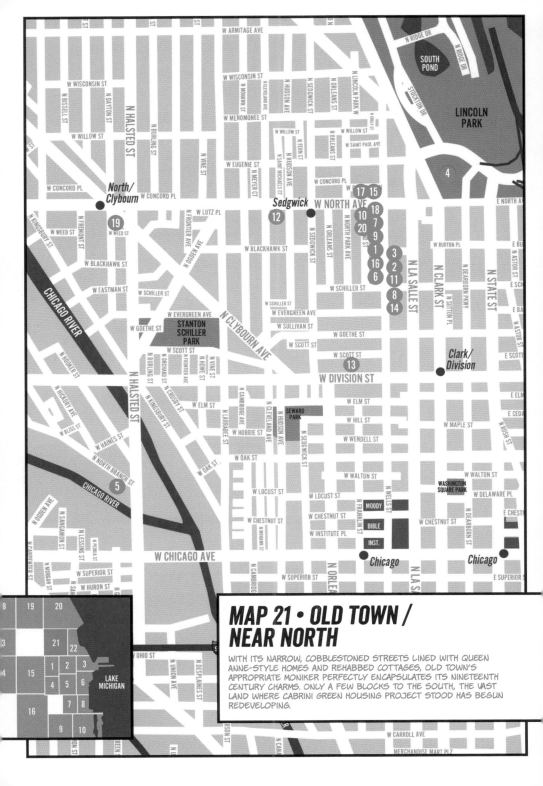

MAP 21 • OLD TOWN / NEAR NORTH

WITH ITS NARROW, COBBLESTONED STREETS LINED WITH QUEEN ANNE-STYLE HOMES AND REHABBED COTTAGES, OLD TOWN'S APPROPRIATE MONIKER PERFECTLY ENCAPSULATES ITS NINETEENTH CENTURY CHARMS. ONLY A FEW BLOCKS TO THE SOUTH, THE VAST LAND WHERE CABRINI GREEN HOUSING PROJECT STOOD HAS BEGUN REDEVELOPING.

1 BENCHMARK
1510 N WELLS ST
DRUNKEN SPORTS BAR WITH A RETRACTABLE ROOF.

2 BISTROT MARGOT
1437 N WELLS ST
GREAT DATE PLACE.

3 BURTON PLACE
1447 N WELLS ST
GREAT LATE NIGHT; GOOD BAR FOOD.

4 CHICAGO HISTORY MUSEUM
1601 N CLARK ST
LEARN THE TRUTH ABOUT THE WINDY CITY.

5 DINING ROOM AT KENDALL COLLEGE
900 N NORTH BRANCH ST
WHEN STUDENTS COOK: GOURMET FOOD, LAYMAN PRICE!

6 THE FIREPLACE INN
1448 N WELLS ST
POPULAR SPOT TO WATCH SPORTS.

7 THE FUDGE POT
1532 N WELLS ST
A CHOCOLATE INSTITUTION.

8 JUDY MAXWELL HOME
1363 N WELLS ST
JOAN CUSACK'S FUNHOUSE OF HYPERBOLIC GIFTS, ART, AND, AHEM, MORE.

9 O'BRIEN'S
1528 N WELLS ST
CHEAP, GOOD FOOD.

10 OLD TOWN ALE HOUSE
219 W NORTH AVE
CRUSTY OLD-TIMERS MEET PERFORMING ARTS CROWD.

11 OLD TOWN POUR HOUSE
1419 N WELLS ST
A BEER LOVER'S DREAM COME TRUE.

12 OLD TOWN SOCIAL
455 W NORTH AVE
LARGE SELECTION OF SPECIALTY BEERS, MEATS, AND CHEESES.

13 SAMMY'S RED HOTS
238 W DIVISION ST
THE SEEDINESS ONLY MAKES IT BETTER.

14 SARA JANE
1343 N WELLS ST
CHIC BOUTIQUE FOR THE LADIES.

15 THE SECOND CITY
1616 N WELLS ST
LEGENDARY IMPROV HOUSE; KINGMAKER OF COMEDY ICONS.

16 THE SPICE HOUSE
1512 N WELLS ST
SPICE UP YOUR COOKING.

17 UP COMEDY CLUB
230 W NORTH AVE
STAND-UP AND IMPROV SEVEN NIGHTS A WEEK.

18 UP DOWN CIGAR
1550 N WELLS ST
ONE STOP SHOPPING FOR THE CIGAR ENTHUSIAST.

19 WEEDS
1555 N DAYTON ST
PINBALL, BRAS, SHOES, POETRY, AND TEQUILA.

20 ZANIES COMEDY CLUB
1548 N WELLS ST
AFTER A FEW DRINKS, EVERYTHING IS FUNNY. WELL, ALMOST.

MAP 22 · GOLD COAST / MAGNIFICENT MILE

GUCCI, CHANEL, BARNEY'S, PRADA; THEY DON'T CALL IT THE GOLD COAST FOR NOTHING. BUT WITH URBAN OUTFITTERS AND H&M, THERE'S PLENTY FOR US REGULAR FOLK AS WELL. PRO-TIP: FOR A GREAT VIEW FROM THE HANCOCK, SKIP THE OBSERVATORY AND HEAD FOR THE BAR AT THE SIGNATURE LOUNGE AT THE 96TH TWO FLOORS ABOVE.

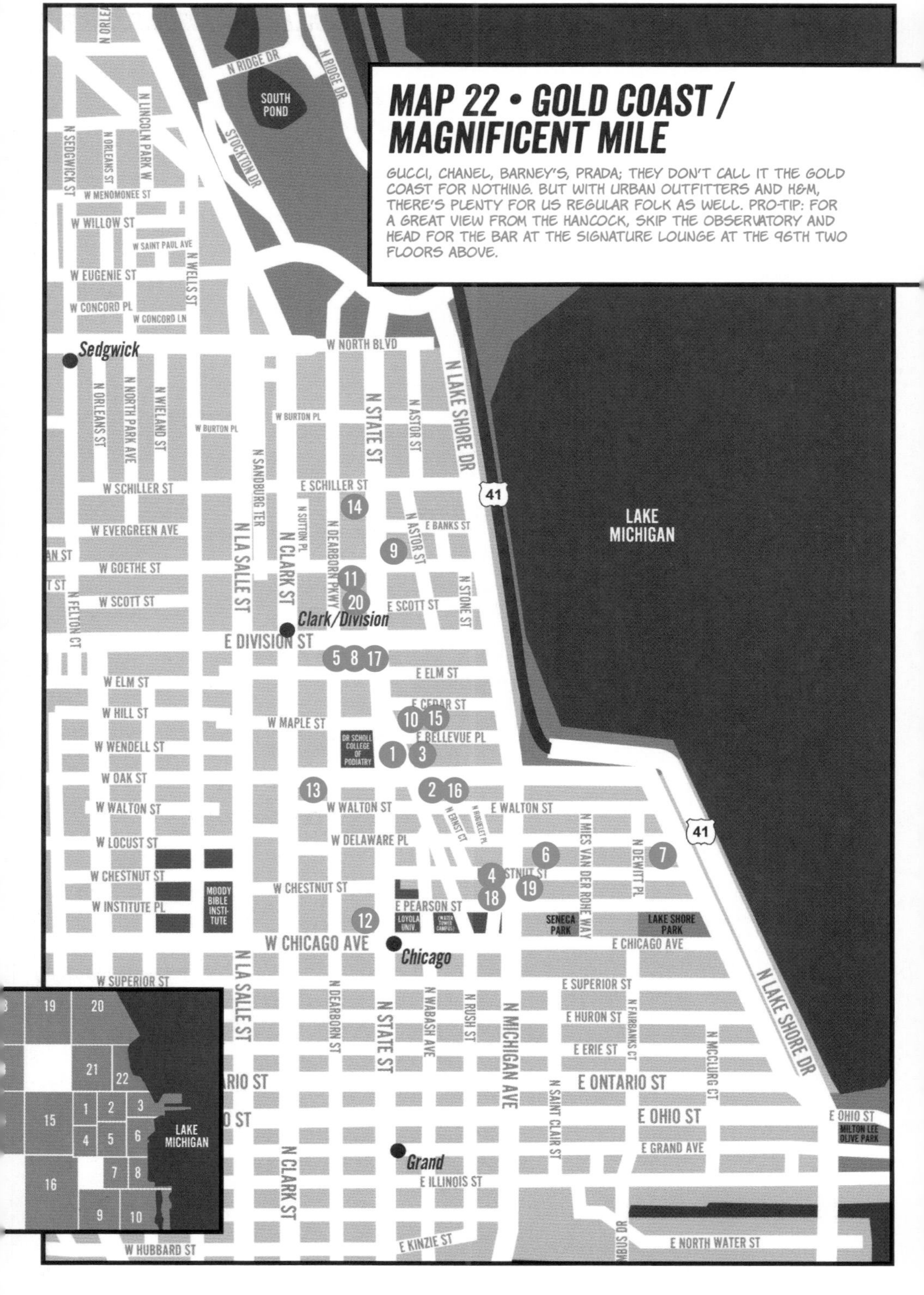

1 DUBLIN'S
1050 N STATE ST
GOLD COAST PUB.

2 THE DRAWING ROOM
937 N RUSH ST
SWANK COCKTAILS AND SIT-DOWN DINING.

3 THE FRYE COMPANY
1007 N RUSH ST
BRICK AND MORTAR FLAGSHIP FOR THOSE BOOTS
YOU'VE BEEN COVETING.

4 H&M
840 N MICHIGAN AVE
EUROPEAN DEPARTMENT STORE STILL TAKING CHICAGO
BY STORM.

5 THE HANGGE UPPE
14 W ELM ST
NO-FRILLS, ALL FUN, DANCING. HIP HOP UPSTAIRS,
'80S CLASSICS DOWNSTAIRS.

6 JOHN HANCOCK CENTER
875 N MICHIGAN AVE
TOURISTS CRAM IN FOR THE GREAT VIEW FROM THE
OBSERVATORY AND THE BAR.

7 LAKE SHORE DRIVE APARTMENTS
860 N LAKE SHORE DR
LESS IS MORE – BY MIES VAN DER ROHE.

8 THE LEG ROOM
7 W DIVISION ST
HUGE SINGLES SCENE.

9 THE LIBRARY
1301 N STATE PKWY
CAFÉ BY DAY, LOUNGE BY NIGHT AT THE PUBLIC
HOTEL.

10 LUXBAR
18 E BELLEVUE PL
BUSTLING RESTAURANT AND BAR.

11 MARIO'S TABLE
21 W GOETHE ST
CLASSIC ITALIAN NEIGHBORHOOD GEM.

12 MR. J'S DAWG & BURGER
822 N STATE ST
MOM & POP BURGER JOINT.

13 THE NEWBERRY
60 W WALTON ST
THERE'S PLENTY ON OFFER AT THIS HISTORIC HUMAN-
ITIES LIBRARY.

14 OLD PLAYBOY MANSION
1340 N STATE PKWY
YOU HAVE NO IDEA WHAT HAPPENED HERE.

15 ORIGINAL PANCAKE HOUSE
22 E BELLEVUE PL
THE APPLE WAFFLE/PANCAKE IS RIGHT!

16 SPRINKLES CUPCAKES
50 E WALTON ST
24-HOUR CUPCAKE ATM!

17 TEAGSCHWENDER
1160 N STATE ST
HIGH-END TEA SHOP SELLS PERFECT GIFTS FOR
TEA-LOVERS.

18 TOPSHOP
830 N MICHIGAN AVE
HIP, TRENDY UK RETAILER.

19 WATER TOWER PLACE
835 N MICHIGAN AVE
HUGE SHOPPING ACROSS SIX FLOORS.

20 ZEBRA LOUNGE
1220 N STATE PKWY
GARISH, CRAMPED PIANO BAR – IN OTHER WORDS,
IT'S A HIT.

MAP 23 • EAST ROGERS PARK

EAST ROGERS PARK IS STITCHED TOGETHER WITH LOYOLA STUDENTS, CIVIC-MINDED YOUNG PROFESSIONALS, NEW IMMIGRANTS, OLD HIPPIES AND BLUE-COLLARED MIDDLE-CLASS DENIZENS. WHILE DENSELY POPULATED AND LIVELY, THE NEIGHBORHOOD'S SEAMS SOMETIMES SHOW AS CRIMES AND GANG ACTIVITY CONTINUES TO BE A PROBLEM. THE DRAW OF EASY ACCESS TO PUBLIC TRANSPORTATION, LAKEFRONT ACCESSIBILITY, CULTURAL DIVERSITY AND LOYOLA'S CAMPUS MAKES EAST ROGERS PARK AN INEXPENSIVE, COLORFUL NEIGHBORHOOD TO RESIDE IN.

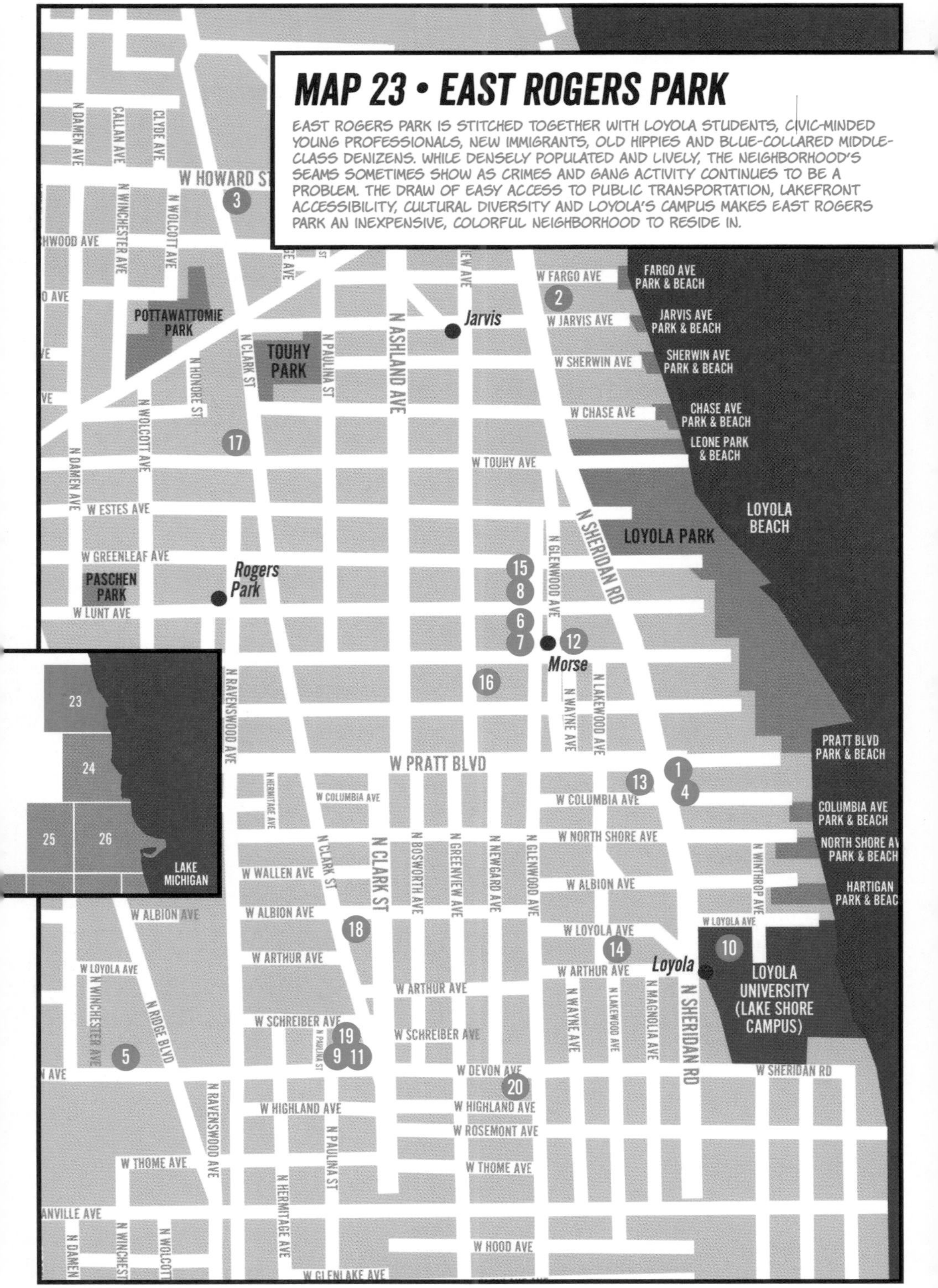

1 THE ARMADILLO'S PILLOW
6753 N SHERIDAN RD
SCORE SOME PAPERBACKS FOR CHEAP.

2 BACH HOUSE
7415 N SHERIDAN RD
ONE OF FRANK LLOYD WRIGHT'S FINAL "SMALL" HOUSES, C. 1915.

3 ETHIOPIAN DIAMOND
7537 N CLARK ST
DELICIOUS ETHIOPIAN FARE.

4 FLATTS & SHARPE MUSIC COMPANY
6749 N SHERIDAN RD
CHEAP GUITARS ($150), OFFERING LESSONS AND MUSIC ACCESSORIES.

5 GHAREEB NAWAZ
2032 W DEVON AVE
CHEAP AND YUMMY INDO-PAKISTANI LUNCH COUNTER OPEN LATE INTO THE NIGHT.

6 THE GLENWOOD
6962 N GLENWOOD AVE
STRAIGHT-FRIENDLY, NEIGHBORHOOD GAY PUB.

7 GLENWOOD ARTS DISTRICT
GLENWOOD AVE AT MORSE AVE
A STRETCH OF MURALS AND QUIRKY STOREFRONTS.

8 HEARTLAND CAFÉ
7000 N GLENWOOD AVE
BROWN RICE, SOCIALIST NEWSPAPERS, AND VEGETARIAN TIDBITS REIGN HERE.

9 JACKHAMMER
6406 N CLARK ST
GAY BAR WITH A WELCOMING NEIGHBORHOOD VIBE.

10 LOYOLA UNIVERSITY OF CHICAGO
1032 W SHERIDAN RD
ONE OF THE LARGEST JESUIT UNIVERSITIES IN THE US.

11 MARJEN FURNITURE
1536 W DEVON AVE
CHEAP FUTONS, DORM FURNITURE.

12 MAYNE STAGE
1328 W MORSE AVE
CATCH A CONCERT AND MORE.

13 NEW 400 THEATER
6746 N SHERIDAN RD
COZY THEATER WITH A BAR.

14 NEWLEAF NATURAL GROCERY
1261 W LOYOLA AVE
ADORABLE ORGANIC GROCERY.

15 RED LINE TAP
7006 N GLENWOOD AVE
BREWS AND BANDS ON THE RED LINE.

16 ROGERS PARK/WEST RIDGE HISTORICAL SOCIETY
1447 W MORSE AVE
PHOTOS, MEMORABILIA, AND HISTORICAL DOCUMENTS OF THE COMMUNITY'S HISTORY DETAILING ITS ETHNIC DIVERSITY.

17 ROMANIAN KOSHER SAUSAGE CO.
7200 N CLARK ST
KOSHER MEAT AND POULTRY.

18 TASTE OF PERU
6545 N CLARK ST
BAREBONES SPOT FOR CHEAP, AUTHENTIC PERUVIAN FOOD.

19 TOUCHE
6412 N CLARK ST
DRUNKEN GAY LEATHER BAR.

20 UNCOMMON GROUND
1401 W DEVON AVE
GREEN RESTAURANT THAT GROWS ITS VEGGIES ON THE ROOF.

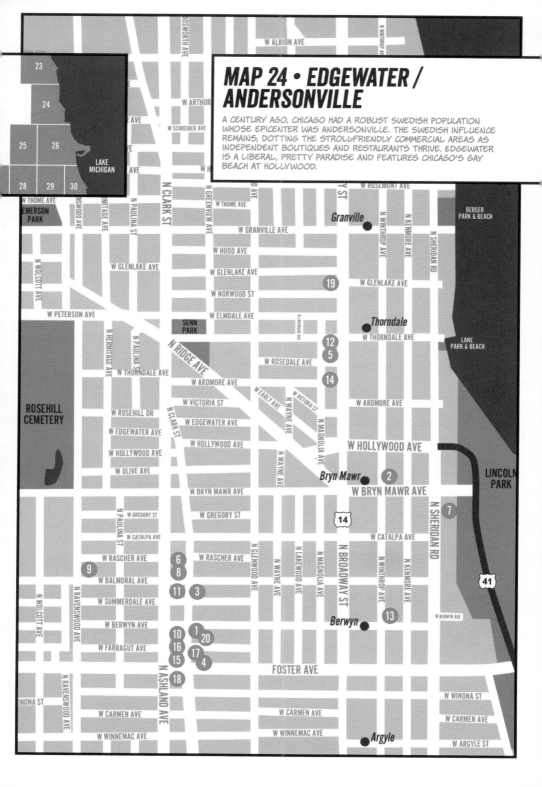

MAP 24 • EDGEWATER / ANDERSONVILLE

A CENTURY AGO, CHICAGO HAD A ROBUST SWEDISH POPULATION WHOSE EPICENTER WAS ANDERSONVILLE. THE SWEDISH INFLUENCE REMAINS, DOTTING THE STROLL-FRIENDLY COMMERCIAL AREAS AS INDEPENDENT BOUTIQUES AND RESTAURANTS THRIVE. EDGEWATER IS A LIBERAL, PRETTY PARADISE AND FEATURES CHICAGO'S GAY BEACH AT HOLLYWOOD.

1 ANDERSONVILLE GALLERIA
5247 N CLARK ST
INDIE MALL WITH OVER 90 VENDORS.

2 BELLE SHORE APARTMENT HOTEL
1062 W BRYN MAWR AVE
FORMER HOMES OF ROARING 1920S NIGHTLIFE, NOW HISTORIC LANDMARKD RESTORED TO THEIR FORMER GLORY AS APARTMENTS.

3 BIG JONES
5347 N CLARK ST
HIGH FALUTIN' SOUTHERN CHOW.

4 BRIMFIELD
5219 N CLARK ST
ECLECTIC DESIGN SENSIBILITY FAVORING PLAID.

5 BROADWAY CELLARS
5900 N BROADWAY ST
WINE AND DINE IN A BRICK-LINED BISTRO.

6 THE BROWN ELEPHANT
5404 N CLARK ST
GREAT RESALE SHOP BENEFITS LOCAL HIV CLINIC.

7 EDGEWATER BEACH APARTMENTS
5555 N SHERIDAN RD
THE BIG PINK BUILDING SYMBOLIZING THE END OF THE LAKESHORE BIKE PATH.

8 HAMBURGER MARY'S
5400 N CLARK ST
FLAMBOYANT BURGER JOINT POPULAR WITH FAMILIES AND THE GAYS.

9 JOIE DE VINE
1744 W BALMORAL AVE
CASUAL WINE BAR POPULAR WITH LOCAL LESBIANS.

10 LADY GREGORY'S
5260 N CLARK ST
IRISH BITES AND BEER.

11 MARTY'S MARTINI BAR
1511 W BALMORAL AVE
COMPACT AND CLASSY GAY BAR.

12 MOODY'S PUB
5910 N BROADWAY ST
BEST BEER GARDEN IN THE CITY WITH THE BEST BURGERS.

13 OLLIE'S LOUNGE
1064 W BERWYN AVE
LIVELY DIVE ON A QUIET STREET.

14 RAS DASHEN
5846 N BROADWAY ST
TRADITIONAL ETHIOPIAN COMFORT FOOD; VEG-AN-FRIENDLY.

15 SIMON'S TAVERN
5210 N CLARK ST
THRIFT-STORE-ATTIRED HIPSTERS AND SWEDISH NAUTICAL THEME IN THIS CLASSIC DIVE.

16 SVEA
5236 N CLARK ST
ADORABLE, TINY SWEDISH DINER.

17 SWEDISH AMERICAN MUSEUM
5211 N CLARK ST
EVERYTHING YOU WANT TO KNOW ABOUT SWEDISH CULTURE, WHICH IS MORE THAN YOU THOUGHT.

18 TASTE OF LEBANON
1509 W FOSTER AVE
DINGY ROOM, ROCK-BOTTOM PRICES, ABOVE-AVERAGE MID-EAST FARE.

19 TRUE NATURE FOODS
6034 N BROADWAY ST
PICK UP YOUR WEEKLY CSA BOX OF FRUITS AND VEGGIES FROM YOUR LOCAL FARMERS.

20 WOMEN & CHILDREN FIRST
5233 N CLARK ST
SPACIOUS FEMINIST BOOKSHOP.

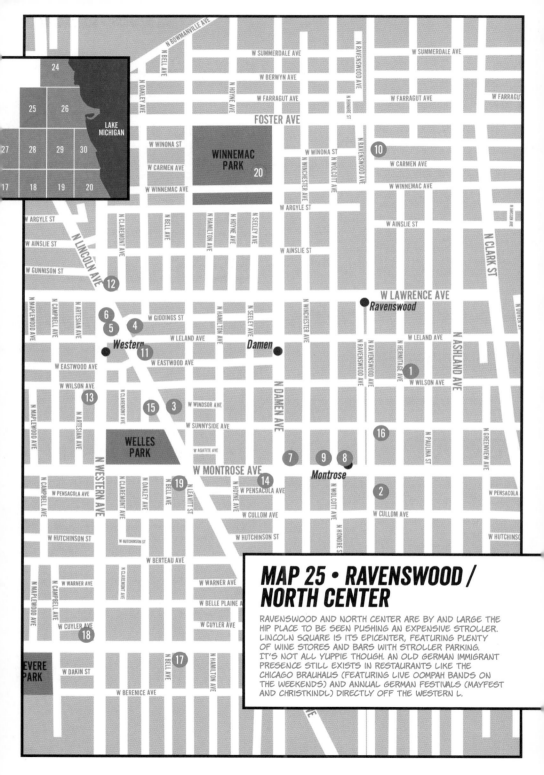

MAP 25 • RAVENSWOOD / NORTH CENTER

RAVENSWOOD AND NORTH CENTER ARE BY AND LARGE THE HIP PLACE TO BE SEEN PUSHING AN EXPENSIVE STROLLER. LINCOLN SQUARE IS ITS EPICENTER, FEATURING PLENTY OF WINE STORES AND BARS WITH STROLLER PARKING. IT'S NOT ALL YUPPIE THOUGH. AN OLD GERMAN IMMIGRANT PRESENCE STILL EXISTS IN RESTAURANTS LIKE THE CHICAGO BRAUHAUS (FEATURING LIVE OOMPAH BANDS ON THE WEEKENDS) AND ANNUAL GERMAN FESTIVALS (MAYFEST AND CHRISTKINDL) DIRECTLY OFF THE WESTERN L.

1 ABBOTT HOUSE
4605 N HERMITAGE AVE
COMELY QUEEN ANNE PAINTED-LADY BUILT IN 1891 FOR ABBOTT LABS FOUNDER.

2 ARCHITECTURAL ARTIFACTS
4325 N RAVENSWOOD AVE
RENOVATOR'S DREAM.

3 BAD DOG TAVERN
4535 N LINCOLN AVE
FOOD, FIREPLACE AND FOLK MUSIC.

4 CAFÉ SELMARIE
4729 N LINCOLN AVE
BRIGHT, CLEAN BAKERY/CAFÉ SERVING WINE AND BEER.

5 CHICAGO BRAUHAUS
4732 N LINCOLN AVE
MORE GERMAN THAN GERMANY...IN OKTOBER.

6 FLEET FEET SPORTS
4762 N LINCOLN AVE
RUNNER'S MECCA.

7 FOUNTAIN HEAD
1970 W MONTROSE AVE
SERIOUSLY EXTENSIVE BEER LIST.

8 GLENN'S DINER
1820 W MONTROSE AVE
FISH-FOCUSED AMERICAN FARE AND CEREAL ALL DAY.

9 HAZEL
1902 W MONTROSE AVE
STYLISH GIFTS AND JEWELRY PLUS AN EXTENSIVE STATIONERY SECTION.

10 KOVAL DISTILLERY
5121 N RAVENSWOOD AVE
TOUR, SIP AND MIX IN THE WHISKEY WONDERLAND.

11 LAURIE'S PLANET OF SOUND
4639 N LINCOLN AVE
FUNKY CD SHOP WITH UNPRETENTIOUS SERVICE.

12 LINCOLN SQUARE
4800 N LINCOLN AVE
A VIRTUAL TOUR THROUGH A EUROPEAN-STYLE NEIGHBORHOOD.

13 LOS NOPALES
4544 N WESTERN AVE
CREATIVE, CHEAP MEXICAN BYOB.

14 NEIGHBORLY
2003 W MONTROSE AVE
YOUR FRIENDLY PRINT, DESIGN AND GIFT SHOP.

15 OLD TOWN SCHOOL OF FOLK MUSIC
4544 N LINCOLN AVE
NORTHERN EXPANSION OF THE BELOVED CHICAGO INSTITUTION. CLASSES AND CONCERT VENUE.

16 SPACCA NAPOLI
1769 W SUNNYSIDE AVE
NEAPOLITAN STYLE PIZZA IN RAVENSWOOD.

17 ST. BENEDICT PARISH & SCHOOL
2215 W IRVING PARK RD
NAMESAKE OF THE ST. BEN'S NEIGHBORHOOD.

18 STICKY RICE
4018 N WESTERN AVE
THAI STOREFRONT OFFERING DISHES BEYOND THE TYPICAL PAD THAI.

19 TINY LOUNGE
4352 N LEAVITT ST
SMALL ON NAME, BIG ON COCKTAILS.

20 WINNEMAC PARK
5001 N LEAVITT ST
HUGE FAMILY-FRIENDLY NEIGHBORHOOD PARK.

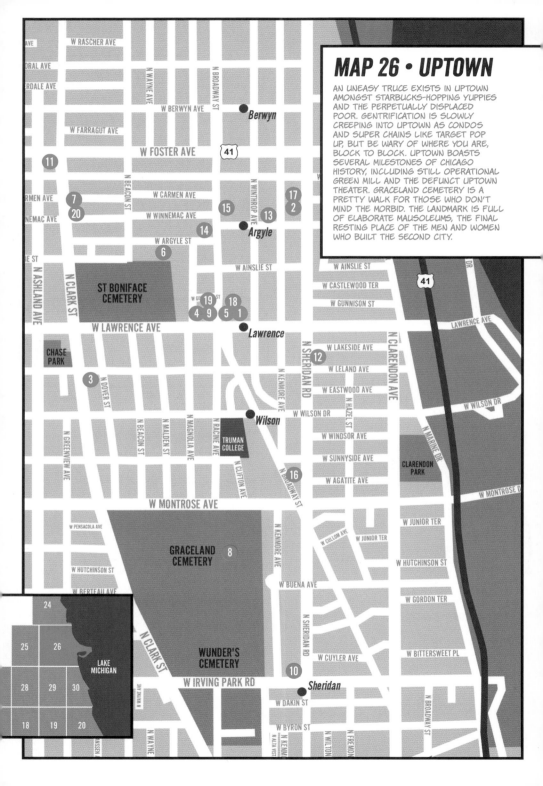

MAP 26 · UPTOWN

AN UNEASY TRUCE EXISTS IN UPTOWN AMONGST STARBUCKS-HOPPING YUPPIES AND THE PERPETUALLY DISPLACED POOR. GENTRIFICATION IS SLOWLY CREEPING INTO UPTOWN AS CONDOS AND SUPER CHAINS LIKE TARGET POP UP, BUT BE WARY OF WHERE YOU ARE, BLOCK TO BLOCK. UPTOWN BOASTS SEVERAL MILESTONES OF CHICAGO HISTORY, INCLUDING STILL OPERATIONAL GREEN MILL AND THE DEFUNCT UPTOWN THEATER. GRACELAND CEMETERY IS A PRETTY WALK FOR THOSE WHO DON'T MIND THE MORBID. THE LANDMARK IS FULL OF ELABORATE MAUSOLEUMS, THE FINAL RESTING PLACE OF THE MEN AND WOMEN WHO BUILT THE SECOND CITY.

1 ARAGON BALLROOM
1106 W LAWRENCE AVE
ONE OF THE BETTER SMALLER MUSIC VENUES IN THE CITY.

2 BIG CHICKS
5024 N SHERIDAN RD
FRIENDLY GAY BAR WITH FABULOUS ART COLLECTION.

3 CAROL'S PUB
4659 N CLARK ST
HILLBILLIES GONE YUPPIE...THANKS TO A LITTLE PRESS.

4 CREW BAR
4804 N BROADWAY ST
GAY SPORTS BAR WITH 50 BEERS A SEVERAL TELEVISIONS.

5 DEMERA
4801 N BROADWAY ST
NEIGHBORHOOD ETHIOPIAN.

6 ESSANY STUDIOS
1333 W ARGYLE ST
FORMER SILENT FILM STUDIO; CHARLIE CHAPLIN AND GLORIA SWANSON MADE MOVIES HERE.

7 FOURSIDED
5061 N CLARK ST
FRAMING AND MORE AT THIS FUNKY SHOP.

8 GRACELAND CEMETERY
4001 N CLARK ST
CHICAGO'S FAMOUS BURIED IN A MASTERPIECE OF LANDSCAPE ARCHITECTURE.

9 GREEN MILL
4802 N BROADWAY ST
LIVE JAZZ SEVEN NIGHTS A WEEK. CAPONE DRANK HERE.

10 HOLIDAY CLUB
4000 N SHERIDAN RD
THE RAT PACK IS BACK!

11 HOPLEAF
5148 N CLARK ST
GREAT FOOD AND EVEN BETTER BEER SELECTION.

12 INSPIRATIONS KITCHENS
4715 N SHERIDAN RD
UPTOWN CAFÉ PROVIDES JOB TRAINING FOR THE HOMELESS.

13 LA PATISSERIE P
1052 W ARGYLE ST
THE EUROASIAN BAKERY OF YOUR DREAMS.

14 PHO XE TANG
4953 N BROADWAY ST
VIETNAMESE AND CHINESE CUISINE ALL DAY.

15 SUN WAH BBQ
5039 N BROADWAY ST
NOTABLE FOR THE BARBEQUED DUCKS HANGING IN THE WINDOW.

16 TATTOO FACTORY
4441 N BROADWAY ST
HIGH-PROFILE PLACE TO GET INKED.

17 TWEET
5020 N SHERIDAN RD
ONE OF THE BEST BRUNCH SPOTS IN THE CITY.

18 UPTOWN LOUNGE
1136 W LAWRENCE AVE
FORMER DUMP BECOMES TRENDY LOUNGE IN UP-AND-COMING NEIGHBORHOOD.

19 UPTOWN THEATRE
4816 N BROADWAY ST
BEEN LOOKING FOR A SAVIOR SINCE 1981, WHILE THE REST OF THE CITY PRAYS IT FINDS ONE BEFORE THE BULLDOZER TAKES IT AWAY.

20 THE WOODEN SPOON
5047 N CLARK ST
HEAVEN FOR FOODIES.

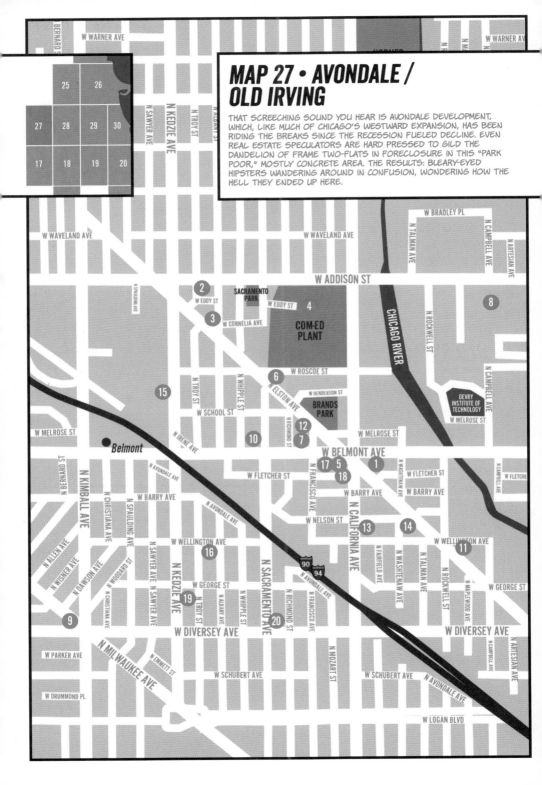

MAP 27 • AVONDALE / OLD IRVING

THAT SCREECHING SOUND YOU HEAR IS AVONDALE DEVELOPMENT, WHICH, LIKE MUCH OF CHICAGO'S WESTWARD EXPANSION, HAS BEEN RIDING THE BREAKS SINCE THE RECESSION FUELED DECLINE. EVEN REAL ESTATE SPECULATORS ARE HARD PRESSED TO GILD THE DANDELION OF FRAME TWO-FLATS IN FORECLOSURE IN THIS "PARK POOR," MOSTLY CONCRETE AREA. THE RESULTS: BLEARY-EYED HIPSTERS WANDERING AROUND IN CONFUSION, WONDERING HOW THE HELL THEY ENDED UP HERE.

1 BEER TEMPLE
3185 N ELSTON AVE
SHOP FOR YOUR FAVORITE OBSCURE CRAFT BREW.

2 BURRITO HOUSE
3145 W ADDISON ST
FOR THOSE (REALLY) LATE NIGHTS.

3 CHIEF O'NEILL'S
3471 N ELSTON AVE
CELTIC MUSIC AND TRADITIONAL IRISH PUB FARE.

4 COMED PLANT
N CALIFORNIA AVE AND W ROSCOE ST
WHAT'S THAT HUMMING SOUND IN AVONDALE? MUST BE
THIS GINORMOUS ELECTRICAL PLANT.

5 DRAGON LADY LOUNGE
3188 N ELSTON AVE
KOREAN DIVE BAR WITH GREAT VEGAN BUFFET.

6 HONEY BUTTER FRIED CHICKEN
3360 N ELSTON AVE
WHOLESOME. SUSTAINABLE. FRIED CHICKEN.

7 KUMA'S CORNER
2900 W BELMONT AVE
HEAVY METAL BAR WITH FAMOUS BURGERS AND LOTS
OF INK.

**8 LANE TECHNICAL COLLEGE PREP
HIGH SCHOOL**
2501 W ADDISON ST
MASSIVE GOTHICSTYLE PUBLIC HIGH SCHOOL.

9 MORRIS B. SACHS BUILDING
2800 N MILWAUKEE AVE
HISTORIC FLATIRON BUILDING AND BURGEONING ART
CENTER.

10 MR POLLO
3000 W BELMONT AVE
SOUTH AMERICAN CHICKEN JOINT. GET A GUANABANA
SHAKE.

11 Ñ
2977 N ELSTON AVE
ARGENTINIAN FLAIR AND ELECTRO GROOVES.

12 NELLY'S SALOON
3256 N ELSTON AVE
ROMANIAN HANGOUT WITH OCCASIONAL LIVE MUSIC.

13 ORBIT ROOM
2959 N CALIFORNIA AVE
GRAB A CRAFT COCKTAIL ON THE SUNNY PATIO.

14 REVIVE HOME & GARDEN
3046 N ELSTON AVE
PLANT NURSERY AND GIFT SHOP.

15 REVOLUTION BREWERY
3340 N KEDZIE AVE
GRAB A PINT AND GLIMPSE BEHIND THE SCENES OF
THE LOCAL BREWER.

16 SMALL BAR
2956 N ALBANY AVE
GREAT DOMESTIC BREWS, IMPORTED BOOZE AND A
CHILL VIBE.

17 SQUARE BAR & GRILL
2849 W BELMONT AVE
A BURGER SHOWDOWN IN AVONDALE.

18 TAQUERIA TRASPASADA
3144 N CALIFORNIA AVE
TASTY, CHEAP TACOS AND SALSA.

19 YUSHO
2853 N KEDZIE AVE
AFFORDABLE RAMEN HOT SPOT.

20 ZEN TECAS
2934 W DIVERSEY PKWY
TYPICAL TAQUERIA.

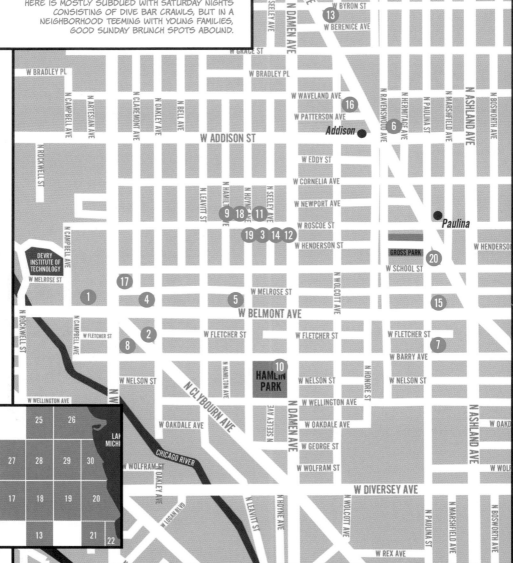

MAP 28 • NORTH CENTER / ROSCOE VILLAGE / WEST LAKEVIEW

THE TAN, FIT, STROLLER-PUSHING SET RULE IN
ROSCOE VILLAGE AND WEST LAKEVIEW. THE NORTH
SIDE JEWEL IS POPULATED WITH GRAY- AND
BROWNSTONES, LUSH, TINY GREEN LAWNS, FUNKY
BOUTIQUES, EXPENSIVE GROCERY STORES AND
COZY NEIGHBORHOOD RESTAURANTS. THE NIGHTLIFE
HERE IS MOSTLY SUBDUED WITH SATURDAY NIGHTS
CONSISTING OF DIVE BAR CRAWLS, BUT IN A
NEIGHBORHOOD TEEMING WITH YOUNG FAMILIES,
GOOD SUNDAY BRUNCH SPOTS ABOUND.

1 19TH DISTRICT
2452 W BELMONT AVE
GOING TO "WESTERN & BELMONT" USED TO BE SYNONYMOUS WITH BEING IN DEEP SH#*.

2 90 MILES CUBAN CAFÉ
3101 N CLYBOURN AVE
CASUAL CUBAN, COUNTER SEATING ONLY.

3 A PIED
2037 W ROSCOE ST
FUNKY SHOE BOUTIQUE SHOWCASING EUROPEAN BRANDS.

4 ANDY'S MUSIC
2300 W BELMONT AVE
KNOCK YOURSELF OUT BROWSING THE EXOTIC MUSICAL INSTRUMENTS SOLD HERE.

5 BEAT KITCHEN
2100 W BELMONT AVE
HIP MUSIC SPOT AND BAR.

6 CAFÉ ORCHID
1746 W ADDISON ST
AUTHENTIC TURKISH FOOD SERVED IN A ROMANTIC HIDEAWAY.

7 CODY'S PUBLIC HOUSE
1658 W BARRY AVE
NAMED AFTER THE OWNER'S DOG. GREAT BACKYARD PATIO.

8 CONSTELLATION
3111 N WESTERN AVE
LINKS HALL&MIKE REED PARTNERSHIP IN FORMER VIADUCT THEATRE.

9 FIXTURE
2108 W ROSCOE ST
GIFT SHOP FEATURING LOCAL DESIGNERS.

10 HAMLIN PARK FIELDHOUSE
3035 N DAMEN AVE
A CHICAGO PARK DISTRICT FACILITY AT ITS BEST.

11 HUBBA HUBBA
2040 W ROSCOE ST
BOUTIQUE JEWELRY AND CLOTHING AT MODERATE PRICES.

12 KITSCH'N ON ROSCOE
2005 W ROSCOE ST
CLEVER RETRO FOOD AND TIKI BAR. FRIENDLY STAFF.

13 MARTYRS'
3855 N LINCOLN AVE
GREAT STAGE FOR LIVE ACTS.

14 ORANGE RESTAURANT
2011 W ROSCOE ST
COZY BRUNCH SPOT.

15 SCOOTER'S FROZEN CUSTARD
1658 W BELMONT AVE
THE TASTIEST CUSTARD THIS SIDE OF ST. LOUIS.

16 SURPLUS OF OPTIONS
3664 N LINCOLN AVE
EVERYTHING YOU WANTED THAT GRANDMA GAVE UP.

17 UNDERBAR
3243 N WESTERN AVE
THERE ARE MORE DEPRESSING 4AM BARS.

18 VICTORY'S BANNER
2100 W ROSCOE ST
VEGETARIAN BRUNCH SERVED BY TOGA-CLAD SRI CHIMNOY FOLLOWERS.

19 VILLAGE TAP
2055 W ROSCOE ST
NEIGHBORHOOD ICON WITH A TOUCH OF CLASS.

20 WISHBONE
3300 N LINCOLN AVE
LAKEVIEW FLOCKS TO THIS SOUTHERN-FOCUSED SPOT FOR SUNDAY BRUNCH.

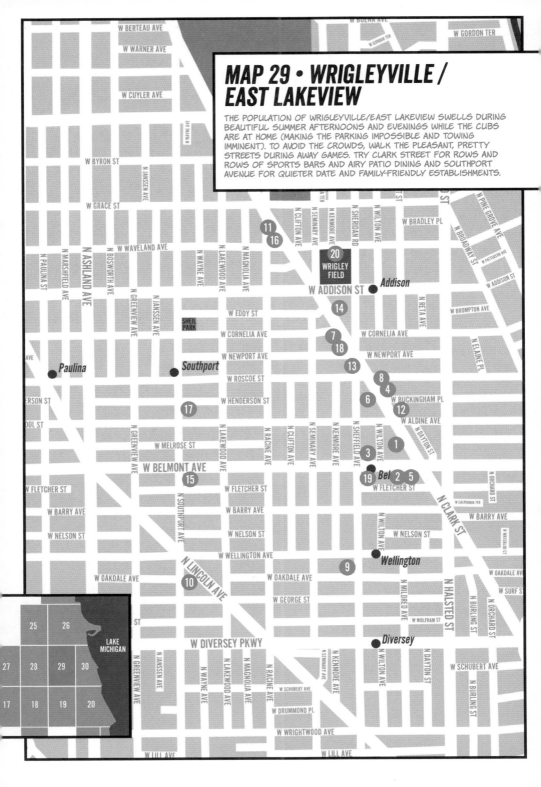

MAP 29 • WRIGLEYVILLE / EAST LAKEVIEW

THE POPULATION OF WRIGLEYVILLE/EAST LAKEVIEW SWELLS DURING BEAUTIFUL SUMMER AFTERNOONS AND EVENINGS WHILE THE CUBS ARE AT HOME (MAKING THE PARKING IMPOSSIBLE AND TOWING IMMINENT). TO AVOID THE CROWDS, WALK THE PLEASANT, PRETTY STREETS DURING AWAY GAMES. TRY CLARK STREET FOR ROWS AND ROWS OF SPORTS BARS AND AIRY PATIO DINING AND SOUTHPORT AVENUE FOR QUIETER DATE AND FAMILY-FRIENDLY ESTABLISHMENTS.

① THE ALLEY
3228 N CLARK ST
SKULLS, TATTOOS, BIG BOOTS.

② ANN SATHER
909 W BELMONT AVE
HUGE CINNAMON ROLLS AND SWEDISH COMFORT FOOD.

③ BERLIN
954 W BELMONT AVE
TINY, CLASSIC, "PANSEXUAL" DANCE CLUB.

④ BLOKES AND BIRDS
3343 N CLARK ST
YUMMY TRADITIONAL ENGLISH FARE.

⑤ BELMONT ARMY
855 W BELMONT AVE
MOSTLY FASHION; LITTLE BIT OF MILITARY.

⑥ BOLAT
3346 N CLARK ST
WEST AFRICAN CUISINE.

⑦ BOOKWORKS
3444 N CLARK ST
USED AND RARE BOOKS.

⑧ HOUNDSTOOTH SALOON
3369 N CLARK ST
SOUTHERN HOSPITALITY AND CRIMSON TIDE ALUMNI
AND FANS.

⑨ KIRKWOOD
2934 N SHEFFIELD AVE
DRINK LIKE A FISH OR OUT OF A FISH BOWL AT THIS
HAVEN FOR HOOSIER ALUMNI.

⑩ LAS TABLAS COLOMBIAN STEAKHOUSE
2942 N LINCOLN AVE
CHIM CHIM-NEY, CHIM CHIM-NEY…CHIMICHURRI.

⑪ METRO
3730 N CLARK ST
INTERNATIONALLY RENOWNED VENUE FOR TOP
LOCAL AND TOURING ROCK MUSIC.

⑫ MIA FRANCESCA
3311 N CLARK ST
CONTEMPORARY ITALIAN DATE PLACE.

⑬ PICK ME UP
3408 N CLARK ST
24 HOUR CAFÉ; OVERFLOWS AFTER THE BARS CLOSE.

⑭ RED IVY
3525 N CLARK ST
PART SPORTS BAR, PART PIZZERIA, PART SPEAKEASY.

⑮ SCHUBAS
3159 N SOUTHPORT AVE
TOP LIVE MUSIC STAPLE WITH ATTACHED RESTAURANT.

⑯ SMART BAR
3730 N CLARK ST
CLUB KIDS UNITE!

⑰ SOUTHPORT LANES & BILLIARDS
3325 N SOUTHPORT AVE
CUTE PLACE WITH REAL, LIVE PINSETTERS.

⑱ STRANGE CARGO
3448 N CLARK ST
HIP, AFFORDABLE THREADS.

⑲ THE VIC
3145 N SHEFFIELD AVE
DRINK, WATCH FILMS, AND TAKE IN AN OCCASIONAL
BAND AT THIS OLD THEATRE.

⑳ WRIGLEY FIELD
1060 W ADDISON ST
CHARM-FILLED BALLPARK THAT REMAINS INDIFFERENT
TO WINS OR LOSSES.

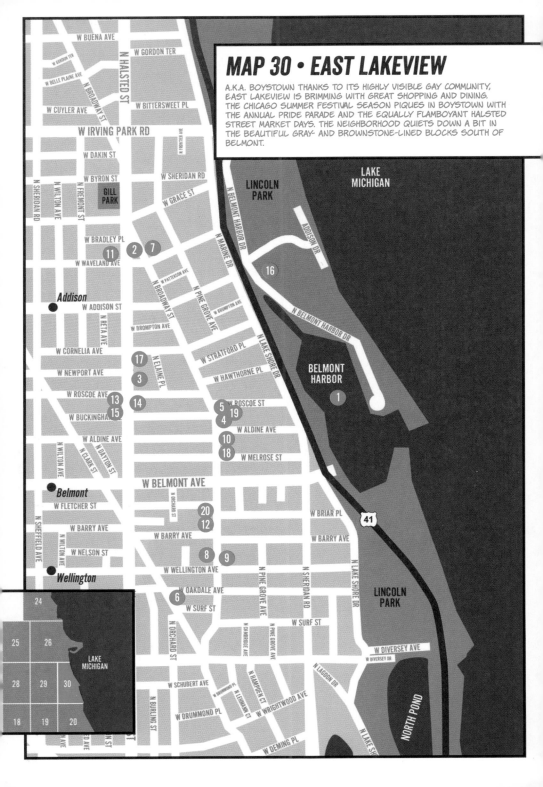

MAP 30 · EAST LAKEVIEW

A.K.A. BOYSTOWN THANKS TO ITS HIGHLY VISIBLE GAY COMMUNITY, EAST LAKEVIEW IS BRIMMING WITH GREAT SHOPPING AND DINING. THE CHICAGO SUMMER FESTIVAL SEASON PIQUES IN BOYSTOWN WITH THE ANNUAL PRIDE PARADE AND THE EQUALLY FLAMBOYANT HALSTED STREET MARKET DAYS. THE NEIGHBORHOOD QUIETS DOWN A BIT IN THE BEAUTIFUL GRAY- AND BROWNSTONE-LINED BLOCKS SOUTH OF BELMONT.

1 BELMONT HARBOR
3600 RECREATION DR
HOME TO THE CHICAGO YACHT CLUB SAILING SCHOOL.

2 CHARLIE'S CHICAGO
3726 N BROADWAY ST
GAY COUNTRY AND WESTERN BAR. THAT'S RIGHT.

3 THE CHICAGO DINER
3411 N HALSTED ST
A VEGETARIAN INSTITUTION.

4 THE CLOSET
3325 N BROADWAY ST
BOY-FRIENDLY, LESBIAN BAR; 4 AM LICENSE.

5 CRAM FASHION
3331 N BROADWAY ST
GOOD FASHION DOESN'T HAVE TO COST SO MUCH.

6 DUKE OF PERTH
2931 N CLARK ST
SHADES OF EDINBURGH, ALONG WITH REQUISITE
WHISKIES AND FISH & CHIPS.

7 F. O'MAHONY'S
3701 N BROADWAY ST
FOOD WHEN YOU NEED IT (LATE!) AND A SEASONAL
MENU.

8 FRIAR TUCK
3010 N BROADWAY ST
ENTER THROUGH A BARREL. YUP, A BARREL.

9 JOHNNY SPROCKETS
3001 N BROADWAY ST
CATERING TO ALL YOUR BICYCLE NEEDS.

10 JOY'S NOODLES & RICE
3257 N BROADWAY ST
STANDARD NOODLES, SOUP, OR FRIED RICE; IMPRES-
SIVELY SIMPLE.

11 KIT KAT LOUNGE
3700 N HALSTED ST
DRAG SHOWS WHILE YOU DINE.

12 RECKLESS RECORDS
3126 N BROADWAY ST
OLDIES AND NEW RELEASES ON VINYL.

13 ROSCOE'S
3356 N HALSTED ST
CAVERNOUS MINGLING FOR THE GAY SWEATER SET.

14 SIDETRACK
3349 N HALSTED ST
POPULAR SHOWTUNE SING-A-LONGS!

15 TOWN HALL PUB
3340 N HALSTED ST
UNASSUMING, MIXED CLIENTELE AND LIVE MUSIC.

16 TOTEM POLE
3600 N LAKE SHORE DR
WHERE DID IT COME FROM? WHY IS IT THERE? NOBODY
KNOWS.

17 TULIP TOY GALLERY
3459 N HALSTED ST
WOMAN-OWNED, INVITING SEX PARAPHERNALIA SHOP.

18 UNABRIDGED BOOKSTORE
3251 N BROADWAY ST
HELPFUL BOOKSTORE WITH GREAT TRAVEL, KIDS,
DISCOUNT AND GAY SECTIONS.

19 WAKAMONO
3317 N BROADWAY ST
SUSHI AND JAPANESE SMALL PLATES.

20 WILDE
3130 N BROADWAY ST
UPSCALE IRISH WITH GOOD FOOD AND PLENTY OF
AMBIENCE.

BEVERLY/MORGAN PARK

OVERVIEW

Beverly Hills, best known simply as Beverly, is the stronghold of Chicago's heralded "South Side Irish" community. An authentic medieval castle, baronial mansions, rolling hills, and plenty of pubs compose Chicago's Emerald Isle.

Once populated by Illinois and Potawatomi Indian tribes, Beverly became home to clans of Irish-American families after the Great Chicago Fire. Famous residents include Andrew Greeley, Brian Piccolo, George Wendt, the Schwinn Bicycle family, and decades of loyal Chicago civil servants. Proud and protective of their turf, these close-knit South Siders call Beverly and its sister community, Morgan Park, "the Ridge." The integrated neighborhood occupies the highest ground in Chicago, 30 to 60 feet above the rest of the city atop Blue Island Ridge. Although the Ridge is just 15 miles from the Loop, most North Siders only trek there for the South Side Irish Parade (www.southsideirishparade.org), which attracts hundreds of thousands of people each year around St. Patrick's Day.

And there is more to Beverly than green beer and craic. The Ridge Historic District is one of the country's largest urban areas on the National Register of Historic Places. Beverly and Morgan Park encompass four landmark districts including the Ridge Historic District, three Chicago Landmark Districts, and over 30 Prairie-style structures.

ARCHITECTURE

Within approximately a nine-mile radius, from 87th Street to 115th Street and Prospect Avenue to Hoyne Avenue, one can view a vast collection of homes and public buildings representing American architectural styles developed between 1844 and World War II. The 109th block of Prospect Avenue, every inch of Longwood Drive, and the Victorian train stations at 91st Street, 95th Street, 99th Street, 107th Street, 111th Street, and 115th Street are all great Chicago landmarks. Walter Burley Griffin Place on W 104th Street has Chicago's largest concentration of Prairie School houses built between 1909 and 1913 by Griffin, a student of Frank Lloyd Wright and designer of the city of Canberra in Australia.

Beverly Area Planning Association (www.bapa.org) provides a good architectural map; history buffs and researchers should get in contact with the Ridge Historical Society (www.ridgehistoricalsociety.org).

CULTURE & EVENTS

The Beverly Arts Center is the epicenter of Ridge culture. The $8 million facility provides visual and performance art classes for all ages as well as events and festivals (2407 W 111th St, 773-445-3838; www.beverlyartcenter.org). Historic Ridge homes open their doors to the public in the fall for the annual Home Tour, Chicago's oldest such tour. Sites are chosen for their diverse architectural styles and historical significance. The Home Tour is organized by the Beverly Area Planning Association (www.bapa.org), and guided trolley tours are also offered for an additional fee.

WHERE TO EAT AND DRINK

• **Rainbow Cone**, 9233 S Western Ave. Ice cream. People line up day and night in the summer.

• **Top Notch Beefburger**, 2116 W 95th St. Burgers really are top notch at this '50s-style grill.

• **Lanigan's Irish Pub**, 3119 W 111th St. Live celtic music from time-to-time.

• **Mrs. O'Leary's Dubliner**, 10910 S Western Ave. One of the many Irish pubs lining Western Avenue.

BROOKFIELD ZOO

GENERAL INFORMATION

ADDRESS: **31ST ST & FIRST AVE, BROOKFIELD, IL 60513**

PHONE: **708-688-8000**

WEBSITE: **WWW.BROOKFIELDZOO.ORG**

TWITTER **@BROOKFIELD_ZOO**

HOURS: **OPEN MONDAY–FRIDAY 10 AM–5 PM AND SATURDAY & SUNDAY 10 AM–6 PM**

ADMISSION: **$16.95 ADULTS, $11.95 CHILDREN 3-11, SENIORS OVER 65, FREE FOR CHILDREN TWO AND UNDER**

OVERVIEW

While Lincoln Park Zoo is free, Brookfield offers a far more comprehensive wild animal experience with a strong emphasis on conservation education. 216 acres of creepy critters make for a memorable day trip. We'll skip the analogy with the Joliet Riverboat Casino.

HAMILL FAMILY PLAY ZOO

This interactive play area is dedicated solely to kids (just what a zoo needs: more kids). Children get to interact in a variety of ways, including donning costumes to play "zoo keeper" or "ring-tailed lemur," creating and frolicking in their own simulated habitats, planting seeds in the greenhouse, or spotting creepy insects in the outdoor bug path. Think a grownup would look silly dressed like a lemur? We want to play! Admission $2.50.

REGENSTEIN WOLF WOODS

The zoo's impressive wolf exhibit allows visitors to follow the progress of a small pack of endangered male wolves as they do the wolfy things wolves do — when they're not sleeping, of course. One-way glass allows spectators to get up close and personal with the wolves without freaking them out. So far, the mirrors have been 100% unsuccessful in detecting any wolf shoplifting.

OTHER EXHIBITS

Of course the zoo is full of exhibits, some more fascinating than others. Among them are the seasonal butterfly exhibit and the dragonfly marsh. Here are some other worthwhile sights:

• *Habitat Africa!*: This is broken up into two sections: The Forest, with small antelopes and other quiet animals and The Savannah, with our favorite, the giraffes.

• *Tropic World:* Visit Kamba, the gorilla born in front of a captivated, slightly disgusted crowd of zoo visitors (mother Koola now knows how Marie Antoinette felt when she shared the delivery of her offspring with the French peasantry) and Bakari, who was born to mother Binto.

• *Stingray Bay:* 50 cownose rays swim in a 16,000-gallon saltwater tank, ready for slimy cuddles! Get up close and personal with the creatures as they glide underneath your fingertips. Admission is $4 for adults, $2.50 for seniors 65 and over and children 3 to 11.

• *Big Cats:* Visit lions, tigers, and snow leopards and they prance, purr, and prowl. Part of The Fragile Kingdom exhibit, the Big Cats are impressive and beautiful in their natural habitat.

• *Great Bear Wilderness:* The Great Bear Wildness features two iconic North American animals: Polar bears and Grizzly Bears.

HOW TO GET THERE

By Car: From the Eisenhower or Stevens Expressway, exit at First Avenue. From there, signs will direct you the short distance to the zoo. Lot parking is $10.

By Train: From downtown Chicago, take the Burlington Northern Metra line to Zoo Stop/Hollywood Station.

By Bus: Pace buses 304 and 331 stop right at the zoo's gates.

PHOTO: ERIC DANLEY

CHICAGO BOTANIC GARDEN

GENERAL INFORMATION

ADDRESS: 1000 LAKE COOK RD, GLENCOE, IL 60022
PHONE: 847-835-5440
WEBSITE: WWW.CHICAGOBOTANIC.ORG OR @CHICAGOBOTANIC
HOURS: OPEN 365 DAYS, HOURS VARY SEASONALLY BASED ON DAYLIGHT
ADMISSION: FREE

OVERVIEW

Occupying 385 acres, the serene and lovely Chicago Botanic Garden has been the backdrop for many a chi-chi wedding since they opened the gates in 1972. The Botanic Garden is comprised of 26 gardens and four natural area. Among them are a specialized Japanese garden, a rose garden, a bulb garden, a greenhouse full of tropical vegetation, a waterfall garden, and several beds solely dedicated to indigenous plants and flowers. Constructed around nine islands with six miles of lake shoreline, the Botanic Garden is one of a select group of public gardens accredited by the American Association of Museums.

The Garden hosts changing exhibits and events, including its popular Model Railroad Garden which features American landmarks made from plant material. Both the Ikebana Society and Macy's sponsor flower shows throughout the year; check the events schedule online to see what's going on before visiting. The Chicago Botanic Garden also offers lifestyle/wellness classes, including yoga and tai chi. Availability and times vary; check the website or call for more information.

The Botanic Garden serves food at the Garden View Café, which offers breakfast and café fare with a focus on local and sustainable plus barista-helmed coffee. The Garden Grille serves up burgers and other grillables in season. Also in season, enjoy a beverage overlooking the roses at the Rose Terrace Café. Picnicking is allowed in the Picnic Glen, by Parking Lot 2.

HOW TO GET THERE

By Car: Take I-90/94 W (The Kennedy) to I-94 (The Edens) and US 41. Exit on Lake Cook Road, then go a half-mile east to the garden. Parking costs $25 per car and $10 for seniors on Tuesdays.

By Train: Take the Union Pacific North Line to Braeside Metra station in Highland Park. Walk west about one mile along Lake Cook Road (aka County Line Road). If you ride the train to the Glencoe station, you can take a trolley directly to the garden. Round-trip tickets cost $2, free for children five and under.

By Bus: The Pace bus 213 connects at Davis Street in Evanston, and the Park Avenue Glencoe and Central Street Highland Park Metra stops. Buses don't run on Sundays and holidays.

By Bicycle: The Chicago Bikeway System winds through the forest preserves all the way up to the garden. Join it near the Billy Caldwell Golf Club at 6200 N Caldwell. A bicycle map is available on the Botanic Garden website.

CHICAGO CULTURAL CENTER

GENERAL INFORMATION

NFT MAPS: *5, 6*

ADDRESS: *78 E WASHINGTON ST, CHICAGO, IL 60602*

WEBSITE: *WWW.CHICAGOCULTURALCENTER.ORG OR @ CHICULTURCENTER*

HOURS: *MON–THURS 9 AM–7 PM, FRI 9 AM–6 PM, SAT 9 AM–6 PM, SUN 10 AM–6 PM*

OVERVIEW

The Chicago Cultural Center is the Loop's public arts center. Free–that's right, we said FREE–concerts, theatrical performances, films, lectures, and exhibits are offered daily. Admission to the Cultural Center and its art galleries are all free, too, as is its WiFi, in case you're in a bind.

The building itself, constructed in 1897, is a neoclassical landmark featuring intricate glass and marble mosaics on its walls and grand stairways. Once the city's central public library, the Cultural Center boasts the world's largest Tiffany dome in Preston Bradley Hall. Free (there's that lovely word again) 45-minute architectural tours are held on Wednesdays, Fridays, and Saturdays at 1:15 pm. Tours meet at the Randolph Street lobby and are limited to the first 20 people. The building is also home to one of the city's popular Visitor Information Centers, which provide custom itineraries for tourists, multilingual maps, and concierge services. You can also find "InstaGreeters" from the Chicago Greeter Program, who will give on-the-spot walking tours. The Greeters also offer free two- to four-hour walking tours with chatty and knowledgeable guides around one of any number of neighborhoods throughout the city; book in advance via www.chicagogreeter.com.

PERFORMANCES

The Chicago Cultural Center offers a number of daytime concerts around the year for all ages in various genres in its Preston Bradley Hall.

ART GALLERIES

A permanent exhibit in the Landmark Gallery, "Stand Up for Landmarks! Protests, Posters & Pictures " is a stunning black-and-white photographic survey of Chicago architecture. Five additional galleries regularly rotate exhibits, showcasing work in many media by renowned and local artists. Tours of current exhibits are ongoing.

HOW TO GET THERE

By Car: Travel down Michigan Avenue to Randolph Street. From Lake Shore Drive, exit at Randolph Street.

By Train: From the Richard B. Ogilvie Transportation Center, travel east to Michigan Avenue on CTA buses 20, 56, 60, and 157. From Union Station, take CTA buses 151 and 157. From the Randolph Street station below Millennium Park, walk west across Michigan Avenue.

By L: Take the Green, Brown, Orange, Purple, or Pink Line to the Randolph stop. Walk east one block.

By Bus: CTA buses : 3, 145, 147, 151 stop on Michigan Avenue in front of the Cultural Center.

HAROLD WASHINGTON LIBRARY CENTER

GENERAL INFORMATION

NFT MAP: *5*
ADDRESS: *400 S STATE ST, CHICAGO, IL 60605*
PHONE: *312-747-4300*
WEBSITE: *WWW.CHIPUBLIB.ORG OR @CHIPUBLIB*
HOURS: *MON–THURS 9 AM–9 PM, FRI–SAT 9 AM–5 PM, SUN 1 PM–5 PM*

OVERVIEW

The massive Harold Washington Library Center is named for Harold Washington (1925–1987), Chicago's first African American mayor, who served from 1983 until he died in office (literally in office–he was in meeting about school issues at the time) in 1987. Said to be the world's largest public library, the 756,640-square-foot neoclassical architectural monstrosity has over 70 miles of shelves storing more than 9 million books, microforms, serials, and government documents. Notable works of sculpture, painting, and mosaics liven up the building's ample wall space and open areas.

Harold Washington's popular library, containing current general titles and bestsellers, is easy to find on the ground floor. The library's audio-visual collection (including an impressive collection of books on tape as well as videos, DVDs, and popular music CDs) is also housed here. The second floor is home to the children's library, and the general reference library begins on the third floor where the circulation desks are located. Among the notable features of the library is the eighth floor Music Information Center housing sheet music and printed scores, 150,000 recordings, the Chicago Blues Archives, eight individual piano practice rooms, and a chamber music rehearsal room. The ninth floor Winter Garden, with its olive trees and soaring 100-foot high ceilings is a popular site for special events. If you have your sights set on getting hitched here, leave your priest or rabbi at home–the library's status as a civic building precludes religious services on its premises.

Frequent free public programs are held in the lower level's 385-seat auditorium, video theater, exhibit hall, and meeting rooms; check the online Events page for more details.

RESEARCH SERVICES

To check the availability or location of an item, search the library's Online Catalog on www.chipublib.org. The Chat With a Librarian feature is available Mon–Fri 9 am–12 noon, or try emailing (response within two days). For faster answers to common research questions, check out the website's selection of free online resources.

COMPUTER SERVICES

The Chicago Public Library's High Speed Wireless Internet System provides free access; all you need is a wireless enabled laptop computer,

tablet PC, or PDA. The Library's network is open to all visitors free of charge and without filters. No special encryption settings, user names, or passwords are required.

The library's computers with Internet access and word processing, desktop publishing, graphic presentation, and spreadsheet applications are located on the third floor in the Computer Commons. Computer use is free and available on a first-come-first-served basis. You can reserve computers online and for up to two one-hour sessions per day. For downloads, bring your own flash drive or purchase one at the library for a fee. Laser printing is also provided for 15 cents a page.

THOMAS HUGHES CHILDREN'S LIBRARY

The 18,000-square-foot Thomas Hughes Children's Library on the second floor serves children through eighth grade. A British citizen and member of Parliament, Thomas Hughes was so taken by news of the tragic Chicago Fire that he started a book collection for Chicago. His collection resulted in the 8,000 titles that composed the first Chicago Public Library. In addition to more than 120,000 children's books representing 40 foreign languages, there is a reference collection on children's literature for adults. Computers with

Internet connections are also available. Children's programs are hosted weekly.

SPECIAL COLLECTIONS

The library's Special Collections & Preservation Division's highlights include: Harold Washington Collection, Civil War & American History Research Collection, Chicago Authors & Publishing Collection, Chicago Blues Archives, Chicago Theater Collection, World's Columbian Exposition Collection, and Neighborhood History Research Collection. The collections' reading room is closed Wednesday, Thursday, and Sunday.

HOW TO GET THERE

By Car: The library is at the intersection of State Street and Congress Parkway in South Loop. Take I-290 E into the Loop.

By L: The Brown, Purple, Orange, and Pink Lines stop at the Library Station. Exit the Red Line and O'Hare Airport Blue Line at Van Buren Station; walk one block south. Change from the Harlem/Lake Street Green Line to the northbound Orange Line at Roosevelt Road station; get off at Library Station.

By Bus: CTA buses that stop on State Street in front of the library are the 2, 6, 10, 29, 36, 62, 151, 145, 146, and 147.

OVERVIEW

Bordering the city to the north and surrounded by beautiful lakeshore scenery and affluent suburbs, Evanston may seem a world away. Truth be told, this town is only 12 miles from Chicago's bustling Loop. Spacious Victorian and Prairie Style homes with mini-vans and Mercedes parked on tree-lined streets overlook Lake Michigan and surround the quaint college town's downtown. Unlike other development-minded and sub-divided suburbs, Evanston still maintains a Chicago-esque feel and remains one of its most attractive bordering municipalities. Of course, Evanston residents still walk with their noses in the air and even charge their city neighbors to visit their beaches. We wonder what their tax base would look like without the city. Once home to Potawatami Indians, Evanston was actually founded after the establishment of the town's most well-known landmark, Northwestern University. Plans for the school began in 1851, and after the university opened for business four years later, its founder John Evans (along with a bunch of other Methodist dudes) proposed the establishment of the city, and so the town was incorporated as the village of Evanston in 1863. Today, residents are as devoted to cultural and intellectual pursuits as the morally minded patriarchs were

to enforcing prohibition. The sophisticated, racially diverse suburb of roughly 75,000 packs a lot of business and entertainment into nearly eight square miles. Superb museums, many national historic landmarks, parks, artistic events, eclectic shops, and theaters make up for any subpar seasons by Northwestern University's Wildcats in the competitive Big Ten conference.

CULTURE

Evanston has several museums and some interesting festivals that merit a visit. Besides Northwestern's Block Museum of Art (www.blockmuseum. northwestern.edu), the impressive Mitchell Museum of the American Indian (www.mitchellmuseum.org) showcases life of the Midwest's Native Americans. The 1865 home of Frances E. Willard, founder of the Women's Christian Temperance Union and a women's suffrage leader, is located at 1730 Chicago Avenue (www.franceswillardhouse. org). Tours of the historic home are offered on the afternoons of every first and third Sunday of each month. Admission costs $10 for adults and $5 for children 12 and under.

FESTIVALS & EVENTS

• *April:* Evanston goes Baroque during Bach Week, www.bachweek.org

• *June:* Fountain Square Arts Festival and free Starlight Concerts hosted in many of the city's parks through August

• *July:* Ethnic Arts Festival

NATURE

Evanston is blessed with five public beaches open June through Labor Day. Non-residents should remember their wallets to pay for beach passes. For hours, fees, and boating information, contact the City of Evanston's Recreation Division (www.cityofevanston.org). The town's most popular parks encircle its beaches: Grosse Point Lighthouse Park, Centennial Park, Burnham Shores Park, Dawes Park, and South Boulevard Beach Park. All are connected by a bike path and fitness trail. On clear days, Chicago's skyline is visible from Northwestern's campus. West of downtown, McCormick, Twiggs, and Herbert Parks flank the North Shore Channel. Bicycle trails thread along the shore from Green Bay Road south to Main Street. North of Green Bay Road is Canal Shores Golf Course, a short 18-hole, par 60 public links at 1031 Central Street (www.canalshores.org) and the Evanston Ecology Center and Ladd Arboretum, located at 2024 McCormick Boulevard (www.evanstonenvironment.org).

HOW TO GET THERE

By Car: Lake Shore Drive to Sheridan Road is the most direct and scenic route from Chicago to Evanston. Drive north on LSD, which ends at Hollywood; then drive west to Sheridan and continue north. Near downtown, Sheridan becomes Burnham Place briefly, then Forest Avenue. Go north on Forest, which turns into Sheridan again by lakefront Centennial Park.

Parking: Watch how and where you park. The rules and regulations are strict and fiercely enforced. Remember...Evanston police do not have much to do.

By Train: Metra's Union Pacific North Line departing from the Richard B. Ogilvie Transportation Center in West Loop stops at the downtown Davis Street CTA Center station, 25 minutes from the Loop. This station is the town transportation hub, where Metra and L trains and buses interconnect.

By L: The CTA Purple Line Express L train travels direct to and from the Loop during rush hours. Other hours, ride the Howard-Dan Ryan Red Line to Howard Street, and transfer to the Purple Line for free.

By Bus: From Chicago's Howard Street Station, CTA and Pace Suburban buses serve Evanston.

GARFIELD PARK

OVERVIEW

Since 1908 the historic West Side has been home to an equally historic botanical gem–Garfield Park Conservatory. The mid 1990s saw major restoration efforts, along with the creation of The Garfield Park Conservatory Alliance, an organization that has raised money for various programs involving the Conservatory. The rest of the vast 185-acre park boasts fishing lagoons, a swimming pool, an ice rink, baseball diamonds, and basketball and tennis courts. Garfield Park's landmark Gold Dome Building houses a gymnasium, fitness center, boxing center, grand ballroom, and various meeting rooms.

Garfield and its sister parks–Humboldt Park (1400 N Sacramento Ave, 312-742-7549) and Douglas Park (1401 S Sacramento Dr, 773-762-2842)–constitute a grand system of sprawling green spaces linked by broad boulevards designed in 1869 by William Le Baron Jenney (better known as the "father of the skyscraper"). However, Jenney's plan didn't bear fruit until almost 40 years later (after the uprooting of corrupt park officials), when Danish immigrant and former park laborer Jens Jensen became chief landscape architect. In 1908, Jensen completed the parks and consolidated their three small conservatories under the 1.8-acre Garfield Park Conservatory's curvaceous glass dome meant to evoke a "great Midwestern haystack."

GARFIELD PARK CONSERVATORY

ADDRESS: *300 N CENTRAL PARK AVE, CHICAGO, IL 60624*
PHONE: *312-746-5100*
WEBSITE: *WWW.GARFIELD-CONSERVATORY.ORG OR @GPCONSERVATORY*
HOURS: *9 AM–5 PM DAILY, WED UNTIL 8 PM*
ADMISSION: *FREE*

One of the nation's largest conservatories, Garfield Park has six thematic plant houses with 1,000 species and more than 10,000 individual plants from around the world. Plants Alive!, a 5,000-square-foot children's garden, has touchable plants, a soil pool for digging, a Jurassic Park-sized bumble bee, and a two-story, twisting flower stem that doubles as a slide. School groups often book the garden for field trips, so check first to determine public access hours. Annual Conservatory events include the Spring Flower Show, Azalea/Camellia Show, Chocolate Festival, Summer Tropical Show, Chrysanthemum (Chicago's city flower) Show, and Holiday Garden Show. Visit online for program scheduling. There is a farmers market at the park on Sundays 11 am–4 pm from June through October.

FISHING

Garfield Park's two lagoons at Washington Boulevard and Central Park Avenue and those at Douglas and Humboldt Parks are favorite West Side fishing holes. Seasonally, they are stocked with bluegill, crappie, channel catfish, and largemouth bass. Eating the fish is another matter. Kids can participate in free fishing sessions at the park lagoons during the summer through the Chicago Park District.

NATURE

The Chicago Park District leads free nature walks and has created marked trails with information plaques at the city's bigger parks, Garfield, Douglas, and Humboldt Parks included. Seasonally, visitors can view as many as 100 species of colorful butterflies at the formal gardens of the three parks. The parks' lagoons are officially designated Chicago birding parks, so take binoculars (see also the Chicago Ornithological Society for more information: www.chicagobirder. org). Picnics for 50 people or more, or tent set-up, require party-throwers to obtain permits issued by the Chicago Park District.

HOW TO GET THERE

By Car: Garfield Park is ten minutes from the Loop. Take I-290 W; exit on Independence Boulevard and drive north. Turn east on Washington Boulevard to Central Park Avenue. Go north on Central Park Avenue two blocks past the Golden Dome field house and Lake Street to the Conservatory. A free parking lot is on the building's south side, just after Lake Street. Street parking is available on Central Park Avenue, Madison Street, and Washington Boulevard.

By L: From the Loop, take the Green Line west to the Conservatory-Central Park Drive stop, a charming renovated Victorian train station at Lake Street and Central Park Avenue.

By Bus: From the Loop, board CTA 20 Madison Street bus westbound. Get off at Madison Street and Central Park Avenue. Walk four blocks north to the Conservatory.

GRANT PARK

OVERVIEW

Grant Park, where grass meets glass, is Chicago's venerable "front lawn." Spanning the Lake Michigan shoreline from N Randolph Street to S Roosevelt Road and west to Michigan Avenue, it's safe to say there's not a more trafficked park this side of New York City's Central Park. Grant Park is a study in contrasts: on the one side featuring massive summer festivals (such as the annual homage to obesity known as Taste of Chicago) that turn the park into Chicago's dirty doormat; but during the rest of the year, a quiet place to relax, play, and count the number of panhandlers who ask if you can "help them out with a dollar."

The park's history can be traced back to 1835 when concerned citizens lobbied to prevent development along their pristine waterfront. Little did they know that when the State of Illinois ruled to preserve the land as "public ground forever to remain vacant of buildings" this meant for everyone, including the wealthy elite who were literally perched on the lofty balconies of the tawny palaces that lined the downtown shores of Lake Michigan. Be careful what you wish for, yes? Architect and city planner Daniel Burnham laid the groundwork for the park and made plans to erect museums, civic buildings, and general park attractions along the waterfront. This plan got somewhat sidetracked by the Great Chicago Fire of 1871. Interestingly enough, remaining debris from the fire was pushed into the lake and now forms part of the foundation for much of Grant Park and Chicago's famous shoreline. Chicagoans can thank local land-lover and legendary mail-order magnate Aaron Montgomery Ward for pressuring the State of Illinois in 1911 to preserve the land as an undeveloped open space.

NATURE

Grant Park's lawns, gardens, lakefront, and bench-lined paths attract a mixed crowd of lunching office workers, exercise fanatics, readers, gawking tourists, homeless and not-so-homeless vagabonds, and just your run-of-the-mill idiots. South and north of famous Buckingham Fountain are the formal Spirit of Music Garden and Rose Garden, respectively. There are also a multitude of sculptures, ranging in form and style, strewn with abandon throughout the park, so expect to see art appreciators and imitators alike milling about as well.

SPORTS

Much of the sports areas in Grant Park are on the south end of the park. Baseball diamonds and tennis courts are available on a first-come basis unless they are reserved for league play. There is also a skate park, volleyball courts and a field house.

MAGGIE DALEY PARK

Covering 20 acres in Grant Park's northeast corner, the evolution of what had been Daley Bicentennial Plaza into Maggie Daley Park—named in honor and memory of Chicago's beloved former first lady—came about after the garage underneath needed substantial renovations that necessitated removing the existing plaza. A growing Lakeshore East population and proximity to Millennium Park to the north informed the new park's design, which seamlessly links some of Chicago's top attractions while providing recreation and open space opportunities for Lakeshore residents. Among other things, the plan contains a rock climbing area, a curvy ice skating "ribbon," skate park, and a boffo-brilliant "play garden" ("ground" just seems so...beneath us!) that blows minds with its multi-themes, oversize equipment, slide crater, and water area.

BUCKINGHAM FOUNTAIN

Buckingham Fountain is Grant Park's spouting centerpiece at the intersection of Congress Parkway and Columbus Drive, and was the original starting point of Route 66. Designed by Edward Bennett, the fountain is an homage to Lake Michigan and houses four statues that represent the Lake's four surrounding states (Illinois, Indiana, Michigan, and Wisconsin, ya big idiot). It has been showering onlookers with wind-blown spray since 1927 and, unfortunately, is notable for its role in the opening sequence of the sitcom Married... with Children. In warm weather months, the center basin blasts water 150 feet into the air every 20 minutes all day long. Lights and music accompany the skyrocketing water display during evening hours. Food concessions and restrooms can be found nearby.

FESTIVALS & EVENTS

Chicagoans used to gather at the Petrillo Music Shell for free Grant Park Orchestra and Chorus concerts during the summer months. Now they go to the Jay Pritzker Pavilion in Millennium Park, located between Michigan and Columbus Avenues that, in and of itself, is worth a visit. Concerts take place June through August (www. grantparkmusicfestival.com or @gpmf). You can't always pass up a free headliner concert at Grant Park's monstrous summer festivals. If at all possible, avoid the gut-to-gut feeding frenzy that is the Taste of Chicago. If you must go, hit it on a weekday afternoon; go on the weekend and you'll understand why. In June, get your groove on at the Chicago Blues Fest. If you're really a diehard fan, spend a full paycheck for a three-day pass to Lollapalooza in August. Extra deodorant required. For a complete event schedule, contact the Chicago Department of Cultural Affairs and Special Events at www.cityofchicago.org/dcase.

HOW TO GET THERE

By Car: Exits off Lake Shore Drive west to Grant Park are Randolph Street, Monroe Drive, Jackson Drive, Balbo Drive, and Roosevelt Road. Also, enter the park from Michigan Avenue heading east on the same streets. The underground East Monroe Garage is off Monroe Drive. Columbus Drive runs through Grant Park's center and has metered parking.

By Train: From the Richard B. Ogilvie Transportation Center, travel east to Michigan Avenue and Grant Park on CTA buses 20, 56, 60, and 157. From Union Station, board CTA buses 7 and 126.

Metra trains coming from the south stop at the Roosevelt Road station on the south end of Grant Park before terminating at the underground Millennium Station at Randolph Street.

By L: Get off at any L stop in the Loop between Randolph Street and Van Buren Street. Walk two blocks east to Grant Park.

By Bus: CTA buses 3, 4, 6, 7, 126, 147, and 151 stop along Michigan Avenue in front of Grant Park.

HISTORIC PULLMAN

GENERAL INFORMATION

HISTORIC PULLMAN FOUNDATION: *WWW.PULLMANIL.ORG*
HISTORIC PULLMAN VISITOR CENTER: *11141 S COTTAGE GROVE AVE, 773-785-8901*
HOURS: *TUES–SUN, 11 AM–3 PM*
ADMISSION: *$5 ADULTS, $4 STUDENTS UNDER 18, $4 SENIORS*

OVERVIEW

Although railroad magnate George Pullman's utopian community went belly-up, the Town of Pullman he founded 14 miles south of the Loop survives as a National Landmark Historic District. Built between 1880 and 1885, Pullman is one of America's first planned model industrial communities.

The "workers' paradise" earned Pullman humanitarian hoorahs, as well as a 6% return on his investment. Pullman believed that if laborers and their families lived in comfortable housing with gas, plumbing, and ventilation—in other words, livable conditions—their productivity would increase, as would his profits. Pullman was voted "the world's most perfect town" at the Prague International Hygienic and Pharmaceutical Exposition of 1896.

All was perfect in Pullman until a depression incited workers to strike in 1894, and the idealistic industrialist refused to negotiate with his ungrateful workers. While George Pullman's dream of a model community of indentured servitude died with him in 1897, hatred for him lived on. Pullman's tomb at Graceland Cemetery is more like a bomb shelter. To protect his corpse from irate labor leaders, Pullman was buried under a forest of railroad ties and concrete.

The grounds and buildings that make up Pullman went through most of the twentieth century stayed intact until 1998, when a man who heard voices in his head torched several of the site's primary buildings. Fortunately, die-hard Pullmanites have banded together to maintain the remaining structures, and for anyone interested in labor history or town planning, the city is worth a train or bus ride down from the Loop.

ARCHITECTURE & EVENTS

Architect Solon Beman and landscape architect Nathan Barrett based Pullman's design on French urban plans. Way back when, Pullman was made up of mostly brick rowhouses (95% still in use), several parks, shops, schools, churches, and a library, as well as various health, recreational, and cultural facilities.

Today, the compact community's borders are 111th Street (Florence Drive), 115th Street, Cottage Grove Avenue (Pullman Drive), and S Langley Avenue (Fulton Avenue). If you're interested in sightseeing

within the historic district, we suggest you start at the Pullman Visitor Center, housed in the historic Arcade Building. There you can pick up free, self-guided walking tour brochures and watch an informative 15-minute film on the town's history. Check online for additional specialty tour information and lecture details.

Along with self-guided tours, the Visitor Center offers 90-minute guided tours on the first Sunday of the month from May to October; key tour sites include Hotel Florence, Greenstone Church (interior), Market Square, the stables, and the fire station. Tours start at 1:30 and cost $10 for adults, $7 for seniors, and $7 for students. Reservations not required. The annual House Tour in mid-October is a popular Pullman event where several private residences open their doors to the public from 11 am to 5 pm on Saturday and Sunday.

WHERE TO EAT

7 Seas Submarine (11216 S Michigan Ave, 773-785-0550): Dine in or take out at this tiny sandwich shop.

Cal Harbor Restaurant (546 E 115th St, 773-264-5435): Omelettes, burgers, etc. at this family grill.

HOW TO GET THERE

By Car: Take I-94 S to the 111th Street exit. Go west to Cottage Grove Avenue and turn south, driving one block to 112th Street to the Visitor Center surrounded by a large, free parking lot.

By Train: Metra's Electric Main Line departs from Millennium Station (underground) at Michigan Avenue between S Water Street and Randolph Street. Ride 30 minutes to Pullman Station at 111th Street. Walk east to Cottage Grove Avenue, and head south one block to 112th and the Visitor Center.

By L: From the Loop, take the Red Line to the 95th Street station. Board CTA 111 Pullman bus going south.

By Bus: CTA 4 bus from the Randolph Street Station travels south to the 95th Street and Cottage Grove stop. Transfer to 111 Pullman bus heading south, which stops at the visitors center.

JACKSON PARK

OVERVIEW

Historic Jackson Park, named for Mary Jackson, original owner of the land and cousin to president Andrew Jackson, borders Lake Michigan, Hyde Park, and Woodlawn, and was, for a long time, an unused tract of fallow land. The 543-acre parcel was eventually transformed into a real city park in the 1870s thanks to Frederick Law Olmsted and Calvert Vaux of Central Park fame. The Midway Plaisance connects Jackson Park to Washington Park.

Jackson Park experienced its 15 minutes of worldwide fame in 1893 when it played host to the World's Fair Columbian Exposition. Today, the Museum of Science and Industry and La Rabida Children's Hospital and Research Center occupy two of the former fair structures. Situated along the lake, the park features three harbors and beaches. The park is also home to the first golf course west of the Allegheny Mountains.

MUSEUM OF SCIENCE AND INDUSTRY

ADDRESS: 57TH ST & LAKE SHORE DR, CHICAGO, IL 60637

PHONE: 773-684-1414

WEBSITE: WWW.MSICHICAGO.ORG OR @MSICHICAGO

HOURS: 9:30 AM–4 PM DAILY, WITH EXTENDED HOURS UNTIL 5:30 DURING HIGH-TRAFFIC TIMES

Admission: $18 for adults, ($15 for Chicagoans); $11 for children 3-11, ($10 for Chicagoans); $17 for seniors, ($14 for Chicagoans) (Note: The Museum offers free admission to Illinois residents on what seem to be arbitrary days, and hours vary month to month, so check the website regularly.)

The 1893 World's Fair Arts Palace is home to the Museum of Science and Industry. The mammoth 350,000-square-foot bastion is one of the largest science museums in the world. Generations of Chicagoans and visitors have been wowed by a vast array of exhibits, including hatching baby chicks and the U-505 (the only World War II German submarine captured). The model railroad, another favorite exhibit, has been expanded to the now 3,500-square-foot Great Train Journey, which depicts the route from Chicago to Seattle. Other popular attractions include the coal mine, the Fairy Castle, and the Omnimax Theater's five-story, domed, wrap-around theater.

NATURE

Two lagoons surround Wooded Island, a.k.a. Paul H. Douglas Nature Sanctuary. Osaka Garden, a serene Japanese garden with an authentic tea house and entrance gate, sits at the island's northern tip. The ceremonial garden, like the golden replica of Statue of the Republic on Hayes Avenue, recalls the park's 1893 Exposition origins. The Chicago Audubon Society (www.chicagoaudubon.org) conducts bird walks in the park. These sites and the Perennial Garden at 59th Street and Cornell Drive are also havens for butterflies.

SPORTS

Back in the very beginning of the 20th century, the Jackson Park Golf Course (312-245-0909 or jacksonpark.cpdgolf.com) was the only public course in the Midwest. Today, the historic 18-hole course is certified by the Audubon Cooperative Sanctuary and has beautiful wilderness habitats. (Or are those scruffy fairways?) Greens fees are $28 during the week and $31 on weekends (all rates are discounted for residents). A driving range is adjacent to the course.

The city's park fitness facilities are a great deal, the facility at the Jackson Park field house included. The fitness center is open Mon–Fri 9 am–9:30 pm, Sat 9 am–4:30 pm, and Sun 11 am–4:30 pm. Adult membership passes cost $17 a month or $150 for the year. From Hayes Drive north along Cornell Avenue are outdoor tennis courts, baseball diamonds, and a running track. Tennis courts are on the west side of Lakeshore Drive at 63rd Street. Jackson Park's beaches are at 57th Street and 63rd Street (water playground, too). Inner and Outer Harbors allow shore fishing.

NEIGHBORING PARKS

North of Jackson Park at 55th Street and Lake Shore Drive is Promontory Point, a scenic lakeside picnic spot. Harold Washington Park, 51st Street and Lake Shore Drive, has a model yacht basin and eight tennis courts on 53rd Street.

To the west, 460-acre Washington Park (5531 S Martin Luther King Dr, 773-256-1248) has an outdoor swimming pool, playing fields, and nature areas. It's also worth stopping by to see Lorado Taft's 1922 Fountain of Time sculpture and the DuSable Museum of African-American History (740 E 56th Pl, 773-947-0600; www.dusablemuseum.org).

At 71st Street and South Shore Drive are South Shore Beach, with a harbor, bird sanctuary, and South Shore Cultural Center (7059 South Shore Dr, 773-256-0149). South Shore Golf Course is a nine-hole public course. Greens fees are $17 weekdays and $19 on weekends (southshore.cpdgolf.com).

HOW TO GET THERE

By Car: From the Loop, drive south on Lake Shore Drive, exit west on 57th Street. From the south, take I-94 W. Exit on Stony Island Avenue heading north to 57th Drive. The museum's parking garage entrance is on 57th Drive. The Music Court lot is behind the museum. A free parking lot is on Hayes Drive.

By Bus: From the Loop, CTA buses 6 and 10 (weekends and daily in summer) stop by the museum.

By L: (the quickest way to get to Jackson Park): Take the Green Line to the Garfield Boulevard (55th Street) stop; transfer to the eastbound 55 bus.

By Train: Sporadic service. From the Loop's Millennium Station at Randolph Street and Van Buren Street stations, take Metra Electric service. Trains stop at the 55th, 56th, and 57th Street Station platform. Walk two blocks east.

LINCOLN PARK

OVERVIEW

The largest of Chicago's 500-plus parks, Lincoln Park stretches 1,208 acres along the lakefront from the breeder cruising scene at the North Avenue Beach to the gay cruising scene at Hollywood Beach. The park boasts one of the world's longest bike trails, but thanks to an ever-increasing abundance of stroller pushers, leashless dogs, and earbud-wearing wheely-doodlers, the path proves treacherous for cyclists and pedestrians alike. Nonetheless, sporty types and summertime dawdlers still find satisfaction indoors and out at Lincoln Park. Take a break from winter inside the Lincoln Park Conservatory, a tropical paradise full o' lush green plants no matter what the thermometer reads. Public buildings, including animal houses at the Lincoln Park Zoo, Café Brauer, Peggy Notebaert Nature Museum, and vintage beach bath houses, make the park as architecturally attractive as it is naturally beautiful.

Much of southern Lincoln Park is open green space populated by football, soccer, dog play, and barbecue grills. Paths shaded by mature trees lead to stoic statues. Until the 1860s, Lincoln Park was nothing more than a municipal cemetery filled with the shallow graves of cholera and smallpox victims, and it was concern about a public health threat that instigated the creation of the park. Although the city attempted to relocate all the bodies in the cemetery-to-park conversion of 1869, digging doggies may unearth more than picnickers' chicken bones.

NATURE

In spring, bird watchers flock to Lincoln Park's ponds and nature trails. Addison Bird Sanctuary Viewing Platform north of Belmont Harbor overlooks five fenced-in acres of wetlands and woods. Birding programs around North Pond are run by the Lincoln Park Conservancy (www.lincolnparkconservancy.org) and the Chicago Ornithological Society (www.chicagobirder.org). More than 100 species of birds have been identified at the 10-acre pond. Free guided walks are held on most Wednesdays during the year starting at 7 am. Bring binoculars and a canteen of coffee. The Fort Dearborn Chapter of the Illinois Audubon Society hosts park and zoo bird walks (www.fort-dearbornaudubon.org). Migratory birds gather around the revamped 1889 Alfred Caldwell Lily Pool at Fullerton Parkway and North Cannon Drive. Next to the Conservatory, Grandmother's Garden and the more formal French-style garden across the street are favorites for both wedding party photos and the homeless during the warmer months.

SPORTS

Baseball diamonds on the park's south end are bordered by La Salle Drive and Lake Shore Drive, next to the field house and NorthStar Eatery. Bicyclists and runners race along Lincoln Park Lagoon to the footbridge over Lake Shore Drive to North Avenue Beach, Chicago's volleyball mecca. To reserve courts and rent equipment, go to the south end of the landmark, boat-shaped bath house. Just north of the bath house is a seasonal rollerblade rink and fitness club. North of Montrose Harbor on the North Wilson Drive lakefront is a free skateboard park.

The 9-hole Sydney R. Marovitz Public Golf Course (3600 Recreation Dr) hosts hackers year-round. Snail-slow play allows plenty of time to enjoy skyline views from this lakefront cow pasture, which is always crowded. Greens fees are $26 weekdays, $29 on weekends, and you can rent clubs. Reserve tee times online at sydneymarovitz.cpdgolf. com or show up at sunrise. The starter sits in the northeast corner of the clock tower field house. For those who want to take it even more leisurely, check out the Diversey Miniature Golf Course (diversey.cpdgolf.com), which offers an 18-hole course complete with waterfalls and footbridges. Diversey mini-golf rates are $10 adults, $8 juniors/seniors. Also nearby is the Diversey Golf Range (141 W Diversey Ave), open year-round (large bucket $16, small bucket $10).

Four clay tennis courts, the last ones left in Chicago, are open 7 am–8 pm and cost $18 per hour; tennis shoes are required. For reservations and further information, call 312-742-7821. There courts on Recreation Drive at Waveland are free, and first come, first, uh, served.

An archery range on the north end of Belmont Harbor is where the Lincoln Park Archery Club (www.lincoln-parkarcheryclub.org) meets. They offer a number of clinics throughout the summer for newcomers to the sport.

Members of the Lincoln Park Boat Club row in Lincoln Park Lagoon. Rowing classes for the public are offered May through September (www. lpbc.net).

The Nature Boardwalk surrounds the South Pond at the Lincoln Park Zoo. Take a walk or jog through the urban oasis which acts as a natural haven for native birds, frogs, fish, and turtles. The Patio at Café Brauer (2021 North Stockton) is sunny spot to take in the view and sip on a specially brewed Boardwalk Blue blueberry-infused golden ale from Goose Island.

GREEN CITY MARKET

ADDRESS: *1750 N CLARK ST, CHICAGO, IL 60614*
PHONE: *773-880-1266*
WEBSITE: *WWW.CHICAGOGREENCITYMARKET.ORG OR @ GREENCITYMARKET*
HOURS: *MAY–OCTOBER, WED & SAT 7 AM–1 PM (OFF-SEASON EVERY OTHER SATURDAY AT PEGGY NOTEBAERT NATURE MUSEUM)*

No Lincoln Park experience would be complete without visiting a quintessential yuppie hotspot–the farmers market. What began in an alley next to the Chicago Theatre in 1998 has since become Chicago's only year round sustainable market, showcasing local farmers selling everything from organic produce and cheese to elk meat and microgreens. Free chef demonstrations take place every Wednesday and Saturday at 10:30 am, a different fruit or vegetable is featured every month according to what's in season.

LINCOLN PARK ZOO

ADDRESS: *2200 N CANNON DR CHICAGO, IL 60614*
PHONE: *312-742-2000*
WEBSITE: *WWW.LPZOO.ORG OR @LINCOLNPARKZOO*
HOURS: *APRIL-MAY 10 AM-5 PM; MEMORIAL DAY-LABOR DAY 10 AM-5 PM ON WEEKDAYS, 10 AM-6:30 PM ON WEEKENDS; SEPTEMBER-OCTO-BER 10 AM-5 PM; NOVEMBER-MARCH 10 AM-4:30 PM*
ADMISSION: *FREE*

Lions and tigers and bears and kids, oh my! We're not sure which scares us most. Established in 1868, Lincoln Park Zoo is the country's oldest free zoo, and still a leader in wildlife conservation. National TV shows Zoo Parade and Ray Rayner's Ark in the Park were filmed here. Look for some family (or, at least, in-law) resemblance at the 29,000-square-foot Regenstein Center for African Apes. Come early and hear the white-cheek gibbons, the smallest of the ape family, mimic car alarms in their morning song to mark their territory. You may even catch one peeing off his tree before a captivated audience. Flanking the zoo's northwest side is the free Lincoln Park Conservatory, a fantastic source of oxygen renewal recommended for hangover sufferers. The Pritzker Family Children's Zoo simulates a North American woods.

PEGGY NOTEBAERT NATURE MUSEUM

ADDRESS: *2430 N CANNON DR, CHICAGO, IL 60614*
PHONE: *773-755-5100*
WEBSITE: *WWW.NATUREMUSEUM.ORG OR @NATUREMUSEUM*
HOURS: *MON–FRI 9 AM–5 PM, SAT–SUN 10 AM–5 PM*
ADMISSION: *$9 ADULTS, $7 SENIORS & STUDENTS, $6 CHILDREN AGES 3–12; THURSDAYS SUGGESTED DONATION FOR ILLINOIS RESIDENTS*

The Peggy Notebaert Nature Museum succeeds in making Illinois' level landscape interesting. The contemporary version of the 1857 Chicago Academy of Sciences, this hands-on museum depicts the close connection between urban and natural environments and represents global environmental issues through a local lens. A flowing water lab and flitting butterfly haven invite return visits. A must-see for anyone with a passion for taxidermy and/or Silence of the Lambs. You can also discover

how pollutive you are in your every-day life—and how to change it—in their Extreme Green House exhibit. Get back to nature with a full class and summer camp schedule.

CHICAGO HISTORY MUSEUM

ADDRESS: 1601 N. CLARK ST & NORTH AVE, CHICAGO, IL 60614
PHONE: 312-642-4600
WEBSITE: WWW.CHICAGOHISTORY.ORG OR @CHICAGOMUSEUM
HOURS: MON–SAT 9:30 AM–4:30 PM, SUN 12 NOON–5 PM
ADMISSION: $14 ADULTS, $12 SENIORS & STUDENTS, CHILDREN UNDER 12 FREE; FREE DAYS FOR ILLINOIS RESIDENTS VARY, VISIT WEBSITE FOR FULL SCHEDULE

The Chicago History Museum holds over 20 million primary documents relating to the history of the Chicago area. Exhibits about the city's pioneer roots, architecture, music, fashion, neighborhoods, windy politics, and oral histories breathe life into an otherwise dry history. Locals can access the excellent research center (open Tuesday through Friday, $10/day; students through grade 12 are free) for genealogical information and housing history. North & Clark Café explores Chicago's love of food.

PERFORMANCES

Lincoln Park Cultural Center (2045 N Lincoln Park W, 312-742-7726) stages plays, theater workshops, and family-friendly performances year-round. While Theater on the Lake (Fullerton Ave & Lake Shore Dr, 312-742-7994) is best known for its summer schedule of alternative drama, it hosts events throughout the calendar year. Lincoln Park Zoo hosts outdoor summer concerts and events as well. See their events calendar online.

HOW TO GET THERE

By Car: Lake Shore Drive exits to Lincoln Park are Bryn Mawr Avenue, Foster Avenue, Lawrence Avenue, Wilson Drive, Montrose Drive, Irving Park Parkway, Belmont Avenue, Fullerton Avenue, and North Avenue.

Free parking lots are at Recreational Drive near Belmont Harbor and Simonds Drive near Montrose Harbor. Paid lots are located at North Avenue Beach, Chicago Historical Society, Lincoln Park Zoo, and Grant Hospital Garage. Stockton Drive and Cannon Drive have free street parking. A metered lot is on Diversey Parkway, next to the golf range.

By Bus: CTA buses 151, 156, and 146 travel through Lincoln Park.

By L: Get off the Red Line at any stop between Fullerton and Bryn Mawr Avenues, then head one mile east. On the Brown Line, all stops between Sedgwick and Belmont are about a mile east of the park as well.

MCCORMICK PLACE

GENERAL INFORMATION

NFT MAP: *11*
MAILING ADDRESS: *2301 S LAKE SHORE DR, CHICAGO, IL 60616*
PHONE: *312-791-7000*
WEBSITE: *WWW.MCCORMICKPLACE.COM OR @MCCORMICK_PLACE*
SOUTH BUILDING: *EXHIBIT HALL A*
NORTH BUILDING: *EXHIBIT HALLS B AND C; METRA TRAIN STATION*
LAKESIDE CENTER (EAST BUILDING): *EXHIBIT HALLS D AND E;
4,267-SEAT ARIE CROWN THEATER (LEVEL 2)*
WEST BUILDING: *EXHIBIT HALL F; TRANSPORTATION CENTER;
PARKING LOT A*

OVERVIEW

When it comes to the convention business, size matters. With 2.6 million square feet of exhibit space spread over four buildings, McCormick Place is the largest convention center in the country and one of the largest in the world. The center hosts more than three million visitors every year for trade shows, including the Chicago Auto Show, and public exhibitions in the South Building, North Building, Lakeside Center (East Building) and West Building. McCormick Place also includes the Arie Crown Theatre, one of the largest theaters in Chicago according to seating capacity, which hosts a variety of plays, concerts, and seminars. McCormick Place's growth continues to bolster the rapid development of South Loop, and with each expansion the complex's overall aesthetic appeal steadily improves. But despite major renovations, Chicagoans still refer to the complex as "the mistake on the lake." Mayor Daley called the black boxy behemoth the "Berlin Wall" that separates Chicagoans from their beloved lakefront.

FINDING YOUR WAY AROUND

Getting to McCormick Place is the easy part. Then you have to navigate the inside. The main entrance is off Martin Luther King Drive, next to the Hyatt Hotel. If you're totally lost, there are Visitor Information Centers in each building.

HOW TO GET THERE

By Car: From the Loop, take Lake Shore Drive south; from the southeast, travel north on Lake Shore Drive. Signage to McCormick Place on Lake Shore Drive is frequent and clear. There are three main lots: Parking Lot A is for events in the North, South and West Buildings; Lot B serves the South Building and offers a pre-paid express pass option; Lot C is for events at Lakeside Center and Arie Crown Theater. There is also parking at the Hyatt and an additional lot north of McCormick Place at Soldier Field.

By Bus: From the Loop and within walking distance of many hotels, CTA bus 3 stops at McCormick Place. From Richard B. Ogilvie Transportation Center, take buses 20, 56, 60, or 157 to Michigan Avenue; transfer to a southbound 3. From Union Station, board eastbound bus 7 to Michigan Avenue; transfer to a southbound 3.

During major shows, countless charter buses circle downtown hotels, transporting conventioneers to McCormick Place for free. Charter buses travel on an express busway from Randolph Street to the South Building in less than ten minutes. For schedules, check with the hotels and at McCormick Place information desks.

By Train: A Metra train ride from the Loop's Millennium Station at Randolph Street and Van Buren Street stations to the McCormick Place Station takes nine minutes. Escalators to the train platform are on the west side of the Grand Concourse (Level 2.5).

OAK PARK

GENERAL INFORMATION

VISIT OAK PARK: 888-625-7275; WWW.VISITOAKPARK.COM OR @VISITOAKPARK

OVERVIEW

You can thank Oak Park for Prairie Style architecture, A Moveable Feast, McDonald's, and, yes, Tarzan. The creators of each called this charming suburb their home: Frank Lloyd Wright, Ernest Hemingway, Ray Kroc, and Edgar Rice Burroughs, respectively. Best known for its architectural gems and strong public schools, Oak Park is a happy hunting ground for home buyers seeking upscale, integrated living ten miles from the Loop. Less impressed than most with his picture-perfect hometown, Hemingway famously described Oak Park as "a village of wide lawns and narrow minds."

ARCHITECTURE

Oak Park harbors the nation's largest concentration of Frank Lloyd Wright buildings, 25 in the village and another six in neighboring River Forest. The village's must-see sites are located in a compact area bordered by Division Street, Lake Street, Forest Avenue, and Ridgeland Avenue. Designs by Wright, William Drummond, George W. Maher, John Van Bergen, and E. E. Roberts are represented throughout.

You can ground yourself in Prairie Style architectural principles at the brilliant Frank Lloyd Wright Home and Studio. Maintained by the Frank Lloyd Wright Trust, guided tours of the designer's personal space are offered daily 10 am–4 pm (951 Chicago Ave, 312-994-4000; flwright.org or @FLWTrust). Tickets can be purchased on the foundation's website or on-site (early arrival recommended) at a cost of $17 for adults, $15 for students, seniors and military, and free for children 3 and under (photography allowed with extra $5 pass). Excellent walking tours of the surrounding streets are also offered: $15 for adults, $12 students, seniors and military, and free for children 3 and under. Worth every penny.

Completed in 1908, Unity Temple (875 Lake St, 708-383-8873; www.utrf.org) was Wright's first commissioned public building; today it houses Oak Park's Unitarian-Universalist congregation. Guided tours and self-guided audio tours of Unity Temple are offered Monday through Saturday through the Frank Lloyd Wright Trust (flwright.org): $15 for adults, $12 students, seniors and military, and free for children 3 and under.

The Oak Park Visitors Center (1010 Lake St, 708-848-1500) offers maps, books and souvenirs and tickets to the Hemingway's Birthplace Home and Museum, and Pleasant Home.

CULTURE & EVENTS

Once a year in May, the public gets to snoop inside Wright-designed private residences during the popular Wright Plus Housewalk organized by the Frank Lloyd Wright Trust (flwright.org).

Get your fill of he-man author Hemingway at the Hemingway Birthplace Home & Museum (www.ehfop.org or @EHFOP). The museum, housed in the Arts Center of Oak Park, is open Sunday through Friday 1 pm–5 pm, and Saturday 10 am–5 pm (200 N Oak Park Ave, 708-848-2222; $10 adults, $8 students and seniors). His birthplace, also included with the price of admission, is located just up the street at 339 N Oak Park Avenue.

MILLENNIUM PARK

OVERVIEW

Only four years behind schedule (who's counting?) and hundreds of millions of dollars over budget (okay, this we counted), Millennium Park finally launched itself in July 2004 as the cultural epicenter Mayor Daley promised us it would be back in 1997. Even if it did take myriad stopgap funding measures resembling yesteryear Al Capone strong-arm tactics to eternally endow us with the AT&T Plaza, McCormick Tribune Plaza & Ice Rink, and the Chase Promenade, locals and tourists alike agree it was well worth it. Even staunch, longtime local naysayers have come to acknowledge that, when all is said and done, the end result really is an amazing addition to Grant Park's north point and is, without a doubt, one of downtown Chicago's crowning jewels.

The park is built on land that was controlled by the Illinois Central Railroad from the 19th century until 1997. In some ways, the wait was worth it: the park's design is entirely modern and completely unmoored from "classic" park design. The starchitects and artists involved have contributed some of their most high-profile, impressive work. The overall experience is fun and vital, and it's not for nothing that Millennium Park immediately became one of the city's most visited attractions. And if you're visiting for the first time, a good starting point is the park's Welcome Center, which is open daily and located at 201 E Randolph Street.

JAY PRITZKER PAVILION

The centerpiece of Millennium Park is the Pritzker Pavilion. It seems the whole park may have very well been conceived to give Frank Gehry's architectural masterpiece an appropriate setting. The pavilion's innovative trellis structure of stainless steel ribbons doubles as the sound system, which replicates the acoustics of an indoor space. The pavilion's stage area is as big as Orchestra Hall across the street and can accommodate a 120-person orchestra and a 150-person choir. Seating for the free concert events includes a 4,000-seat terrace and an additional 95,000-square-foot lawn area that can accommodate 7,000 picnickers. The pavilion is the home of the summer-long Grant Park Music Festival, which features a full-slate of classical concerts.

HARRIS THEATER FOR MUSIC & DANCE

Several dance and theatrical troupes share the 1,500-seat underground space behind Gehry's behemoth bandshell, including Hubbard Street Dance Chicago (not to be missed, but good luck getting tickets!), the Chicago Children's Choir, and the Jazz Institute of Chicago. Two underground parking garages flank the theater, and as with all parking in this area, it's first come/ first served and a bit of a mess on the weekends. Tickets and schedule available at www.harristheaterchicago.org

NATURE & SCULPTURE

The park has several different defined spaces: Wrigley Square, with its neoclassical epistyle; the Chase Promenade, gearing up to house art fairs and ethnic festivals; and the AT&T Plaza (between the skating rink and promenade), which is home to Anish Kapoor's 100-ton stainless steel jelly-bean sculpture, Cloud Gate (be sure to take a picture of yourself staring into it–not exactly original, but so hard to resist). Flanking the skating rink to the south is the modernist Crown Fountain, which features two glass brick towers, 50 feet in height, with projected video images of the faces of actual Chicago residents. The Lurie Garden, a ridiculously conceptual assemblage of seasonal foliage, offers a beautiful public gathering space as well as more contemplative environments. The BP Bridge, a 925-foot-long winding bridge–Frank Gehry's first–connects Millennium Park to Maggie Daley Park just east of the park. Clad in brushed stainless steel panels, the BP Bridge complements the Pritzker Pavilion in function as well as design by creating an acoustic barrier for traffic noise. It's well worth the walk.

SPORTS

The 15,910-square-foot McCormick Tribune Ice Rink opens annually in November. On Saturdays in the summer, take part in free fitness classes on the Great Lawn. The options range from tai chi to yoga, with some more danceable aerobics as well. The park also houses a state-of-the-art, heated bicycle garage, which provides parking for 300 bikes, showers, a repair facility, and a café.

DINING

The 300-seat Park Grill (consistently one of top burgers in the city) overlooking the skating rink offers burgers, steaks, and salads year round. In the summer, carry-away grub is available from a variety of kiosks throughout the park.

HOW TO GET THERE

No matter your mode of travel, approach the area around Millennium Park with patience and allow extra time.

By Car: Exits off Lake Shore Drive west to Millennium Park are at Randolph Street and Monroe Drive. Also, enter the park from Michigan Avenue heading east on the same streets. If you choose to drive, underground parking is available in several areas. Access the Grant Park North Garage from Michigan Avenue. Enter Millennium Park Garage from the lower levels of Randolph Street and mid-level of Columbus Drive. Parking is also available at the Grant Park South and East Monroe Garages.

By Train: Metra trains coming from the south terminate at the underground Millennium Park Station at Randolph Street. From the Richard B. Ogilvie Transportation Center, travel east to Michigan Avenue and Millennium Park on CTA buses 20, 56, 60, and 157. From Union Station, board CTA buses 60 or 151.

By L: Get off at any L stop in the Loop between Randolph Street and Monroe Street. Walk two (or three) blocks east to Millennium Park.

By Bus: CTA buses 3, 4, 6, 14, 20, 56, 60, 124, 151, 157 and 173 serve the park.

MUSEUM CAMPUS

OVERVIEW

Museum Campus is the ultimate destination for educational field trips. South of Grant Park at the intersection of Roosevelt Road and Lake Shore Drive, Museum Campus's 57 acres of uninterrupted lakefront parkland connect three world-renowned Chicago institutions: The Field Museum, Shedd Aquarium, and Adler Planetarium & Astronomy Museum. You've got Mayor Daley to thank for all of this beautiful space; it was the bossman himself who championed the rerouting of Lake Shore Drive to the west to consolidate the land around Museum Campus, which opened in 1998. Chicagoans, take note: although none of the museums that make up the museum campus are shouting from rooftops about it, all three offer reduced admission rates to locals. Be sure to ask for it.

THE FIELD MUSEUM

ADDRESS: *1400 S LAKE SHORE DR, CHICAGO, IL 60605*
PHONE: *312-922-9410*
WEBSITE: *WWW.FIELDMUSEUM.ORG OR @FIELDMUSEUM*
HOURS: *OPEN DAILY 9 AM–5 PM, EXCEPT CHRISTMAS*
ADMISSION: *BASIC ADMISSION IS $18 ADULTS, $15 STUDENTS & SENIORS, $13 CHILDREN AGES 3–11. ADDITIONAL ADMISSION FEES APPLY FOR FULL MUSEUM EXPERIENCE. FREE DAYS FOR ILLINOIS RESIDENTS VARY, VISIT WEBSITE FOR FULL SCHEDULE.*

The massive, Greek Revival-style museum constructed in 1921 houses over 20 million artifacts. From dinosaurs, diamonds, and earthworms to man-eating lions, totem poles, and mummies, there is just too much to savor in a single visit. The permanent Evolving Planet exhibit features an interactive stroll through 4 billion years of evolution, from single-celled organisms through dinosaurs, hominids, and finally to human beings. Another noteworthy permanent exhibit is Sue, the largest, most complete, and best preserved Tyrannosaurus Rex discovered to date. Complete with a half-smoked pack of Marlboros, since we now know that's what killed the dinosaurs. As with most museums, some temporary exhibits cost additional bucks on top of normal museum fees. Free museum tours are available; check website for times.

JOHN G. SHEDD AQUARIUM

ADDRESS: *1200 S LAKE SHORE DR, CHICAGO, IL 60605*
PHONE: *312-939-2438*
WEBSITE: *WWW.SHEDDAQUARIUM.ORG OR @SHEDD_AQUARIUM*
HOURS: *MEMORIAL DAY–LABOR DAY: DAILY, 9 AM–6 PM; LABOR DAY–MEMORIAL DAY: MON–FRI, 9 AM–5 PM; SAT–SUN: 9 AM–6 PM. CLOSED CHRISTMAS.*
ADMISSION: *BASIC ADMISSION IS $8 ADULTS, $6 CHILDREN AGES 3–11. ADDITIONAL ADMISSION FEES APPLY FOR FULL MUSEUM EXPERIENCE. FREE DAYS FOR ILLINOIS RESIDENTS VARY, VISIT WEBSITE FOR FULL SCHEDULE.*

Opened in 1929, the Beaux Arts-style aquarium's six wings radiate from a giant, circular coral reef tank. The museum features revolving exhibits with a special focus on marine ecology and preservation. Popular favorites include Wild Reef, where you can get up close and personal with the sharks. During the summer the Shedd hosts weekly "Jazzin at the Shedd" events featuring live jazz, cocktails overlooking the downtown skyline, fireworks, and full access to the aquarium until 10 pm.

BURNHAM PARK

Burnham Park, the site of the 1933 Century of Progress exhibition, encompasses McCormick Place, Burnham Harbor, the former Merrill C. Meigs Airport (closed in a political coup by Mayor Daley in 2003), and Soldier Field. A free skateboard park is located at Lake Shore Drive and 31st Street. The 12th Street Beach, especially popular with swimmers and divers because of the deep water east of the beach, is on

Northerly Island. Other beaches are at 31st Street and 49th Street. Outdoor basketball courts are east of Lake Shore Drive around 35th Street and 47th Street. Fishing is welcome along Solidarity Drive and Burnham Harbor shore. The wilderness Nature Area at 47th Street attracts butterflies and birds.

ADLER PLANETARIUM

ADDRESS: *1300 S LAKE SHORE DR, CHICAGO, IL 60605*

PHONE: *312-922-7827*

WEBSITE: *WWW.ADLERPLANETARIUM.ORG OR @ADLERSKYWATCH*

HOURS: *MON–FRI 9:30 AM–4 PM, SAT–SUN 9:30 AM–4:30PM; THIRD THURSDAYS (21+ ADLER AFTER DARK) 6:30 PM–10:30 PM; CHECK WEBSITE FOR SPECIAL EXTENDED SUMMER HOURS*

ADMISSION: *BASIC ADMISSION IS $12 ADULTS, $8 CHILDREN 3–11. ADDITIONAL ADMISSION FEES APPLY FOR FULL MUSEUM EXPERIENCE. FREE DAYS FOR ILLINOIS RESIDENTS VARY, VISIT WEBSITE FOR FULL SCHEDULE.*

The Adler Planetarium & Astronomy Museum offers interactive exhibits explaining space phenomena and intergalactic events; its 2,000 historic astronomical and navigational instruments form the western hemisphere's largest collection. On the first Friday of every month, weather permitting, amateur astronomers young and old are invited to bring their own telescopes to the Planetarium lawns. Roving scientists offer tips and instructions on telescope usage and observational features. Come summer, the 21+ Alder After Dark events are great, nerdy date nights featuring both kinds of cosmos. Chicago skyline views from the planetarium grounds are out of this world any day of the week, and are always worth the trip.

HOW TO GET THERE

By Car: From the Loop, take Columbus Drive south; turn east on McFetridge Drive. From the south, take Lake Shore Drive to McFetridge Drive. Area parking lots are near Soldier Field, Field Museum, Adler Planetarium, and McCormick Place. Standard $19 rate for parking in the lot adjacent to the Adler and $19 in the Soldier Field lot. Fees are higher on days when there's Park District-sponsored special events. Metered parking is available on Solidarity Drive.

By Bus: CTA buses 2, 6, 10, 12, 14, 127, 130, and 146 serve the area.

By L: Ride the Orange, Red, or Green Lines to the Roosevelt Road stop. Walk east through the pedestrian underpass at Roosevelt Road.

By Train: From Richard B. Ogilvie Transportation Center, travel east on CTA bus 20 to State Street; transfer to the 146. From Union Station take CTA bus 1, 126, or 151; transfer at State Street to the 10 or 146. From La Salle Street station, take the 146. South Shore and Metra trains stop at the Roosevelt Road station.

On Foot: Walk south through Grant Park past bobbing boats and the gushing Buckingham Fountain to the Museum Campus.

Water Taxis: Seasonally, water taxis operate between Navy Pier and Museum Campus (312-222-9328; www.shorelinesightseeing.com).

NAVY PIER

GENERAL INFORMATION

NFT MAP: *3*
ADDRESS: *600 E GRAND AVE CHICAGO, IL 60611*
PHONE: *312-595-7437*
WEBSITE: *WWW.NAVYPIER.COM OR @NAVYPIER*
PIER HOURS: *SUMMER, 10 AM–10 PM SUN–THUR, 10 AM–10 PM FRI–SAT; OFF-SEASON 10 AM–8 PM SUN–THUR, 10 AM–10 PM FRI–SAT (WINTER CLOSES 7 PM SUN). CLOSING TIMES OF RESTAURANTS, SHOPS, AND ATTRACTIONS VARY BY SEASON, HOLIDAY, AND PUBLIC EXHIBITIONS/EVENTS.*
SKYLINE STAGE: *1,500-SEAT OUTDOOR PERFORMANCE PAVILION IN PIER PARK, PERFORMANCES ARE MAY THROUGH SEPTEMBER*
IMAX THEATRE: *312-595-5629 OR @NAVYPIERIMAX*
FREE FIREWORKS: *MEMORIAL DAY TO LABOR DAY, WEDNESDAYS (9:30 PM) & SATURDAYS (10:15 PM)*
WBEZ RADIO: *NPR LOCAL AFFILIATE, 312-948-4600; WWW.WBEZ.ORG OR @WBEZ*
EXHIBIT SPACE: *FESTIVAL HALL, LAKEVIEW TERRACE, BALLROOM LOBBY, GRAND BALLROOM; 36 MEETING ROOMS*

OVERVIEW

With nine million visitors a year, Navy Pier is the quintessential Chicago tourist attraction. Yet save for an occasional Skyline Stage concert, speed-boat ride, or high-end nosh at Riva, most Chicagoans reserve Pier visits for those times when you have either very elderly or very young relatives in town. Knocked for years as a glorified mall on the lake, Navy Pier is undergoing a multi-multi-million-dollar "reimagining" that intends to refocus the visitor experience toward something more diverse, local-friendly, sustainable and in touch with the waterfront. With a boutique hotel. Phase I is scheduled for completion in 2015, with funding to follow for subsequent work.

Opened to the public in 1916 as a municipal wharf, the pier has also done time as a) the University of Illinois at Chicago's campus, b) a hospital, c) a military training facility, d) a concert venue, and e) a white elephant. In 1989, the Metropolitan Pier and Exposition Authority invested $150 million to transform the crumbling pier into an uninspired entertainment-exhibition complex that still somehow attracts three times as many visitors than the Art Institute of Chicago and Willis Tower combined. In addition to convention space (home to the annual Chicago Flower and Garden Show), Navy Pier also houses two museums, Chicago Shakespeare Theater, the Crystal Gardens, an outdoor concert pavilion, a vintage grand ballroom, a 15-story Ferris wheel, an IMAX Theatre, and, just for the hell of it, a radio station.

CHICAGO SHAKESPEARE THEATER

The Chicago Shakespeare Theater has a 510-seat, courtyard-style theater and a 180-seat studio theater that are Chicago's sole venues dedicated to performing wordsmith Willy's works. In addition to the season's plays, the theater produces Shakespeare "shorts" for younger patrons. A bookstore and teacher resource center are also located on-site (312-595-5600; www.chicagoshakes. com or @chicagoshakes).

CHICAGO CHILDREN'S MUSEUM

The Chicago Children's Museum features daily activities, a creative crafts studio, and 15 interactive exhibits ranging from dinosaur digs and waterworks to a toddler tree house, safety town, and construction zone. The museum is open daily from 10 am to 5 pm, and Thursday until 8 pm. Admission is $14 for adults and children, $13 for seniors and children under one. Children 15 and under get in free on the first Sunday of every month under the Free First Sundays program, and Thursdays 5 pm to 8 pm is free admission for all. (312-527-1000; www. chicagochildrensmuseum.org or @ childrensmuseum).

GETTING THERE

By Car: From the north, exit Lake Shore Drive at Grand Avenue; proceed east. From the southeast, exit Lake Shore Drive at Illinois Street; go east. Parking garages are located on the Pier's north side, and plenty of parking lots are just west of Lake Shore Drive in Streeterville.

By Bus: CTA buses 29, 65, 66, and 124 serve Navy Pier.

By L: Take the Green or Red Line to Grand Avenue. Board eastbound CTA Bus 29, or take the free trolley.

By Train: From Richard B. Ogilvie Transportation Center or Union Station, take CTA bus 124.

By Trolley: Free, daily trolleys that typically run every 20 minutes travel between Navy Pier and State Street along Grand Avenue and Illinois Street from Memorial Day to Labor Day. Pick-up points are indicated by "Navy Pier Trolley Stop" signs along the route.

By Boat: Seasonal water shuttles travel between Navy Pier and the Museum Campus and along the Chicago River to the Sears Tower (312-222-9328; www.shorelinesightseeing. com or @ShorelineSights).

SIX FLAGS GREAT AMERICA

GENERAL INFORMATION

ADDRESS: *1 GREAT AMERICA PKWY, GURNEE, IL 60031*

PHONE: *847-249-4636*

WEBSITE: *WWW.SIXFLAGS.COM/GREATAMERICA OR @SFGREAT_AMERICA*

HOURS: *OPEN MAY THROUGH OCTOBER, 10:30 AM UNTIL THE EVENING (AS LATE AS 10 PM IN MIDDLE OF SUMMER), BUT CHECK CALENDAR ON WEBSITE FOR SPECIFIC HOURS AND DATES.*

ENTRY: *FULL PRICE TICKETS ARE $66.99 FOR ADULTS AND $46.99 FOR KIDS UNDER 54"; ONLINE DISCOUNTS AVAILABLE.*

OVERVIEW

Metropolitan Chicago's Six Flags Great America is the seventh facility in the Six Flags amusement park empire, which began in Texas in 1961. Great America opened in 1976 (thus the "Great America") as a Marriott property, and was sold to Six Flags in 1984. Known for its thrill rides, the park is home to the Whizzer, an original park feature that has received recognition from the American Coaster Enthusiasts group.

TICKETS

Reduced rates are available for advanced purchase through the website and via promo codes and other promotions throughout the season. "The Flash" passes are available for impatient riders, offering cuts in line (and, for a price, even deeper cuts) for an extra fee. For die-hard thrill seekers, or if you plan to go more than once a year, season passes offer the best deal.

THRILL RIDES

Every few years, Six Flags tries to outdo itself with an even more death-defying and harrowing ride. Case in point: the Superman-Ultimate Flight ride in which passengers soar through the air head-first as though they were flying, nearly brushing the ground below them on the giant loop-de-loop. Other thrills include the Raging Bull "hyper-twister," where you drop at incredible degrees and speeds into subterranean depths. Batman The Ride allows your feet to dangle free, while riders remain standing, supported by a bicycle seat between the legs (men who desire children, be wary). Also try the equally frightening Vertical Velocity, V2 for short, which propels riders backward and forward up a corkscrew at 70 mph in less than four seconds, suspended by the same paltry harness that barely staves off fatality. Meanwhile, the classic wooden American Eagle coaster offers vintage, but no-less-worrisome, rickety thrills. The Viper, newer and sexier cousin to the geriatric American Eagle, provides a similar timber ride and is modeled after Coney Island's Cyclone. Try The Demon if you're interested in forgetting your name and address. Buccaneer Battle is a pirate-themed raft ride that allows you to soak other people with super-powered soak guns. Cool.

HURRICANE HARBOR WATER PARK

Opened in 2005, Great America's adjoining Hurricane Harbor water park features pools and various thrill slides in case you want to bring your trunks to the park. Open until around 6 p.m. through most of the summer, Hurricane Harbor costs an extra $5 (free for season pass holders) and includes access to shower facilities. Lockers are available for rent. Attractions include Skull Island, a supersoaker interactive water play structure highlighted by a 1,000-gallon-plus water drop that dumps itself upon unsuspecting children every so often. The park has miles of water rides, including the twisty tunnels of Hurricane Mountain and the high-speed tube and bowl slides of Vortex and Typhoon. The Tornado, a combination tube and bowl slide, allows four riders to experience spinning in the 60-foot-wide funnel together. An adventure river, Castaway Creek, offers both exciting adventures complete with geysers, as well as leisurely relaxation under waterfalls and mists.

FRIGHT FEST

Avoid the heat and long lines of the summer season and creep into the park during the month of October (mostly on weekends) among the Halloween-themed décor, haunted houses, and scary music playing over the P.A. This is, by far, our favorite time to go and worth the price of a season pass for the convenience of just dropping by for a few thrills whenever the heck you feel like it (the park is open until midnight on most Saturday nights during Fright Fest). Water rides (dyed blood red–bwahahaha!) in the park are usually less crowded, so take advantage of those to get the pasty white complexion and blue-tinged lip effect that will help you fit in, especially since costumes aren't allowed.

MAKE A NIGHT OF IT

Six Flags partners with many area hotels, including several either within walking distance or accessible via a shuttle bus—saving on parking and avoiding having to drive under the influence of pure joy. See, for example, Grand Hotel & Suites (5520 Grand Ave, 847-249-7777), Hampton Inn (5550 Grand Ave, 847-662-1100), Holiday Inn Gurnee (6161 West Grand Ave, 847-336-6300), KeyLime Cove Indoor Waterpark Resort (1700 Nations Dr, 877-713-4951), or Econo Lodge (3740 Grand Avenue, 224-441-3270). Various other nearby accommodations in neighboring towns also provide shuttle bus service, and some also offer discount tickets. Check the Six Flags website for more details.

HOW TO GET THERE

By Car: Take I-94 or I-294 west, exit at Grand Avenue. Typical driving time is about 45 minutes from Chicago. Be aware that traffic is very congested in July and August! Arrive extra early or extra late to beat the crowds.

By Train & Bus: Take the Metra Union Pacific North Line to Waukegan, where you can catch the Pace bus 565 to Great America. Pace also offers express bus service from Schaumburg and Rosemont on Fridays and weekends during the summer. Note: Public transportation to Great America from the Ogilvie Transportation Center and Madison and Canal takes just over two hours each way.

SKOKIE

GENERAL INFORMATION

WWW.SKOKIE.ORG

OVERVIEW

When Skokie was first incorporated under the moniker Niles Centre in 1888, it was considered to be the rowdy neighbor of temperate Evanston due to the large number of taverns within its borders. By 1940, residents were clamoring for a name change and a PR facelift. In November of that year, the village was renamed Skokie after the nearby Skokie River and canals, which themselves were named after an old Native American word for "swampland." Personally, we'd be more attracted to a party town, but nonetheless, the facelift was a success. With the completion of the Edens Expressway in the 1950s, residential development in Skokie was booming.

A chunk of the growth comprised Eastern European refugees from World War II, many of whom were Jewish. It is estimated that between 1945 and 1955, 3,000 Jewish families resettled in Skokie. Synagogues and Jewish services followed, and the village soon developed a self-perpetuating reputation as a thriving Jewish enclave. Skokie made international headlines in 1977–78 when it contested plans by the National Socialist Party of America, a branch of the American Nazi Party, to march on the village square. The NSPA was defended by the ACLU in a divisive case that brought the contest between free expression and freedom against hate speech into the international fore. As far as the NSPA was concerned, the decision to march in Skokie was an act of political manipulation. Chicago had denied the Nazis' right to march in SW Chicago's Marquette Park, which was the NSPA's home turf. The group then threatened to relocate their planned assembly to Skokie. When the Village of Skokie lost their bid to ban the march, Chicago finally conceded, allowing the Nazis to gather at Marquette Park in June 1978. A handful of Nazis showed up, countered by thousands of anti-Nazi protesters.

As if being the head of a neo-Nazi movement and threatening to march on the front lawns of concentration camp survivors doesn't already make you the world's biggest jackass/creep, NSPA leader Frank Collin secured the title in 1979 when he was arrested and incarcerated on child molestation charges.

CULTURE & EVENTS

In 1988, an urban renewal project to restore the North Shore's decrepit Chicago River waterfront resulted in the two-mile Skokie Northshore Sculpture Park (sculpturepark. org), an outdoor recreation area with walking paths, picnic areas, and featuring more than 60 sculptures by artists of local, national, and international renown. The park, sandwiched between McCormick Blvd and the north branch of the Chicago River, runs the two miles from Touhy to Dempster.

Time travel through history at the Skokie Heritage Museum (8031 Floral Ave, 847-674-1500), an assemblage of historical photos, papers, and artifacts painstakingly gathered by the Skokie Historical Society. The museum, housed in a restored 1887 firehouse, also features the history of Skokie's firefighters. Behind the museum, an authentic 1840s log cabin relocated to this location allows kids a glimpse into the town's pioneer past.

Skokie is the home of the Illinois Holocaust Museum & Education Center (9603 Woods Dr, 847-967-4800; www.ilholocaustmuse-

um.org or @ihmec). Opened in 2009, the facility is not only on a mission to educate future generations about the horrors of the Holocaust but also an attempt to close an upsetting chapter in Skokie's history. The two wings and their respective architecture are meant to evoke the hard edges of the historical record and the soft arches of a hopeful future. It's open to the public weekdays 10 am–5 pm and Thursday evening until 8 pm. Saturday and Sunday from 11 am-4pm. Museum closed Thanksgiving, Christmas, and major Jewish holidays. Admission is $12 for adults, $8 for seniors and students aged 12-22, $6 for children 5-12.

NORTH SHORE CENTER FOR THE PERFORMING ARTS

Home to the Skokie Valley Symphony Orchestra, the Centre East Theater, and, most notably, the highly acclaimed Northlight Theater, the North Shore Center for the Performing Arts (9510 Skokie Blvd, 847-673-6300; www.northshorecenter.org or @NSCPAS) is a state-of-the-art performance venue. Touring artists perform here, world class theater (sometimes featuring ensemble members from Steppenwolf) is mounted here, and it's also a North Shore venue for exhibits and trade shows. Designed by architect Graham Gund in 1996, The North Shore Center for the Performing Arts has given Northeast Illinois culture seekers a reason to come to Skokie besides bagels and lox.

WHERE TO DRINK

Despite its alcohol-fueled history, Skokie is not really known as a place to imbibe socially. Young residents head to youthful watering holes in the vicinity of the Northwestern campus in formerly tee-totaling Evanston (will the ironies never end?). Meanwhile, local drunks hang out at anonymous corner taverns just like anywhere else. Retail workers, middle managers, and the secretarial set mingle and mate at the food and booze joints adjacent to Old Orchard.

WHERE TO EAT

Old Orchard Shopping Center is filled with family-friendly chain options. Happily, Skokie still houses enough locally owned, independent restaurants to add interest and diversity to their dining scene. Folks travel from all over Chicagoland for local delis and kosher fare ever debating the superiority of Kaufman's v. New York Bagel and Bialy as THE place for a bagel and shmear.

HOW TO GET THERE

By Car: Take the Edens Expressway (I-94), and exit at Dempster.

By L: The Skokie Swift Yellow Line runs non-stop between the Howard Street Red Line terminus and the Dempster-Skokie station at 5001 Dempster St. Trains run approximately every 10-15 minutes between 5 am and 11 pm.

COLUMBIA COLLEGE CHICAGO

GENERAL INFORMATION

NFT MAPS: *8, 9, 11*
ADDRESS: *600 S MICHIGAN AVE, CHICAGO, IL 60605*
PHONE: *312-369-1000*
WEBSITE: *WWW.COLUM.EDU OR @COLUMBIACHI*
EVENT INFORMATION: *WWW.COLUM.EDU/CALENDAR*
ENROLLMENT: *10,142 (2013)*
ENDOWMENT: *$123 MILLION (2013)*

OVERVIEW

Named in honor of the World's Columbian Exposition, Columbia College Chicago first opened in 1890 as a women's speech academy. Over time, it has become one of America's most diverse private arts and media schools. It is best known for its film, television, and fiction departments, which turn out prominent professionals. Columbia alumni played key writing and production roles in Barbershop, Real Women Have Curves, Analyze This, Schindler's List, and Leaving Las Vegas. They win Emmy Awards (for art direction on Alias, special effects on Star Trek: Enterprise, animation on Samurai Jack, and cinematography on Carnivale). And they write acclaimed books; celebrated scribblers Joe Meno, Don DeGrazia, and Sam Weller all returned to Columbia's fiction writing department as faculty. Other programs include photography, dance, theater, music, art and design, journalism, fashion design, poetry, education, and management for the arts, entertainment, and media. Columbia's campus is the bustling South Loop, and its colorful student body immerse themselves in the city.

TUITION

Tuition for full-time undergrads hovers around $23,000. There's fees, books, art supplies, CTA passes, and obligatory museum visits, too. And have you heard about the Superdorm (525 S State St)? There, you can live in the middle of the Loop with more than 1,700 of your closest friends. Hey, college is a perpetual slumber party.

CULTURE

Columbia College is one of Chicago's most esteemed cultural arts presenters; more than 300,000 visitors attend Columbia events each year. The college hosts a regular slate of innovative dance performances throughout the year. The Museum of Contemporary Photography is one of just a handful of fully accredited photography museums in the United States. The Story Week Festival of Writers, held in the spring, is among Chicago's top literary draws. The college brings in authors, editors, agents, and publishers for a week of readings, panels, and special events, such as a rock-related literature night at the Metro. Spring also brings Fashion Columbia and the Manifest Urban Arts Festival, celebrating graduate achievements. The college's galleries and theaters feature the work of students alongside notable outside artists. The school's Media Production Center (MPC), located at 1600 S State St, opened in early 2010. Designed by local architects Studio Gang, it's a 35,000 sq. ft. state-of-the-art facility–containing studios, labs and classrooms–which allows for cross-disciplinary collaboration unlike anywhere else in the U.S. at the college/university level.

CENTER FOR BOOK AND PAPER ARTS
1104 S Wabash Ave, 2nd Fl
312-369-6630

MUSEUM OF CONTEMPORARY PHOTOGRAPHY
600 S Michigan Ave
312-663-5554
www.mocp.org or @MoCP_Chicago

A+D GALLERY
619 S Wabash Ave
312-369-8687
www.colum.edu/adgallery or @adgallery

GLASS CURTAIN GALLERY
1104 S Wabash Ave, 1st Fl
312-369-6643

C33 GALLERY
33 E Congress Pkwy, 1st Fl
312-369-6856

DANCE CENTER
1306 S Michigan Ave
312-369-8300
www.colum.edu/dance_center or
@Dance_Center

GETZ, CLASSIC, AND NEW STUDIO THEATERS
72 E 11th St
312-369-6126
www.colum.edu/theater_center

CONCERT HALL
1014 S Michigan Ave
312-369-6240

CENTER FOR BLACK MUSIC RESEARCH
618 S Michigan Ave, 6th Fl
312-369-7559
www.colum.edu/cbmr

MEDIA PRODUCTION CENTER (MPC)
1600 S State St
312-369-3314

DEPARTMENT CONTACT INFORMATION

UNDERGRADUATE ADMISSIONS: *312-369-7130*
GRADUATE ADMISSIONS: *312-369-7260*
SCHOOL OF FINE AND PERFORMING ARTS: *312-369-7964*
SCHOOL OF MEDIA ARTS: *312-369-8211*
SCHOOL OF LIBERAL ARTS AND SCIENCES: *312-369-8211*

DEPAUL UNIVERSITY

GENERAL INFORMATION

LINCOLN PARK CAMPUS: *WELCOME CENTER, 2400 N SHEFFIELD AVE, CHICAGO, IL 60614*
PHONE: *773-325-7000 X5700*
LOOP CAMPUS: *1 E JACKSON BLVD, CHICAGO, IL 60604*
PHONE: *312-362-8000*
NAPERVILLE CAMPUS: *312-476-4500/630-548-9378*
OAK FOREST CAMPUS: *312-476-3000/708-633-9091*
O'HARE CAMPUS: *312-476-3600*
WEBSITE: *WWW.DEPAUL.EDU OR @DEPAULU*
ENROLLMENT: *24,414 (2013)*
ENDOWMENT: *$384 MILLION (2013)*

OVERVIEW

Established in 1898 by the Vincentian Fathers as a school for immigrants, DePaul has become the country's largest Catholic university (with over 24,000 students) and the biggest private educational institution in Chicago, offering nearly 300 undergraduate and graduate programs of study. Of the university's seven campuses in the Chicago area, the Lincoln Park and Loop campuses serve as the core locations. The highly acclaimed Theatre School, College of Liberal Arts and Sciences, School of Music, and School of Education hold down the 36-acre Lincoln Park campus amid renovated historic homes on tree-lined streets.

DePaul's Loop Campus at Jackson Boulevard and State Street is where you'll find the College of Commerce, College of Law, and School of Computer Science, Telecommunications, and Information Systems. Nationally respected Kellstadt Graduate School of Business and DePaul's thriving continuing education program, the School of New Learning, can also be found on the Loop Campus. The heart of the Loop campus is DePaul Center, located in the old Goldblatt Brothers Department Store, now grounded by a university-sanctioned Barnes and Noble. Most students in the Loop campus are adults, so popular hangouts include the Brown Line L, Red Line L, and Metra stations while they're all waiting for the train home. Prominent DePaul alumni include Chicago father-son mayors Richard M. Daley and his dad, the late Richard J. Daley; McDonald's Corporation's former CEO Jack Greenberg; Pulitzer Prize-winning composer George Perle; and actors Gillian Anderson and John C. Reilly.

TUITION

Full-time undergraduate tuition hovers around $34,000.

SPORTS

The DePaul Blue Demons might be named a bit oddly as the athletic ambassadors of the largest Catholic university in the United States, but their teams are strong despite any identity confusion. The Blue Demons play in the Big East Conference and DePaul's teams include men's and women's basketball, cross-country,

soccer, tennis, and track and field, men's golf, and women's softball and volleyball. Its men's basketball team often has solid years and standout players often move on to the NBA.

For tickets, visit the ticket office at the Sullivan Athletics Center (2323 N Sheffield Ave, 773-325-7526, depaulbluedemons.com). The Blue Demons play at McGrath-Phillips Arena (women's basketball and volleyball, 2323 N Sheffield Ave), Allstate Arena (men's basketball, 6920 N Mannheim Rd, Rosemont, IL, 847-635-6601; allstatearena. com), and Wish Field and Cacciatore Stadium (men's and women's soccer and softball, respectively, both on the 900 block of Belden Ave).

CULTURE ON CAMPUS

DePaul's vibrant Theatre School is the oldest of its kind in the Midwest. Founded in 1925 as the Goodman School of Drama, the school stages over 150 performances during its season. The Theatre School performs contemporary and classic plays at its 1,325-seat Merle Reskin Theatre, a French Renaissance-style theater built in 1910 and located at 60 E Balbo Drive in the South Loop. Chicago Playworks and the School of Music's annual opera are also performed at the Merle Reskin Theatre. Best of all, tickets are reasonable—all under $20. For directions and parking ga-

rage locations, call 312-922-1999 or go to theatre.depaul.edu. Take the Red Line to the Harrison Street or Jackson Street stops just southwest of the theater. CTA buses 29, 36, 151, and 146 also stop nearby.

The DePaul Art Museum (museums. depaul.edu), located at 935 W Fullerton, is open Wed–Sun and offers free admission to all visitors. Permanent collections of sculpture and oil paintings from local and international artists adorn the galleries. A pay parking lot is located one block east of the library on N Sheffield Avenue. DePaul's John T. Richardson Library and Loop campus library in DePaul Center (library.depaul.edu) are open to the public year-round, 7 am–11 pm. Take plenty of change for the copy machines as check-out privileges are reserved for students and faculty.

DEPARTMENT CONTACT INFORMATION

LINCOLN PARK CAMPUS ADMISSIONS OFFICE: *773-325-7500*
LOOP CAMPUS ADMISSIONS OFFICE: *312-362-8300*
COLLEGE OF COMMERCE: *312-362-6783*
COLLEGE OF LAW: *312-362-8701*
COLLEGE OF LIBERAL ARTS & SCIENCES: *773-325-7300*
JOHN T RICHARDSON LIBRARY: *773-325-7862*
LOOP CAMPUS LIBRARY: *312-362-8433*
KELLSTADT GRADUATE SCHOOL OF BUSINESS: *312-362-8810*
SCHOOL FOR NEW LEARNING: *312-362-8001*
COLLEGE OF COMPUTING AND DIGITAL MEDIA: *312-362-8381*
SCHOOL OF MUSIC: *773-325-7260*
THEATRE SCHOOL: *773-325-7917*

ILLINOIS INSTITUTE OF TECHNOLOGY

GENERAL INFORMATION

NFT *MAP: 13, 14*
MAIN *CAMPUS: 3300 S FEDERAL ST, CHICAGO, IL 60616*
PHONE: *312-567-3000*
WEBSITE: *WWW.IIT.EDU OR @ILLINOISTECH*
ENROLLMENT: *7,850 (2013)*
ENDOWMENT: *$194 MILLION (2013)*

OVERVIEW

In the 19th century, when higher education was reserved for society's upper crust, meat magnate Philip Danforth Armour put his money to good use and funded an institution dedicated to students who wished to learn a variety of industrial arts. The Armour Institute carried his name until a merger with the engineering school Lewis Institute in 1940 changed the name to Illinois Institute of Technology. Over the next 40 years, the college continued to merge with other small technical colleges, resulting in the IIT we know today. The school is as notable for its Mies Van Der Rohe-designed campus (although it is arguably not his best work) as for its groundbreaking work in aeronautics research. The student center, designed by Dutch architect Rem Koolhaas, includes a space-aged metallic tube through which the local L train travels.

Chicago-Kent College of Law, Stuart School Graduate School of Business, and the Master of Public Administration program are all based in the Loop. The Institute of Design is located near Merchandise Mart. The Rice campus, in west suburban Wheaton, offers undergraduate continuing education and degree programs to working professionals. The National Center for Food Safety and Technology, located on the Moffett Campus in the southwest suburbs, and the IIT Research Institute, housed in IIT's tallest building on its main campus in Bronzeville, are just two of the many research organizations IIT has incorporated since 1936 to serve various needs of private industry and government. IIT grants PhDs and other professional degrees in a vast array of areas including science, mathematics, engineering, architecture, psychology, design, business, and law.

TUITION

Undergrads pay around $40,000 per academic year plus room and board, books, and various fees. Graduate, law and business school tuition varies by program.

SPORTS

IIT competes in NCAA Division III. The Scarlet Hawks field teams in an array of sports, including men's and women's swimming and diving, cross-country, track and field, basketball, soccer, and men's baseball, women's lacrosse, and women's volleyball.

CULTURE ON CAMPUS

Most first-year students live on IIT's architecture-rich campus. The State Street Village student residence, located at State and 33rd Streets, was designed by well-known Chicago-based architect Helmut Jahn. Jahn, a graduate of IIT himself, created the six-building complex across the street from Van Der Rohe's historical landmark, the S.R. Crown Hall. When not diving deep into all manner of stuff that 98 percent of the rest of civilization barely comprehends, IIT students also participate in more than 120 student clubs and organizations and Greek life is not shunned or frowned upon (an IIT fun fact: around 8% of all Greeks get a 4.0 GPA each semester; Bluto Blutarsky these cats ain't). Also, all of Chicago and all it has to offer is accessible via the Red and Green L lines.

DEPARTMENT CONTACT INFORMATION

UNDERGRADUATE ADMISSIONS: *312-567-3025*
GRADUATE ADMISSIONS: *312-567-3020*
ALUMNI OFFICE: *312-567-5000*
ARMOUR COLLEGE OF ENGINEERING: *312-567-3009*
OFFICE OF PROFESSIONAL DEVELOPMENT: *630-682-6035*
CHICAGO-KENT COLLEGE OF LAW: *312-906-5000*
COLLEGE OF ARCHITECTURE: *312-567-3260*
COLLEGE OF SCIENCE: *312-567-3800*
KEATING SPORTS CENTER: *312-567-3296*
INSTITUTE OF DESIGN: *312-595-4900*
LEWIS COLLEGE OF HUMAN SCIENCES: *312-567-3956*
STUART SCHOOL OF BUSINESS: *312-906-6500*

LOYOLA UNIVERSITY (LAKE SHORE CAMPUS)

GENERAL INFORMATION

LAKE SHORE CAMPUS: *1032 W SHERIDAN RD, CHICAGO, IL 60626*
PHONE: *773-274-3000*
WATER TOWER CAMPUS: *820 N MICHIGAN AVE, CHICAGO 60611*
PHONE: *312-915-6000*
HEALTH SCIENCES CAMPUS: *2160 S FIRST AVE, MAYWOOD, IL 60153*
PHONE: *708-216-9000*
WEBSITE: *WWW.LUC.EDU OR @LOYOLACHICAGO*
ENROLLMENT: *15,957 (2014)*
ENDOWMENT: *$463 MILLION (2014)*

OVERVIEW

Loyola University, one of the largest Jesuit universities in the United States, is known throughout the Midwest for its first-rate schools of business and law, as well as for its Medical Center (a well-respected research institution). It was originally established in 1870 as St. Ignatius College and was re-named in 1909.

Lake Shore Campus, the largest campus of Loyola's four campuses, is on the lake in Rogers Park and houses the College of Arts & Sciences, the Graduate School, Niehoff School of Nursing, Mundelein College Adult Education Program, and Cudahy Library. The university's Water Tower campus downtown on Michigan Avenue is home to the Schools of Business, Education, Law, and Social Work and some College of Arts & Sciences courses. Loyola operates the Stritch School of Medicine and the Master's degree programs through the Niehoff School of Nursing at its suburban Maywood campus. The university also has a campus in Rome, one of the largest American campuses in Western Europe, as well as centers in Beijing on the campus of Beijing University and Vietnam. Notable graduates include Sho Yano, who ranks first in the world with the highest known I.Q. Other notable grads include Chicago Bears owner George S. Halas Jr., actor/comedian Bob Newhart, and celebrated authors Sandra Cisneros and Stuart Dybek.

TUITION

Undergraduate tuition costs just over $37,000 (give or take a couple hundred dollars depending on the program of study), including most added fees. All first- and second-year students are required to live on campus and participate in a meal plan.

SPORTS

Represented by their mascot the LU Wolf, the Loyola Ramblers compete in the NCAA Division I Missouri Valley Conference. Loyola rambles in varsity sports such as men's and women's basketball, cross-country, golf, soccer, track and field, and volleyball and women's softball. The Ramblers haven't seen a lot of

recent success, with the exception of the men's volleyball program, which won a national title in 2014. Catch basketball at the Joseph J. Gentile Center on the Lake Shore Campus. For tickets, visit the box office, call 773-508-WOLF or visit www.loyolaramblers.com.

CULTURE ON CAMPUS

Founded in 2005, the Loyola University Museum of Art (LUMA) showcases the famous Martin D'Arcy collection of Medieval, Renaissance and Baroque art. Paintings by masters Tintoretto, Guercino, Bassano, and Stomer, plus sculpture, furniture, jewelry, decorative arts, and liturgical vessels, are part of the over 500-piece collection dating from 1150 to 1750. The museum, located at 820 N Michigan Avenue, is housed in the historic Lewis Towers building on Mag Mile. General admission is $8, $6 for seniors and $2 for non-Loyola students under age 25 (free on Tuesdays or every day with Loyola ID) Hours: Tues, 11 am–8 pm; Wed–Sun: 11 am–6 pm. For more information, call 312-915-7600 or visit www.luc.edu/luma.

The university's Cudahy Library, Lewis Library at the Water Tower Campus, Science Library, Health Sciences Library, and Graduate Business School Library are all open to the public. Checkout privileges, however, are reserved for the university's students and faculty.

The Loyola University Theatre performs at the Kathleen Mullady Theatre (1125 W Loyola Ave, 773-508-3847) in the Centennial Forum/Mertz Hall building on the Lake Shore campus. A second studio stage is active with student productions during the fall and spring term, and a number of Loyola arts alumni events take place every year on campus.

The Loyola Campus also offers a variety of media options for its students. Printwise, there is Inside Loyola, Loyola Magazine and the Loyola Phoenix student newspaper. WLUW (88.7 FM) hosts a variety of shows.

DEPARTMENT CONTACT INFORMATION

UNDERGRADUATE ADMISSION OFFICE: *312-915-6500*
SCHOOL OF CONTINUING AND PROFESSIONAL STUDIES: *312-915-8900*
COLLEGE OF ARTS & SCIENCES: *773-508-3500*
QUINLAN SCHOOL OF BUSINESS: *312-915-8900*
SCHOOL OF EDUCATION: *312-916-6800*
SCHOOL OF LAW: *312-915-7120*
STRITCH SCHOOL OF MEDICINE: *708-216-3229*
NIEHOFF SCHOOL OF NURSING: *773-508-3249*
JOHN FELICE ROME CENTER: *773-508-2760*
SCHOOL OF SOCIAL WORK: *312-915-8900*
GRADUATE SCHOOL OF BUSINESS: *312-915-6124*
THE GRADUATE SCHOOL: *773-508-3396*
UNIVERSITY LIBRARIES: *773-508-2632*

NORTHWESTERN UNIVERSITY (EVANSTON CAMPUS)

GENERAL INFORMATION

EVANSTON CAMPUS: *633 CLARK ST, EVANSTON, IL 60208*

PHONE: *847-491-3741*

CHICAGO CAMPUS: *ABBOTT HALL, 710 N LAKE SHORE DR, CHICAGO, IL 60611*

PHONE: *312-503-8649*

WEBSITE: *WWW.NORTHWESTERN.EDU OR @NORTHWESTERNU*

ENROLLMENT: *21,000 (2014)*

ENDOWMENT: *$7.9 BILLION (2013)*

OVERVIEW

Northwestern University, along with the University of Chicago, likes to think of itself as part of the "Ivy League of the Midwest." While this might seem a little snooty, NU is certainly the cream of the crop in the Big Ten Conference. 21,000 full- and part-time students attend Northwestern's 12 schools and colleges, located in Evanston and downtown Chicago, a far cry from the two original faculty members and ten students in attendance when the school opened in 1855. NU's campus in Doha, Qatar opened in 2008 and offers communication and journalism degrees, along with a certificate in Middle East studies and a minor in politics and media.

Founded in 1851, Northwestern University was established in Evanston by many of the same Methodist founding fathers of the town itself, including the founder of Chicago's Board of Trade. The University's name was derived from its founders' desire to service the citizens of the former Northwest Territory. The 240-acre lakefront campus is bordered roughly by Lincoln Street to the north and extends south to Clark Street and west to Sheridan Road. The Evanston campus houses the Weinberg College of Arts and Sciences; McCormick School of Engineering and Applied Science; the Schools of Music, Communication, Education and Social Policy; the Graduate School; Medill School of Journalism; and J.L. Kellogg School of Management.

The university did a bit of branching out when it purchased land for the Chicago campus in 1920. Located on a 25-acre lot between the lake and Michigan Avenue in the Streeterville neighborhood, the Chicago campus houses the Schools of Law, Medicine, and Continuing Studies. Graduate school and Kellogg courses are also offered at the Chicago campus. Several excellent hospitals and medical research institutions affiliated with the university dominate the northern edge of Streeterville. The Robert H. Lurie Medical Research Center at Fairbanks Court and Superior Street, completed in 2004, has expanded the university's research abilities with nine floors of laboratory space. The Prentice Women's Hospital, completed in 2007, continues to offer comprehensive and innovative treatments bolstering women's and infants' health.

TUITION

The university charges around $47,000 for undergrad tuition only. Room and board rates hover around $15,000 for an undergraduate student living in a double room and on a 14-meal-per-week plan.

SPORTS

The only private school in the Big Ten conference, Northwestern fields eight men's and eleven women's intercollegiate teams along with a host of club teams. A rare powerhouse outside the northeast, the women's

lacrosse team won the NCAA national championship seven times between 2005 and 2012, going undefeated in two of those seasons. The Wildcats' football fortune has been looking up ever since the purple-clad boys broke an epic 33-year losing streak in 2004; subsequent years have seen bowl games and an occasional Top 25 ranking. The Wildcats' home is Ryan Field at 1501 Central Avenue, about three blocks west of the Central stop on the elevated Purple Line of the CTA. Basketball games are held at the Welsh-Ryan Arena behind the stadium. For tickets, visit www.nusports.com or call 888-467-8775 (i.e., "888-GO-PURPLE"). Northwestern students get free admission to any home game with valid NU Wild-CARD ID.

CULTURE ON CAMPUS

The Mary and Leigh Block Museum of Art on the Evanston campus (40 Arts Circle Dr; 847-491-4000; www.blockmuseum. northwestern.edu or @NUBlockMuseum) has 4,000 items in its permanent collection, including Old Masters' prints, architectural drawings, contemporary photographic images, and modern sculpture. The Block is also home to the state-of-the-art Pick-Laudati Auditorium that hosts film festivals and contemporary classics, as well as cinema series and lectures throughout the year. Hours: Tues, 10 am–5 pm; Wed–Fri, 10 am–8 pm; weekends, 10 am–5 pm. Admission is always free, but a suggested donation is appreciated.

The Pick-Staiger Concert Hall (50 Arts Circle Dr, 847-491-5441; www.pickstaiger. com or @pickstaiger), is not only the main stage for the university's musical performances but it is also home to several professional performance organizations such as the Chicago Chamber Musicians, Chicago Philharmonic, Northshore Concert Band, Evanston Symphony Orchestra, and others. Each year, Pick-Staiger Concert Hall also hosts the Segovia Classical Guitar Series and the Winter Chamber Music Festival. Call 847-467-4000 or visit www. pickstaiger.com to purchase tickets.

Student-led A & O Productions (www. aoproductions.net or @aoproductions) has been programming events, hosting films, and bringing comedians, speakers, and bands to campus since 1969. Past performers have included Lupe Fiasco, Tracy Morgan, Snoop Dogg, and Sarah Silverman.

For the upper echelon student interested in art or vandalism, one can visit the famed "Rock" that students began defacing in the 1940s. "Go Cats!," "Rich Kids Can Tag As Well!" and "I'm wasting my parent's money!" have all made brief appearances. Northwestern University also runs a student newspaper, The Daily Northwestern, and a student-run radio station, WNUR 89.3 FM (www.wnur.org or @WNUR893).

DEPARTMENT CONTACT INFORMATION

UNDERGRADUATE ADMISSIONS: *847-491-7271*
GRADUATE SCHOOL (EVANSTON): *847-491-5279*
WEINBERG COLLEGE OF ARTS AND SCIENCES: *847-491-3276*
FEINBERG SCHOOL OF MEDICINE: *312-503-8649*
KELLOGG SCHOOL OF MANAGEMENT: *847-491-3308*
MEDILL SCHOOL OF JOURNALISM: *847-467-2050*
SCHOOL OF COMMUNICATION: *847-491-7023*
SCHOOL OF PROFESSIONAL STUDIES: *312-503-6950*
SCHOOL OF EDUCATION AND SOCIAL POLICY: *847-491-8193*
MCCORMICK SCHOOL OF ENGINEERING AND APPLIED SCIENCE: *847-491-5220*
SCHOOL OF LAW: *312-503-3100*
SCHOOL OF MUSIC: *847-491-7575*

UNIVERSITY OF CHICAGO

GENERAL INFORMATION

NFT MAP: *19*
MAILING ADDRESS: *EDWARD H. LEVI HALL, 5801 S ELLIS AVE, CHICAGO, IL 60637*
PHONE: *773-702-1234*
WEBSITE: *WWW.UCHICAGO.EDU OR @UCHICAGO*
ENROLLMENT: *15,000 (2014)*
ENDOWMENT: *$6.7 BILLION (2013)*

OVERVIEW

Located amid the pleasant tree-lined streets of Hyde Park just seven miles south of downtown Chicago, the University of Chicago is a world-renowned research institution with a winning tradition in Nobel prizes. More than 80 Nobel laureates have been associated with the university as faculty, students or researchers. The university prides itself on its rigorous academic standards and top-ranked programs, while its students thrive in an environment that encourages creative exploring, taking risks, intellectual rigor, and determining the direction and focus of one's own education.

While its business, law, and medical schools are renowned for cranking out brainy gurus with assembly line efficiency, the university also has a long alumni list filled with artists, writers, politicians, film directors, and actors. To name a few: Studs Terkel, Sara Paretsky, Carol Moseley-Braun, Kurt Vonnegut, Susan Sontag, David Auburn, Ed Asner, Saul Bellow, Katharine Graham, Philip Glass, Saul Alinsky, Paul Goodman, Mike Nichols, and Second City improv theater founders Bernard Sahlins and Paul Sills.

Established in 1890, the University of Chicago was founded and funded by John D. Rockefeller. Built on 200 acres donated by Marshall Field and designed by architect Henry Ives Cobb, the university's English Gothic buildings of ivy-clad limestone ooze old money and intellectual achievements. Rockefeller described the university as "the best investment I ever made." We just hope parents footing the bill for their kids' education feel the same.

The University of Chicago operates on a trimester schedule rather than the more common two-semester academic year. Chicago has about 15,000 students, 5,000 of which are undergraduates. About 2,000 of the graduate students attend classes at the downtown riverfront campus Gleacher Center (450 N Cityfront Plaza Dr, 312-464-8787; www.gleachercenter.com), where the popular Graham School of Continuing Liberal and Professional Studies holds most of its continuing education classes.

TUITION

Undergraduate tuition is inching up toward $50,000 a year, not including room and board, although the university makes an effort to graduate two-thirds of its students debt free.

SPORTS

A long time ago, the famous nickname "Monsters of The Midway" belonged to The University of Chicago's football team (not "da Bears"), and the institution garnered football trophies right along with Nobel Prizes. The Maroons racked up seven Big Ten Football championships between 1899 and 1924, but the gridiron glory of yore faded and losing teams became the norm. The bleachers at Stagg Field, where fans once flocked to witness athletic triumphs, earned more fame as the site where Enrico Fermi and university scientists split the atom on Dec. 2, 1942. Four years later, President Robert Maynard Hutchins put in the university's walking papers from the Big Ten and abolished the football team. Perhaps this was a step towards prioritizing scholarly pursuits over athletic achievement, however the catastrophic results of the "controlled release of nuclear energy" might

be to blame. But the school hasn't totally abandoned sports. Varsity football, reinstated in 1969, is back, albeit in a different form. UChicago is a member of NCAA Division III's University Athletic Association and hosts 19 varsity athletic sports in a conference comprised of some of the nation's leading research institutions, and since 1990 has won team championships in men's basketball, women's cross country, football, men's and women's soccer, softball, men's indoor track & field, and wrestling. The campus also boasts over 45 club sports and hundreds of intramural teams.

CULTURE ON CAMPUS

The Reva and David Logan Center for the Arts is the University of Chicago's state-of-the art multidisciplinary arts center. Opened in 2012, the 184,000-square-foot building integrates a dynamic mix of spaces to create a rich environment for arts and scholarship for the university, the South Side and greater Chicago. Visit logan.uchicago.edu for the calendar of events.

The Robie House, located at 5757 S Woodlawn Ave, is Frank Lloyd Wright's residential ode to all things horizontal and structurally organic (312-994-4000; flwright.org). This Prairie-style masterpiece is considered one of the most important buildings in the history of American architecture. Adult tickets cost $17, students and seniors pay $14.

Two must-see but often overlooked free museums on campus are the Oriental Institute Museum (1155 E 58th St, 773-702-9520; oi.uchicago.edu or @orientalinst) and the Smart Museum of Art (5550 S Greenwood Ave, 773-702-0200; smartmuseum.uchicago.edu or @SmartUChicago). Showcasing ancient treasures from university digs since the 1900s (and yes, Indiana Jones did his undergraduate studies at U of C), the Oriental Institute houses permanent galleries

devoted to ancient Egypt, Nubia, Persia, Mesopotamia, Syria, Anatolia, the ancient site of Megiddo, along with a rotation of special exhibits. The Smart Museum boasts a permanent collection of 10,000 fine art objects spanning five millennia of both Western and Eastern civilizations–so yes, it'll be enough to look at for that afternoon you have to kill.

To satisfy your inner cineaste, take in a picture show at Doc Films (Ida Noyes Hall, 1212 E 59th St, 773-702-8574; docfilms.uchicago.edu or @DocFilmsChicago), the largest continuously running student film society in the nation. The screenings at their state-of-the-art theater range from foreign art house fare to documentaries to Hollywood classics, and feature companion lectures and Q&A with professors, actors, directors, and producers. If you're jonesing for a music fix, University of Chicago Presents is one of the city's landmark classical music presenters and features a variety of performers in the elegant, Victorian-style Mandel Hall (chicagopresents.uchicago.edu or @chicagopresents).

The university's Equity playhouse Court Theater continues its national reputation of staging critically acclaimed contemporary and classical productions by renowned playwrights (5535 S Ellis Ave, 773-753-4472; www.courttheatre.org or @courtchicago).

DEPARTMENT CONTACT INFORMATION

UNDERGRADUATE STUDENT ADMISSIONS: *773-702-8650*
DIVINITY SCHOOL: *773-702-8200*
BOOTH SCHOOL OF BUSINESS: *773-702-7743*
GRAHAM SCHOOL OF CONTINUING LIBERAL AND PROFESSIONAL STUDIES: *773-702-1722*
HARRIS GRADUATE SCHOOL OF PUBLIC POLICY STUDIES: *773-702-8400*
LAW SCHOOL: *773-702-9494*
PRITZKER SCHOOL OF MEDICINE: *773-702-1939*

UNIVERSITY OF ILLINOIS AT CHICAGO

GENERAL INFORMATION

NFT *MAP: 26*
ADDRESS: *1200 W HARRISON ST, CHICAGO, IL 60680*
PHONE: *312-996-7000*
WEBSITE: *WWW.UIC.EDU OR @UICNEWS*
ENROLLMENT: *28,000 (2014)*
ENDOWMENT: *$675 MILLION (2013)*

OVERVIEW

With over 27,000 students, the University of Illinois at Chicago (UIC) is the largest university in the city. Located on the Near West Side, UIC is ethnically diverse and urban to the core. It is a leading public research university and home to the nation's largest medical school. Its legacy as a builder in Chicago, however, is a bit spotty. In the mid-1960s, the school leveled most of what was left of a vibrant Italian-American neighborhood to build its campus next to the Eisenhower Expressway.

Today, UIC continues to consume city blocks south of Roosevelt Road in further developing the South Campus. The expansions have all but erased the colorful, landmark Maxwell Street flea market area (this bustling mess of market now takes place only on Sundays along nearby S Canal Street). Of course, not everyone is crying over the loss of the eyesore market or the decrepit, crumbling buildings and homes that comprised the area, although we question whether a community of pricey cookie-cutter townhomes really constitutes much of an improvement. One thing that everyone seems to agree on is that many of the campus' original, ugly cement slab structures are kissing the wrecking ball as well. Even with the multi-million-dollar improvements, the campus is still fairly average; unless you're going to class or the doctor, a lone trip to UIC to see the Jane Addams Hull-House Museum is sufficient.

TUITION

In-state undergraduate tuition and fees ranges from approximately $11,000 to $14,000 .

SPORTS

The UIC Flames, named after the Great Chicago Fire of 1871, are, uh, hot these days. The men's basketball team competes in the NCAA tournament, and the women's gymnastics, tennis squad, and softball teams have all advanced to NCAA tournament play in recent years. Other Flames

men's and women's teams include swimming & diving and cross-country/track & field. UIC also has men's tennis, gymnastics, baseball, and soccer, as well as women's basketball and volleyball. Basketball games and women's volleyball matches are played at UIC Pavilion at the corner of S Racine Avenue and Harrison Street. For tickets, call 312-413-8421, or visit www.uicflames.com.

Too bad the NCAA doesn't have a bowling tournament because UIC would be a strong contender. The campus has its own alley located at 750 S Halsted Street (312-413-5170) where the public is welcome to sling balls and swig beers with students.

CULTURE ON CAMPUS

Jane Addams Hull-House (800 S Halsted St, 312-413-5353; www.uic.edu/jaddams/hull or @JAHHM), America's first settlement house, opened in 1889. The free museum documents the pioneering organization's social welfare programs that supported the community's destitute immigrant workers. Jane Addams was cool. Way cool. Museum hours are 10 am to 4 pm Tuesday through Friday and noon to 4 pm on Sunday, closed on Mondays and Saturdays.

DEPARTMENT CONTACT INFORMATION

ADMISSIONS AND RECORDS: *312-996-4350*
GRADUATE COLLEGE: *312-413-2550*
SCHOOL OF ARCHITECTURE: *312-996-3335*
COLLEGE OF APPLIED HEALTH SCIENCES: *312-996-2079*
COLLEGE OF BUSINESS ADMINISTRATION: *312-996-2700*
COLLEGE OF EDUCATION: *312-996-4532*
COLLEGE OF ENGINEERING: *312-996-2400*
COLLEGE OF LIBERAL ARTS AND SCIENCES: *312-413-2500*
COLLEGE OF MEDICINE: *312-996-3500*
COLLEGE OF NURSING: *312-996-7800*
COLLEGE OF PHARMACY: *312-996-7240*
SCHOOL OF PUBLIC HEALTH: *312-996-6620*
COLLEGE OF SOCIAL WORK: *312-996-7096*
COLLEGE OF URBAN PLANNING AND PUBLIC AFFAIRS: *312-413-8088*
OFFICE OF CONTINUING STUDIES: *312-996-8025*
UNIVERSITY OF ILLINOIS MEDICAL CENTER: *800-842-1002*

BIKING

GENERAL INFORMATION

ACTIVE TRANSPORTATION ALLIANCE: *9 W HUBBARD ST, STE 402,*
WWW.ACTIVETRANS.ORG OR @ACTIVETRANS; 312-427-3425
CHICAGO CYCLING CLUB: *WWW.CHICAGOCYCLINGCLUB.ORG OR*
@CCC_SCOOP; 773-509-8093
DIVVY BIKES: *WWW.DIVVYBIKES.COM OR OR @DIVVYBIKES;*
855-553-4889
DOT CHICAGO COMPLETE STREETS: *CHICAGOCOMPLETESTREETS.ORG*
THE CHAINLINK: *WWW.THECHAINLINK.ORG*

OVERVIEW

During the Emanuel administration, the city set forth a comprehensive strategy to make Chicago the best big city for bicycling. By 2020, the plan is for a 645-mile network of biking facilities in order to provide a bicycle accommodation within a half-mile of every Chicagoan. In addition, the plan calls for more bikeways where more people live and to build more infrastructure where ridership is high, while establishing a strong backbone of infrastructure where ridership is currently lower.

In short, the bicycling situation in Chicago has improved, but there is still a long way to go. Bike riders still need to carefully navigate the city streets and trails as residents learn to adjust to the city's bicycle initiatives. Currently, Chicago has more than 200 miles of bike lanes—and not just painted lanes on busy thoroughfares where double parking is endemic but also on-street protected and buffered lanes; a recent initiative was to make a two-way, protected bike lane on

Dearborn Street through the Loop. There are more than 36 miles of trails, including the 18.5 mile Lakefront Trail, which does not always require you battle headphone-wearing roller bladers, leashless dogs, and shoulder-to-shoulder stroller pushers. Chicago also has more than 13,000 bike racks—more than most big cities—and sheltered, high-capacity bike parking areas at many CTA rail stations, and even a state-of-the-art bike parking garage in Millennium Park (complete with showers!).

Divvy, the city's bike share system, debuted in the spring of 2013. The system is planned for 4,750 bikes available for sharing at 475 locations across the city. Bikes are available 24 hours a day, 7 days a week, 365 days a year for short point-to-point trips. Users pick up a bike from a self-service docking station and return it to any other station nearest their destination. Yearly membership is $75 and day passes are $7, allowing for unlimited trips of up to 30 minutes each. Users can learn more and enroll at www.divvybikes.com.

If you are a cyclist in Chicago, bear in mind that bicycles, like other vehicles of the roads, are subject to the same laws and rights as drivers. You might feel like you're the only biker in the city who comes to a full stop at a sign, but fastidiously sticking to the laws is a good way to make a case for drivers to accept bikers.

This includes the right to take a lane and the obligation to hand signal for turns. It goes without saying that you should always ride defensively (but don't bike on sidewalks: you can be ticketed). Helmets are still optional, but you'd have to have a pretty thick head to tempt fate without one. The many white "ghost bikes" set up throughout the city serve as vigils for fallen bikers, and remind riders of the need to buy and wear a helmet. Besides, one of the many perks of cycling is that no matter how goofy you may feel in your gear, there is always someone who looks much, much stupider beside you. The same goes for an adequate assortment of chains and u-locks, as bike thievery is rampant in every neighborhood in the city. The police department offers a bike registration service, so you'll have legal recourse if you stumble upon your stolen bike somewhere out there. The Active Transportation Alliance does its best to raise awareness with events like Bike the Drive in May (no cars on Lake Shore Drive for a whole morning!) and Bike to Work Week in June.

BIKES ONBOARD MASS TRANSIT

Bicycles are permitted (free) on all L trains at all times except rush hour (7 am–9 am and 4 pm–6 pm on weekdays). Use the accessible turnstile or ask an attendant to open an access gate. Don't try to take your bike through the tall steel gates–not least of which because it will get stuck. Only two bikes per carriage are allowed, so check for other bikes before you get on. The CTA has equipped all of its buses with front exterior bike racks, which are much less intimidating to use than they appear. If your bike is the first to be loaded, lower the rack and place it in position with the front wheel facing the curb. If there is already a bike on the rack, place your bike's rear wheel toward the curb. If two bikes are already loaded, wait for the next bus (whenever that may be). Bus-traveling bicyclists be warned, horror stories abound about bikes falling off racks, and there are even hit-by-bus-while-trying-to remove-bike rumors. Always tell the driver that you are going to be loading or removing your bike, and ask for help if you need it– not all bus drivers are as gruff as they appear. On Metra commuter trains, bikes are allowed on all weekday trains arriving in Chicago after 9:30 am and leaving Chicago before 3 pm and after 7 pm, and on all weekend trains (with the exception of some major events). There is a maximum number of bikes allowed per rail car (it varies by line–check the Metra website for your planned route), so follow the conductor's instructions if he or she asks you to board a different car.

BILLIARDS AND BOWLING

BILLIARDS

The city's affluent "nesters" may be more interested in big-screen TVs than pool tables these days. The game's popularity goes in cycles. It spiked in the '80s thanks largely to *The Color of Money*, the pool-themed film starring Paul Newman and Tom Cruise, part of which was shot at **Chris's Billiards** on the city's Northwest side. With two-dozen tables, no booze and no nonsense, this Jefferson Park institution remains the most credible spot among Chicago's seasoned players, although it sometimes intimidates newcomers. (We wouldn't call it "sleazy," but we wouldn't eat off the floor, either.) **Uno Billiards** is an oasis of seediness in the otherwise upscale Albany Park area. The equipment's not in tip-top shape, but cut this place and it bleeds character. **Chicago Billiard Cafe** is also a hike from downtown, but it's a pleasant atmosphere with a full food menu.

Somewhat hipper environs can be found at **City Pool Hall**, a well-kept room also noted for its delectable burgers, and **Pressure Billiards & Café**, which boasts regulation tournament tables and, on weekends, one of the city's least hack-prone standup comedy nights. If racking the balls ever gets seriously trendy again, you can bet that the folks at **G Cue Billiards** will be the first to know. Professional player Tom Karabatsos was the original owner of this two-level lounge, which accommodates more hangers-out than pool purists.

BOWLING

Bowling is supposed to be the most blue-collar of all sports, so in the City of Big Shoulders, you'd expect comb-overs, beer frames, unfashionable wrist guards, and visible plumber's cracks to abound. In the '90s, several local alleys jazzed it up for the teenagers with rock music and late-night fog-and-light shows, and we can live with that.

Today, high-end lounges like **10 Pin Bowling Lounge**, mash-up retro kitsch with modern glam. And the upscale, Hollywood-themed chain, **Lucky Strike Lanes**, is a good place to kill time if you're waiting to catch a movie at the adjacent AMC River East.

If you prefer not to define your bowling experience as "sophisticated" or "cutting edge," we recommend the newly-renovated **Lincoln Square Lanes** in Ravenswood, the city's only second-floor alley, which has been open since 1918. Climb a flight of stairs above Matty K's Hardware store and you'll get twelve lanes with old-school wood floors, live blues and rockabilly music on weekends, and a balcony from which to watch the action. Other good choices for an authentic Chicago bowling adventure include **Diversey-River Bowl**, where there's an eclectic mix of league fanatics and hipster rockers ordering bottles of Bud shaped like bowling pins, or the only-slightly-grungy **Waveland Bowl**, which has been open 24 hours a day, seven days a week since 1969. For a place that successfully maintains a vibe of "real deal" authenticity while welcoming newcomers, head to the **Timber Lanes**, where hand scoring still reigns amid wood-paneled walls, a pinball machine, and a well-stocked bar.

GOLF

Weather permitting, golfers can tee up all year round in Chicago. The Chicago Park District's public courses are open daily, dawn to dusk. At **Jackson Park's** premier 18-hole facility, the scenery alone will make you forget the bustle of the city. The nine-hole **Sydney R. Marovitz (Waveland) Golf Course** is usually busy, but it has great views of the lake. And **Robert A. Black's** nine-hole, 2,339-yard, par-33 layout was designed by the renowned Dick Nugent. In addition, the park district operates three driving ranges and three learning centers, including one for juniors at Douglas Park.

The Forest Preserve District of Cook County offers 11 public courses in and around the Northwest Side. **Indian Boundary's** huge fairways and fast-moving greens make for fun play and golfers often catch glimpses of visiting deer. At **Edgebrook**, bordered by mature trees along the Chicago River, the signature fifth hole–a 93-yard par three with an elevated green–offers a serious test of skill. Just 10 minutes from downtown, Billy Caldwell's sharply undulating greens make it a great place to play a quick nine. Many of the city's courses offer twilight specials, so bring your glow-in-the-dark balls if you're looking to save some cash.

And, for a real urban golf experience, the privately owned **Harborside International** on the South Side, host to some Illinois PGA events, offers two tricky 18-hole, Scottish-links courses open to the public in season. Private courses in the city include the Beverly, Ridge, and Ridgemoor country clubs and Riverside Golf Club. However, if you want to see Tiger Woods play, you'll have to head out to the suburbs; the PGA tour visits clubs like Cog Hill in southwest Lemont and the members-only Medinah Country Club in the western 'burbs.

If you prefer your golf a little smaller, in-the-know mini-golfers head to the Park District's exceptionally cheap miniature golf course at **Diversey**, or the free mini golf course at **Douglas Park**. or head down south to the ultimate in windmill-dodging action, supernatural-themed Haunted Trails Amusement Park. **Navy Pier** also has a course, but the throngs of tourists with multi-colored balls makes it hard to recommend for the putt-putt purist.

RECREATIONAL PATHS

GENERAL INFORMATION

CHICAGO PARK DISTRICT: **WWW.CHICAGOPARKDISTRICT.COM**
OR **@CHICAGOPARKS**, 312-742-PLAY (7529)
ACTIVE TRANSPORTATION ALLIANCE: **WWW.ACTIVETRANS.ORG**
OR **@ACTIVETRANS**, 312-427-3325
CHICAGO AREA RUNNER'S ASSOCIATION: **WWW.CARARUNS.ORG**
OR **@CARARUNS**, 312-666-9836

OVERVIEW

Greater Chicago offers more than 250 recreational off-road paths that allow bikers, skaters, walkers, and joggers to exercise without worrying about vehicular traffic.

LAKEFRONT TRAIL

Chicago has one of the prettiest and most accessible shorelines of any city in the US–this is the 500-pound gorilla of recreational paths in Chicago. Use one of Lake Shore Drive's over/underpasses (generally available every half mile or so) and you'll discover 15 miles of bathing beaches and over 20 miles of bike paths–just don't anticipate being able to train for the Tour de France during summer weekends, when the sheer number of people makes it impossible to bike along the path at faster than a snail's pace. But thanks to Burnham and Bennett's 1909 "Plan for Chicago," at least we can count on the shoreline remaining non-commercial, with great cycling, jogging, blading, skating, and swimming opportunities for all.

MAJOR TAYLOR TRAIL

If you've ever wanted to take in a slice of Chicago's southwestern-most corner (and let's face it, who hasn't?), try the six-mile bike route that begins at Dawes Park at 81st and Hamilton Streets near Western Avenue. The route incorporates an abandoned railroad right-of-way and runs to the southeast through Beverly and Morgan Park, ending up at the Cook County Forest Preserve near 130th and Halsted Streets. The trail was named in honor of cycling legend Marshall "Major" Taylor, one of the first African American cyclists, who lived out the final years of his life in a YMCA in Chicago.

NORTH BRANCH TRAIL

To access the northern end of the trail, take Lake Cook Road to the Chicago Botanic Garden, located east of I-94. You can also start from any of the forest preserves as the path winds southward. To access the southern end of the trail in Chicago, take Milwaukee Avenue to Devon Avenue and head a short way east to the Caldwell Woods Preserve. The North Branch winds along the Chicago River and the Skokie Lagoons, but unlike most of the other trails, this one crosses streets, so be careful and look out for cars as you approach. Still, it represents a great way to get out of the city–and if you make it all the way to the Botanic Garden, admission is free as you won't have to pay for parking!

BURNHAM GREENWAY

The 11-mile stretch of the Burnham Greenway, which extends from 104th Street on the city's south side all the way down to Lansing in the south suburbs, has a bit of a checkered past (the former railroad right-of-way was once cited for major pollution), but now the paved route is great for biking, skating, and pedestrians. Expect to find all of northern Illinois' major ecosystems, from wetlands to prairies to a Ford Motor plant in close proximity to one another.

NORTH SHORE CHANNEL TRAIL

This trail follows the North Shore Channel of the Chicago River from Lawrence Avenue through Lincolnwood, Skokie (where you'll find a bizarre sculpture park lining the trail), and Evanston to Green Bay Road at McCormick Boulevard. Not all of the seven miles of the trail are paved bike paths and you'll have to switch back and forth between path and street. Skokie paved the trail segment between Oakton and Howard Streets, but there are still many missing links in the route, much to the chagrin of Friends of the Chicago River (FOCR), who are trying to extend and improve the Channel Trail. The Green Bay Trail branches off to the north from the North Shore Channel Trail and will take you past multi-million dollar houses, cute suburban downtowns, and the Ravinia Festival.

CHICAGO PARK DISTRICT

Many of the parks under the jurisdiction of the Chicago Park District have paths dedicated to cycling, jogging, walking, rollerblading, and skating. The Chicago Area Runner's Association is so committed to lobbying for runners' rights that it successfully petitioned to have the Lincoln Park running paths plowed and salted through the winter so they could continue their running activities (though prepare to find water fountains that are shut off and bathrooms that are locked). This calls into question the sanity of such masochistic dedication, but we can only assume that the entire year is needed to prepare for the Chicago Marathon, held annually in October.

THE 606 TRAIL

The long-awaited elevated path is slated to open in June 2015 on the tracks of the former Bloomingdale Line. The corridor adds nearly three miles of safe, recreational green space to Wicker Park, Bucktown, Logan Square and Humboldt Park. As construction progresses and gentrification spreads west, real estate developers are already tripping over themselves to build, gut or reno every property within view of the trail.

SKATING

GENERAL INFORMATION

CHICAGO PARK DISTRICT: 312-742-PLAY (7529);
WWW.CHICAGOPARKDISTRICT.COM OR @CHICAGOPARKS

OVERVIEW

Due to the temperature extremes that Chicago experiences, its residents can enjoy both ice skating and inline skating at various times of the year. Ice skating can be a fun, free, winter activity if you have your own skates, and if you don't, many rinks rent them. Skateboarding is also a popular pastime and a number of parks throughout the city are equipped with skating facilities.

INLINE SKATING

Paths and streets fill up in the summertime with these one-row rollers. Similar to bike riding, inline skating in Chicago serves dual purposes. If you plan on strapping on the blades to get from A to B, be super-careful navigating the streets. As it is, Chicago drivers tend to have difficulty seeing cyclists, and chances are they won't notice you until you've slammed into their open car door. Wear protective gear whenever possible, especially a helmet, and learn to shout loudly so that people can anticipate your approach. If recreational skating is more your speed, Chicago has many recreational paths with cool places to skate.

ROLLER DERBY

If watching skating seems far more interesting than actually lacing up, catch the Windy City Rollers, Chicago's premier all-female roller derby league. Featuring tattooed beauties beating the crap out of each other while skating the circular track, the WCR is unlike any other Chicago sporting event out there. Plenty of beer is served, and the atmosphere is fun and loose, while still retaining the competitive spirit that makes the Derby the Derby.

SKATE PARKS

If you're more interested in adrenaline than exercise, grab your blades or board and a couple of buddies and head down to the magnificent Burnham Skate Park (east of Lake Shore Drive at 31st St). With amazing grinding walls and rails, vert walls, and banks, Burnham Park presents hours of fun and falls. *Logan Blvd Skate Park* is a shared board-bike facility, and features a bowl corner with a spine, smaller quarters with hips, funbox with small flat and down rail, smaller spine and some hips. There are also places to skate in Lincoln, Piotrowski, and Grant Parks.

ICE SKATING

The Park District's seven outdoor rinks offer free admission and reasonably priced skate rentals, making ice skating an excellent way to turn bitterly frozen winter lemons into recreational lemon ice. The city-owned *McFetridge Sports Complex* offers indoor skating year round The Olympic-sized skating rink and warming-house complex at *Midway Plaisance* offer a South Side venue for dropping precise one-footed salchows on an unsuspecting public.

If you, like the rest of Chicago, have recently caught hockey fever, try your hand at one of the many adult and child leagues run year round at *Johnny's Ice House*,

The McCormick Tribune Ice Rink at Millennium Park is another option: admission is free and rentals run $10. The Winter Wonderfest at Navy Pier also features a seasonal rink (www.winterwonderfest.com), as does Wrigley Field's *The Rink at Wrigley*.

SWIMMING AND TENNIS COURTS

SWIMMING GENERAL INFORMATION

CHICAGO PARK DISTRICT: *312-742-PLAY (7529)*;
WWW.CHICAGOPARKDISTRICT.COM OR @CHICAGOPARKS

The Chicago Park District operates more than 50 outdoor pools and more than 25 indoor pools, many of which are equipped with ramps or lifts for disability access. At the top of our list is the 500-person-capacity outdoor wonderment at **Washington Park**, a 50-meter pool that's connected to a large, oval, side pool where fountains spray into a zero-depth entrance. Even better—it's got a 36-foot, theme-park-style water slide. It's overrun with pool rats during open swim periods, but grown folks like the designated lap times, water aerobics classes, and adult swims.

We also like the 30-meter outdoor pool at **River Park**, an Albany Park spot that boasts a diving well, a spacious deck with lounge chairs and umbrella tables, and an interactive kids' water playground. And when the weather gets cold, there's great lap swimming at the **Ida Crown Natatorium** at Eckhart Park. What's a natatorium? It's a pool inside its own building, and this one looks like it might have been designed by Eero Saarinen, but it wasn't.

All outdoor pools are free for the summer (mid-June to Labor Day). During the year, lap swim fees for indoor pools are $25 a month or $40 for three months. Get a complete list of facilities and register for aquatic exercise, diving, lifeguard, underwater hockey, and water polo classes at www.chicagoparkdistrict.com.

TENNIS COURTS

While we admit we're suckers for any sport that includes the word "love" in its scoring system, we try not to think of the significance that it means "zero" in tennis talk. Find love and more at these Chicago tennis courts.

INDOOR FACILITIES

McFetridge Sports Center is the only indoor public facility in the system. All tennis courts are free and open to the public on a first-come-first-served basis. Courts are open daily—check each park for individual hours. **Midtown Tennis Club** offers lessons and competitive programs for kids and adults.

OUTDOOR FACILITIES

In the summer, opt for tennis with a view at several lakeside facilities. Look for newly reconstructed courts in Grant Park's soon-to-be completed Maggie Daley Park in Spring 2015. Waveland Park's Tennis on the Lake provides daily instruction from April through October. A full listing of the Chicago Park District's 120+ facilities is available at www.chicagoparkdistrict.com.

SOLDIER FIELD

GENERAL INFORMATION

NFT MAP: *11*
ADDRESS: *1410 S MUSEUM CAMPUS DR, CHICAGO, IL 60605*
PHONE: *312-235-7000*
WEBSITE: *WWW.SOLDIERFIELD.NET OR @SOLDIERFIELD*
BOX OFFICE: *847-615-BEAR (2327)*
BEARS WEBSITE: *WWW.CHICAGOBEARS.COM OR @CHICAGOBEARS*
TICKETMASTER: *800-745-3000 OR WWW.TICKETMASTER.COM*

OVERVIEW

The gleaming hunk of stadium with the mismatched Doric columns out front is the second iteration of Soldier Field, which first opened October 9, 1924–the 53rd anniversary of the Chicago Fire. Planned just after World War I, the facility was originally known as Municipal Grant Park Stadium before being rechristened in 1925 as Soldier Field. Although it is probably best known as the home of Da Bears, the football team did not even start using Solider Field until 1971. Indeed, the stadium has seen its share of events, from college football to NASCAR to a Martin Luther King, Jr. rally to stadium shows by The Rolling Stones, U2, Madonna, Bruce Springsteen, and Bon Jovi.

In 1985 Soldier Field was listed on the National Register of Historic Places, a sentimental pick. Soon enough, however, with the stadium needing major repair and lacking the requisite pro football amenities like ginormoscreens and luxury boxes, officials began the delicate task of figuring out exactly how to update the landmark. The solution was to basically gut the inside and preserve some of the stadium's distinctive column facade. In 2006 Soldier Field was delisted from the National Register of Historic Places.

Originally constructed for $13 million, the 2003 renovation of Soldier Field cost $632 million. Although the Bears lost to the Green Bay Packers in their first game at the renovated stadium, the finished product was lauded for its forward-looking design. Also, there was more sideline seating, concession stands, and bathrooms–the last of which you can never have too many. And of course the ginormoscreens: two 82-foot-by-23-foot behemoths, which, at 1,886 square feet, offer more space than many American homes.

Public tours are available Mon–Fri 9 am–5 pm. Tours include access to the field, south courtyard, Doughboy statue, grand concourse, colonnades, Skyline Suite and visitors' locker room. Tours cost $15 for adults and $10 for students 10 and over.

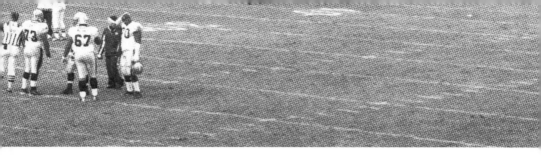

HOW TO GET TICKETS

Single-game tickets are available in July via Ticketmaster. Set your alarm. Season tickets are nearly impossible to come by, unless you're related somehow to Bill Swerski, in which case see if 'ol Uncle Bill will chip in for your Personal Seat License, whose prices seem to rival a freaking taxi medallion. The best way to get great seats (other than by having them left to you in a will) is to use the various online ticket exchanges, either the officially sanctioned Ticketmaster Ticket Exchange resale site or an entity like StubHub.

HOW TO GET THERE

By Car: From the north or south, take Lake Shore Drive; follow the signs to Soldier Field. For parking lots, exit at E McFetridge, E Waldron, E 14th Boulevard, and E 18th Drive. From the west, take I-55 E to Lake Shore Drive, turn north, and follow the signs. Travel east on I-290, then south on I-90/94 to I-55; get on I-55 E to Lake Shore Drive. On non-game days, expect to pay around $22 for the parking lots surrounding Soldier Field, less for Adler Lot, and you can reserve a spot online before you arrive. Rates rise significantly on game days; suffice it to say, you don't even want to know. Visit www.soldierfieldparking.com for detailed information or call the Soldier Field Parking Hotline at 312-235-7701. Two parking and game-day tailgating lots are located south of Waldron Drive. There are also lots on the Museum Campus off McFetridge Drive and near McCormick Place off 31st Street and E 18th Street.

By Train: On game days, CTA Soldier Field Express bus 128 runs non-stop between the Ogilvie Transportation Center and Union Station to Soldier Field. Service starts two hours before the game, runs up to 30 minutes after kickoff, and up to one hour post-game.

By L: Take the Red, Orange, or Green Lines to the Roosevelt station stop. Board eastbound CTA bus 146 to the Museum Campus, and then walk south to Soldier Field. Walking from Roosevelt station would take approximately 15 minutes...an alternative to waiting for the bus.

By Bus: CTA bus 146 stops on McFetridge Drive near Soldier Field. Buses 3, 4, 12, and 18 stop somewhat near the stadium.

US CELLULAR FIELD

GENERAL INFORMATION

NFT *MAP: 13*
ADDRESS: *333 W 35TH ST, CHICAGO, IL 60616*
GENERAL *INFO: 312-674-1000*
TICKET *SALES: 866-SOX-GAME*
WEBSITE: *WWW.WHITESOX.COM OR @WHITESOX*

OVERVIEW

Both of Chicago's major league ball-parks are named for corporations (one famous for gum, the other famous for cell phones) but the similarities end there. Any White Sox fan will tell you: tourists pay big bucks to watch ivy grow in the little place on the North Side, real baseball fans head to see the White Sox play at US Cellular Field.

Straddling the Bridgeport and Bronzeville neighborhoods on Chicago's south side, US Cellular Field opened in 1991 to replace the old Comiskey Park. The new park was built for $167 million—a relative bargain even in 1991. Cost-cutting meant altering the original design, though, and not for the better (though it does preserve a replica of Bill Veeck's signature exploding firework scoreboard from the old yard). What the park lacks in beauty, it makes up for with its friendly staff, terrific sightlines (although the park itself faces the wrong way, wedged uncomfortably between 35th Street and an elementary school) and fabulous food—perennially rated among the best in Major League Baseball. Meat-eaters: follow your nose to the grilled onions and say "Polish with." Better yet, say "Polish witt"—you'll get a sublimely good Polish sausage smothered in caramelized onions. And for the vegetarian, as long as you keep your voice down, you can snag a very tasty veggie dog at several of the Sox's many concession stands. Indeed, look around and you'll notice that most Sox fans do enjoy their food at the ballpark. And if you're hoping to hear about fashion, or business deals, or coffee shops, this ain't the place. Fans here talk about baseball. They love the game, and they love the team that finally brought a World Series trophy to Chicago back in 2005.

HOW TO GET TICKETS

Purchase tickets through the team's website (www.whitesox.com) or at the US Cellular Field Box Office (weekdays: 10 am–6 pm, weekends: 10 am–4 pm). Children shorter than the park's turnstile arm (approximately 36 inches) are admitted free, but must share your seat. Attendance is generally abysmal, so take advantage of desperate specials such as Half-Price Monday tickets, available on select Monday home games (except for big ticket matchups, e.g., Yankees, Cubs). Check the website for Value Days schedules. Pet check is located between Gates 2 and 3, for a $3 fee.

HOW TO GET THERE

By Car: US Cellular Field is located at the 35th Street exit off the Dan Ryan Expressway. Take I-90/94, stay in the local lanes, and exit at 35th Street. If you're parking, exit at 35th Street. Follow signs to "Sox Parking" at lots E, F, and L on the stadium's south side. Fans with red, prepaid season parking coupons exit at 31st Street, and follow signs for "Red Coupons" to lots A, B, and C just north of the stadium. If the 35th Street exit is closed due to heavy traffic, which is often the case on game days, proceed to the 39th Street exit; turn right for "Sox Parking" and left for "Red Coupons." The handicapped parking and stadium drop-off area is in Lot D, west of the field and accessible via 37th Street. If you're planning to tailgate, the lots open two hours before the game and close 30 minutes after everything is said and done.

By Bus: CTA buses 24 and 35 stop closest to the park. Others stopping in the vicinity are the 29, 44, and 39.

By L: Ride the Red Line to the 35th Street-Sox stop just west of the ballpark. Another good option, especially heading north after the game, is the Green Line. The 35th-Bronzeville-IIT (Illinois Institute of Technology) Station is a little longer walk that the 35th Street-Sox stop, but always less crowded.

WRIGLEY FIELD

GENERAL INFORMATION

NFT MAP: *29*
ADDRESS: *1060 W ADDISON ST, CHICAGO, IL 60613*
GENERAL INFO: *773-404-2827*
TICKET SALES: *800-THE-CUBS (843-2827)*
WEBSITE: *WWW.CUBS.COM OR @CUBS*

OVERVIEW

Built in 1914 and originally known as Weeghman Park, the stadium was renamed Wrigley Field in 1926 to honor chewing gum mogul and former Cub owner William Wrigley, Jr. It is the second-oldest ballpark in Major League Baseball (a few years behind Boston's Fenway Park) and is (along with Fenway, in certain years, at least) sometimes more interesting for its rich history than for what's taking place on the field. With its signature ivy-covered walls, manual scoreboard, and view-obstructing columns, Wrigley harks back to a bygone era of baseball stadia—night games weren't even possible at Wrigley until 1988 when lights were finally installed. That said, a multi-hundreds-of-millions-dollar, four-year renovation, will add seating, hoodely-doo amenities, an adjacent multi-use development, and—gasp!—a massive jumbotron in the outfield by 2018. And while the good news is that the changes will be privately financed, the trade off will be more on-field advertising to help pay for it.

Quirks abound at Wrigley. Strange lake-effect wind patterns wreak havoc on batters, especially in the early months of the season. Invading seagulls sometimes make the infield look like a cross between an aviary and Hitchcock's The Birds. And about those nearby buildings with the seats on them—until the 1990s, it was a time-honored tradition for the club to share sightlines. Then building owners got a little greedy, erecting bleacher seats and actually charging people to sit up there. As renovations proceed and precious rooftops sightlines are threatened, tensions between the front office and these business owners continue.

The Cubs haven't won a World Series title since their back-to-back wins over Detroit in 1907 and 1908, and haven't even appeared in the Fall Classic since 1945, yet this lovable losing team has one of the most impressive attendance records in Major League Baseball. Still, Wrigley has still hosted its share of historic moments: Ernie Banks' 500th career home run in 1970, Kerry Wood's twenty strikeouts in 1998, and Sammy Sosa's sixty home runs in 1998, 1999, and 2001. Every year, faithful fans claim this is their year; optimism remains, regardless of record, bad trades, overpaid and underperforming players, bad ownership/management, and ruinously expensive beer. All that aside, a day

at Wrigley is like no other experience in the world, and a must-see for any self-respecting Chicagoan/baseball fan, and there is nothing—nothing!—like singing "Take Me Out to The Ballpark" during the seventh inning stretch inside the friendly confines. Because no matter the score, no matter the curse, we will "root, root, root for the Cubbies."

HOW TO GET TICKETS

Individual game tickets can be purchased from the Cubs' website, by calling 800-843-2827, or in person at Wrigley Field outside of Gate F at the corner of Clark and Addison Streets; open weekdays from 8 am to 6 pm and weekends from 9 am to 4 pm. You can usually score discount tickets to afternoon games Monday through Thursday in April, May, and September, or by waiting around the ballpark until the game starts. Especially when they are in the typical six-game losing skid.

HOW TO GET THERE

By Car: If you must. Remember the old days when Wrigleyville hillbillies used to let you park on their front lawns for five bucks? Well, today traffic on game days is horrendous, and parking prices are sky-high. Post-game spill-out from local bars and dozens of mindless cab drivers freeze traffic as police do their best to prevent drunken revelers from stumbling into the streets. From the Loop or south, take Lake Shore Drive north; exit at Irving Park Road, and head west to Clark Street; turn south on Clark Street to Wrigley Field. From the north, take Lake Shore Drive to Irving Park Road; head west to Clark Street, and turn south. From Chicago's West Side, take I-290 E or I-55 N to Lake Shore Drive, then follow directions above. From the northwest, take I-90 E and exit at Addison Street; travel east three miles. From the southwest side, take I-55 N to I-90/94 N. Exit at Addison Street; head east to the park.

Street parking around Wrigley Field is heavily restricted, nearly impossible and insanely expensive. The Cubs operate several garages around the area, and advance reservations are available up to 24 hours in advance by calling 800-843-2827. On game nights, tow trucks cruise Wrigleyville's streets nabbing cars without a resident permit sticker. On night and weekend games, park smart at the team's free remote lot, which has 1,000 spaces and a free shuttle to Wrigley.

By L: Take the Red line direct to Wrigley Field, get off at the Addison Street stop one block east.

By Bus: CTA buses 22, 8, and 152 stop closest to Wrigley Field.

UNITED CENTER

GENERAL INFORMATION

NFT MAP: *23*
ADDRESS: *1901 W MADISON ST, CHICAGO, IL 60612*
PHONE: *312-455-4500*
WEBSITE: *WWW.UNITEDCENTER.COM OR @UNITEDCENTER*
CHICAGO BULLS: *312-455-4000, WWW.BULLS.COM OR @CHICAGOBULLS*
CHICAGO BLACKHAWKS: *312-455-7000, WWW.CHICAGOBLACKHAWKS.COM OR @NHLBLACKHAWKS*

OVERVIEW

The commanding crown of Chicago's West Town District, the United Center is home to both the NHL's Blackhawks and the NBA's Bulls. The stadium, which seats about 20,000 for both hockey and basketball, is also a theater, convention hall, and concert venue. Opened in 1994, the $175 million stadium was privately funded by deep-pocketed Blackhawks owner William Wirtz and penny-pinching Bulls majority owner Jerry Reinsdorf (a privately funded and owned stadium—what a concept!) and built to replace the beloved but aging Chicago Stadium. The new arena borrows from the old Madhouse on Madison, which stood across the street until 1995: the old building's exterior and even its acoustics are alluded to and echoed in the new facility. And just in case you forget whose "house" this is, the impressive statue of Michael Jordan posterizing an anonymous bronze mass located in front of the main entrance to the United Center is there to remind you (although Blackhawk legends Stan Mikita and Bobby Hull also are honored with statues along Madison, and Jordan wingman Scottie Pippen and coach/broadcaster Johnny "Red" Kerr have bronzes inside the building). When the United Center isn't reveling in all those rings and hoisted cups, it serves as the city's go-to venue for arena rock acts like Springsteen, The Rolling Stones, and U2. In 1996 it hosted the Democratic National Convention.

HOW TO GET TICKETS

Book tickets over the phone or online with Ticketmaster, or visit the United Center box office at Gate 4. On non-game days, box office hours are generally Monday to Saturday, 11 am to 6 pm (Sat until 4 pm). On game days, the box office is open until the first intermission or halftime.

HOW TO GET THERE

By Car: From the Loop, drive west on Madison Street to United Center. From the north, take I-90/94 and exit at Madison Street; head west to the stadium. From the southwest, take I-55 N to the Damen/Ashland exit; head north to Madison Street. From the west, take I-290 E to the Damen Avenue exit; go north to Madison Street.

By L: Take Orange, Green, Purple, or Brown lines to Madison and switch to westbound 20 bus. Or, take the Forest Park Branch of the Blue line to the Medical Center-Damen Avenue Station. Walk two blocks north to United Center.

By Bus: CTA bus 19 United Center Express is the most efficient choice. In service only on event and game days, this express bus travels from Randolph Street south down Michigan Avenue, then west along Madison Street to the United Center. No stops are made between Halsted and the United Center. Service begins 90 minutes before events and continues for one hour after events end. CTA bus 20 also travels Madison Street beginning at Wabash Avenue and has "owl service."

SPORTS LEAGUES AND CLUBS

Even though the city seemingly perennially ranks among the fattest in the country, Chicagoans aren't completely unfamiliar with the concept physical fitness, which is saying something in the land of deep dish pizza and Italian beef. Leagues aren't just limited to stalwarts like basketball and home-grown 16-inch softball; dodgeball and kickball leagues abound, and if you can organize the squad and raise the money necessary to participate, you won't even notice you're working out as you pelt some unsuspecting lame-o in the face with an inflated rubber ball.

GENERAL TIPS

If you're interested in finding a specific league or group for a particular sport, a good place to start is Chicago Athlete magazine. This free publication is also available online at www.mychicagoathlete.com and is distributed around town.

If you're a beginner, before you go spending a ton of money on your sport of choice, check out what the Chicago Park District (www.chicagoparkdistrict.com) has to offer. They offer loads of clubs, training groups, and classes on a wide range of sports from archery to weightlifting to yoga—all on the cheap. Their handy online program guide lets you search by age group, parks, program type, or zip code.

MULTIPLE SPORTS LEAGUES AND CLUBS

Chicago Sport and Social Club (www.chicagosocial.com) is the mother of all of the Windy City leagues. Offering volleyball, basketball, football, floor hockey, soccer, dodge ball, dance, bowling, running, kickball, yoga, softball, rock climbing, kayaking, tennis, boot camp and boxing fitness, and even bar games (such as euchre, darts, and pool), this league has it all.

The non-profit Chicago Metropolitan Sports Association (chicagomsa.leagueapps.com) is the largest gay and lesbian sports organization in the Midwest, offering badminton, bowling, flag football, soccer, co-ed and women's softball, tennis, and volleyball. Even if you're not interested in playing, it's still fun to watch.

RUNNING

By far, most of the area sports groups and clubs are focused on running. If you're training for a running event—everything from your first 5K to the Chicago Marathon—the Chicago Area Runner's Association (www.cararuns.org) has you covered. This organization is for all levels of runners—from the seasoned marathoner to the amateur looking to begin running for the first time.

TRIATHLON

When you're ready to, er, "tri" something a little more intense you can set your sights on a triathlon. The city offers tons of opportunities to get involved with this swim-bike-run race. Clubs run the gamut from volunteer-driven organizations to professional training for a fee. Check out Chicago Endurance Sports (www.chicagoendurancesports.com), Chicago Tri Club (www.chicagotriclub.com), Lakeview YMCA Triathlon Club (www.ymcachicago.org/lakeview), or Together We Tri (www.togetherwetri.com).

RUGBY

If rugby's your game, Chicago has opportunities to join in the fun and violence. Two women's teams dominate the Chicago scene—North Shore Women's Rugby (www.northshorerugby.com) and Chicago Women's Rugby (www.cwrfc.org). For the men, Chicago offers more opportunities: Chicago Griffins Rugby Club (www.chicagogriffins.com), Chicago Lions Rugby Football Club (www.chicagolions.com), Lincoln Park Rugby Football Club (www.lprfc.com), and the South Side Irish (www.southsideirishrugby.com).

O'HARE AIRPORT

GENERAL INFORMATION

ADDRESS: *10000 W O'HARE AVE, CHICAGO, IL 60666*
AIRPORT CODE: *ORD*
PHONE: *773-686-2200/800-832-6352*
WEBSITE: *WWW.OHARE.COM OR @FLY2OHARE*
PARKING: *773-686-7530*
TRAVELER'S AID: *773-894-2427*
POLICE: *773-686-2385*
CUSTOMS INFORMATION: *773-894-2900*

OVERVIEW

Named for Butch O'Hare, the superstar US Navy fighter pilot who earned a Medal of Honor during World War II, O'Hare International Airport is one of the busiest airports in the world, handling more than 66 million passengers each year. For many around the country, O'Hare serves as the source of B-roll for news reports about crazy-making weather-related travel delays, often during the holidays, and for good reason: of the top metropolitan statistical areas in the US, Chicago is probably the one with the worst winter weather. So there's that. But don't let worries of delays and frozen runways keep you grounded.

The airport, located just 17 miles northwest of the Loop, is so close to town that it's actually within Chicago city borders. That said, allow plenty of time to get to the airport, but don't stress too hard about security lines unless you're going to Europe. Or if it's Christmas. Or if you're going to Europe on Christmas. Or if you're taking a puddle jumper to Dubuque. Keep in mind if you're taking a red-eye flight that most eateries and shops are closed at night and early morning, so bring snacks and a novel. A good one.

Expansion spells relief, and the O'Hare modernization and expansion plan begun under former Mayor Daley continues under Mayor Rahm Emanuel, having already opened an additional runway while reconfiguring the existing seven runways. Along with other improvements, when the program is complete, O'Hare's capacity should be doubled, helping the airport keep busy well into the 21st century.

Psst. We'll tell you a secret that will make picking up guests at the airport a lot more pleasant. Sign up online for the airline to notify you of flight information and changes via your cellphone, then park your car, and head to the Hilton bar (located in the airport) to wait out the arrival. Better yet, avoid the stress of driving by taking the train in, then waiting at the Hilton bar for Aunt Sally, and load her and yourself into a cab. You probably shouldn't be driving at this point, anyway.

HOW TO GET THERE

By Car: Strongly consider taking public transit to O'Hare, peek a few inches forward for information on the L. But if you absolutely must drive, pay close attention here. To be on the safe side, allow over an hour just for the drive (more during rush hours).

By Bus: Pace Suburban bus routes 250 (with connections to CTA Yellow and Purple Lines) and 330 (connecting with Amtrak/Metra BNSF Line La Grange Road Station) both stop at the airport.

By Train: As a train with an inbound/outbound rush hour-focus, the odds of the Metra North Central Line schedule conveniently coinciding with your flight time are slim, but it could be worth it if you plan in advance. The North Central Line departs Union Station for Antioch, with a stop at the O'Hare Transfer station several times a day (weekdays only). Fare from Union Station is $4.75 one-way. Travel time is approximately 30 minutes.

By L: The CTA Blue Line train is the easiest and most efficient way to get to O'Hare. Trains run frequently between downtown Chicago and O'Hare 24 hours a day. Travel time from the Loop is 45 minutes. The station is located on the lower level of Terminal 2. From there use the Airport Transit System to reach other terminals. The full fare from O'Hare toward downtown is $5 (back outbound you'll pay the standard single-ride rate).

By Cab: Join the cab queue at the lower level curb-front of all terminals. There are no flat rates, as all of the cabs run on meters, but you probably won't have to spend more than $40. Beware if you're traveling to certain suburbs, though: fare rules allow cabbies to raise your fare for these routes; ask what the fare will be when you enter the cab. Shared ride service is available to downtown ($24 per person), McCormick Place ($24 per person), and Midway International Airport ($37 per person). Cab companies serving O'Hare include American United, 773-327-6161; Flash Cab, 773-561-1444; Yellow Cab, 773-907-0020; and Sun Taxi, 773-736-3883.

By Shuttle: Go Airport Express (888-284-3826 or www.airportexpress.com) provides shared-ride, door-to-door shuttle service between O'Hare and downtown hotels/attractions daily from 4 am until 11:30 pm. Shuttles depart every 10 to 15 minutes from Terminals 1E, 3F, 2D, and 5E. Expect to pay about $30. No reservations necessary (reservations required for other destinations).

Tri State/United Limo (800-248-8747, www.coachusa.com/tristateunitedlimo) offers hourly service between O'Hare and Midway from early morning to evening. The shuttle leaves from the International Terminal's outside curb by Door 5E and from the airport's Bus Shuttle Center in front of the O'Hare Hilton Hotel by Door 4. Allow at least an hour for travel time between the airports and expect to pay $24 for a one-way fare. Tri State/United Limo also serves nearby communities on the South Side and Northwest Indiana, including Notre Dame.

By Limousine: Sounds pricey, but depending on where you're going and how many people you are traveling with, it may be cheaper to travel by limo than by cab or shuttle. Advance reservations recommended.

MIDWAY AIRPORT

GENERAL INFORMATION

ADDRESS: **5757 S CICERO AVE, CHICAGO, IL 60638**
AIRPORT CODE: **MDW**
PHONE: **773-686-2200**
WEBSITE: **WWW.FLYCHICAGO.COM/MIDWAY OR @FLY2MIDWAY**
PARKING: **773-838-0753**
CUSTOMS INFORMATION: **773-894-2900**

OVERVIEW

Named to commemorate the Battle of Midway during World War II, Midway International Airport is located just ten miles southwest of downtown Chicago. Once the world's busiest airport, by the 1960s, Midway eventually lost that title to upstart O'Hare. That said, Midway still ranks as one of the 30 busiest airports in the US, serving 20 million passengers per year. Now considered the city's outlet mall of airports, Midway primarily serves budget carriers like Southwest Airlines. On the positive side, it is an easy alternative to the bigger, badder O'Hare. Plus the bars for pre-flight entertainment aren't as crowded.

The "International" in Midway International Airport returned in 2002 after a 40-year absence, the result of a $739 million terminal development project that added a new terminal building, concourses, parking, and customs facility. The rental car building on 55th Street opened in 2013, and consolidates rental agencies in one spot.

Superstitious travelers beware of flying December 8th. On this date in 1972, a Boeing 737 crashed into a residential area during landing. In 2005, exactly 33 years later another Boeing slid off the runway in a landing attempt on December 8. Spooky.

HOW TO GET THERE

By Car: From downtown, take I-55 S. From the northern suburbs, take I-290 S to I-55 N. From the southern suburbs, take I-294 N to I-55 N. From the western suburbs, take I-88 E to I-294 S to I-55 N. Whether you're traveling north or south along I-55, look for the Cicero Avenue/South/Midway Airport exit.

By Bus: CTA buses 47, 54B, 55, 55A, 55N, 62N, 62H, 63, and 63W all serve the airport. Take the Green Line or the Red Line to the Garfield Station and transfer to bus 55 heading west. If you're coming from the south on the Red Line, get off at the

Escalator Up To: ↗
Ticketing ↴
Baggage Check-In ↑

63rd Street stop and take bus 63 westbound. In addition, Pace suburban routes 379, 382, 383, 384, 385, 386, and 390 travel to the airport.

By L: The most convenient and cost-effective method of travel between Midway Airport and the Loop is a 20-30 minute train ride on the CTA Orange Line. Midway is the terminus of the Orange Line, which circles around the Loop and heads back to the airport. Trains run between 4–4:30 am and approximately 1 am. Trains run frequently during rush hours (approximately every five minutes), less so in the middle of the day, and every 10–15 minutes in the evening and late evening hours. The Orange Line conveniently drops you off inside Midway Airport (a huge plus in winter time!)–allow about 15 minutes to cart yourself and all your accoutrements to the security checkpoint.

By Cab: Cabs depart from the lower levels of the terminals and are available on a first-come-first-served basis. There are no flat rates (all cabs run on meters), but you can plan on paying around $30 to get to the Loop. Shared ride service is available to downtown ($18 per person), McCormick Place ($18 per person), and O'Hare International Airport ($35 per person). Cab companies serving Midway include American United, 773-327-6161; Flash Cab, 773-561-1444; Yellow Cab, 773-907-0020; and Sun Taxi, 773-736-3883.

By Shuttle: Go Airport Express (888-284-3826 or www.airportexpress.com) provides shared ride, door-to-door shuttle service between Midway and downtown hotels/attractions daily from 6 am until 11:30 pm. Shuttles depart approximately every 15 minutes outside the Lower Level Arrivals door #3. Expect to pay about $27 to get to the city.

Tri State/United Limo (800-248-8747, www.coachusa.com/tristateunitedlimo) offers hourly service between O'Hare and Midway from early morning to evening. The shuttle leaves from the Lower Level Arrivals door #3. Allow at least an hour for travel time between the airports and expect to pay $24 for a one-way fare. Tri State/United Limo also serves nearby communities on the South Side and Northwest Indiana, including Notre Dame.

By Limousine: Sounds pricey, but depending on where you're going and how many people you are traveling with, it may be cheaper to travel by limo than by cab or shuttle. Advance reservations recommended.

GENERAL INFORMATION

MAILING ADDRESS: *CHICAGO TRANSIT AUTHORITY, 567 W LAKE ST, CHICAGO, IL 60661*
RTA TRAVEL INFORMATION CENTER: *312-836-7000*
CTA CUSTOMER SERVICE: *888-968-7282*
WEBSITE: *WWW.TRANSITCHICAGO.COM OR @CTA*
VENTRA: *WWW.VENTRACHICAGO.COM OR @VENTRACHICAGO*

OVERVIEW

We may never find a system of public transit free from flaws, but if you need a quick, socially responsible way to get from A to Wrigley, CTA's your guy. Once you figure out its complicated card system, CTA service will get you relatively close to where you need to go (most of the time), and sometimes the city's trains and buses are even on schedule!

For location-to-location CTA directions and schedules, we honestly and without irony, recommend the useful CTA trip planner at tripsweb.rtachicago.com. It is useful in that it includes Pace suburban buses.

FARES AND VENTRA

While buses accept cash and coin, you must use a Ventra card to ride the L. Fare on the L is $2.25. Bus fare is $2 with Ventra card and $2.25 with cash (no transfers with cash fare). On both bus and L, transfers cost 25 cents, up to two additional rides within two hours.

The Ventra Card is a payment system that allows customers to use a single fare card for regional transit through the Chicago area. This means it can be used on CTA and Pace.

THERE ARE THREE WAYS TO USE THE VENTRA SYSTEM:

Ventra Card: Any amount of money can be loaded on to a Ventra Card with cash or online

Ventra Ticket: A disposable, paper card, the Ventra Ticket is for single ride use and day pass unlimited-ride tickets.

Personal bank issued credit cards: Link your personal credit or debit card with RFID chip technology (look for the four nesting parentheses, the universal symbol for information transmitted wirelessly through the ether) to your Ventra account and you add value or purchase passes so you can use your own card as a fare card.

Ventra Cards will have a one-time cost fee of $5 that is refunded as transit value. Disposable, single ride Ventra tickets cost $3, which includes the $2.25 fare, a $.25 transfer and a $.50 limited use ticket fee (since you pay for a transfer whether you take one or not, and you're getting penalized for a single ticket with that $.50, the rational choice is to just get the $5 Ventra Card). You can also use the Ventra Card as a prepaid debit card; just keep in mind the requisite fees associated with most prepaid debit cards.

Ventra Cards are available at Ventra Vending Machines, located at all L stations and at CTA headquarters at 567 West Lake Street. Vending machines are also located at Chicago Union Station, Ogilvie Transportation Center, Millennium Station, Navy Pier, and the Museum of Science & Industry. In addition, retailers across the city both sell and add value to Ventra Cards; check www.ventrachicago.com for a full list of retailers.

UNLIMITED PASSES OFTEN OFFER THE BEST VALUE:

- 1-Day CTA Pass for $10

- 3-Day CTA Pass for $20

- 7-Day CTA Pass for $28

- 7-Day CTA/Pace Pass for $33

- 30-Day CTA/Pace Pass for $100

One-day passes are available as a disposable one-time-only Ventra Card, but other passes require a Ventra Card, though the $5 fee can be applied to the pass cost, depending on how and when you sign up for an account.

Reduced Fares: Reduced fares are available for qualified passengers—people with disabilities, senior citizens, students (during school days/hours only) and children aged 7 through 11 (children under 7 ride free).

CTA BUSES

CTA's buses cart about one million sweaty, crabby passengers around Chicago and its surrounding suburbs everyday; the fleet is the second-largest public transportation system in the US. CTA's 120-plus bus routes mirror Chicago's efficient grid system. The majority of CTA routes run north-south or east-west, and in areas where the streets are numbered, the bus route is usually the same as the street.

The entire CTA bus fleet meets ADA accessibility standards. All buses kneel (or tilt to make the first step less steep). All buses are equipped with wheelchair lifts and secure wheelchair seating. Additionally, as a boon to the visually impaired and those too busy gawking at Chicago's skyscrapers to read the signs on the front of each bus, all buses clearly and loudly announce the bus number and direction at every stop.

Bus Tracker is a helpful online resource helping riders determine "exactly" when a bus will arrive. Accessible via www.ctabustracker.com or via text message, the Bus Tracker gives a damn good estimate of arrival times, cutting down wait times by a significant margin. You'll be grateful in December. And January. And February. And March...

Bus Stops: CTA stops are clearly marked with blue and white signs displaying the name and number of the route, as well as the final destination. Most routes operate from the early morning until 10:30 pm. Night routes, called "Night Owls," are identified on bus stop signage by an owl picture. Owl service runs approximately every half-hour through the night. All bus stop signs are labeled with a "Stop ID number" that you can use to get arrival times by text message. Simply text ctabus [stopID] to 41411 on your cell phone and the bus tracker will text you back with estimated arrival times for all buses at that stop.

Bicycles Onboard: All CTA buses are equipped with bike racks mounted on front grills to carry up to two bikes. The CTA website features tutorial videos that explain how to load a bicycle with the two different systems buses use. Locking your bike to the rack is not allowed, but you are encouraged to sit near the front and keep an eye on your ride.

THE L

OVERVIEW

Whether traveling underground, on street level, or above the sidewalk, Chicagoans refer to their elevated rapid transit system as the "L" (though some prefer to call it the "Smell.") No matter what you call it, nothing says Chicago as loud and clear as the high-pitched whine, guttural grumble, and steely grind of the train itself. L tracks lasso Chicago's heart, creating The Loop, where five of the seven L lines ride side-by-side above the pulsating business and financial district.

FARES

All L trips require a Ventra Card, Chicago's universal fare card. To use cards, tap the reader on top of the turnstile. Standard fare on CTA trains is $2.25, and a 25 cent transfer allows two additional rides within two hours of issuance. Transfer rates are automatically deducted from your fare card when reused within the time limit. Transferring within the rail network is free at determined, connected transfer stations.

FREQUENCY OF SERVICE

CTA publishes schedules that say trains run every 3 to 12 minutes during weekday rush hours and every 6 to 20 minutes all other times. Nice idea, but the truth is service can be irregular, especially during non-rush hours, after-hours, and in bad weather. While the system is relatively safe late at night, buses with Owl night service may be better options in the wee hours. The CTA's Train Tracker app gives station-specific ETAs to minimize the number of times you lean in to the tracks in search of your train.

L LINES

Blue Line: Its 24-hour O'Hare and Forest Park branches service the West and Northwest sides, including getting travelers to and from O'Hare Airport in a jiffy.

Pink Line: Chicago's newest elevated rail line took over the Blue Line's former Cermak/Douglas route with service to the near Southwest Side. The first trains leave the 54th/Cermak terminus at 4:05 am weekdays, and the last train from the Loop leaves 1:30 am daily.

Red Line: Runs north-south from the Howard Street station down to the 95th Street/Dan Ryan station; operates 24-hours.

Brown Line: Starts from the Kimball Street station and heads south with service to the Loop and sometimes just to Belmont Avenue, where you can connect with the 24-hour Red Line.

Orange Line: Service from Midway Airport and Chicago's Southwest Side to and from the Loop.

Green Line: Covers portions of west and south Chicago. The Harlem/Lake Street branch travels straight west to suburban Oak Park, while the Ashland/63rd Street and Cottage Grove branches go south and split east and west.

Purple Line: Shuttles north/south between Linden Place in suburban Wilmette and Chicago's northernmost L station at Howard Street. An express service runs from Linden to the Loop, with no stops between Howard and Belmont, during weekday rush hours.

Yellow Line: Also known as the "Skokie Swift," the Yellow Line runs between the north suburban Skokie Station and Chicago's Howard Street station, with one intermediate stop at Oakton Street.

BICYCLES

Bicycles ride free and are permitted on board at all times except weekdays from 7 am to 9 am and 4 pm to 6 pm. Only two bikes are allowed per car, so survey the platform for other bikes and check out the cars as they pull into the station for two-wheelers already on board.

GREYHOUND BUSES

Greyhound (800-231-2222, www.greyhound.com or @GreyhoundBus) is the rock-bottom traveler's best friend. The bus line offers dirt-cheap fares, the flexibility drifters prefer, "basic" station "amenities," and the gritty, butt-busting experience of traveling America's scenic blue-line highways and rural byways with some colorful characters.

Stations: Greyhound's main train station is south of Union Station at 630 W Harrison St in West Loop (312-408-5821). CTA buses 60, 125, 156, and 157 make stops near the terminal. The closest L stop is on the Blue Line's Forest Park Branch at the Clinton Street Station on Congress Parkway. Additional Chicago-area Greyhound stations are located within L train stations: 14 W 95th St in the Red Line's 95th Street/Dan Ryan Station (312-408-5999), and 5800 N Cumberland Ave on the Blue Line's O'Hare Branch in the Cumberland Station (773-693-2474).

Shipping Services: Greyhound Package Express (www.shipgreyhound.com) offers commercial and personal shipping services and is available at all three Chicago bus stations. Packages are held at the station for pick-up.

Fares: Tickets can be purchased on the phone or online with a credit card, or at a station with cash, travelers' checks, or credit cards. Regular fare pricing applies for both individual advance ticket sales and minutes-before-departure sales.

Discounts are available for children under 12 (up to 25% off regular fares), seniors 62 and older (5% discounts), and military members (10% discounts). Students and veterans can receive discounts via respective membership cards (with associated fees). The cost for an individual return ticket is always deeply discounted if it is purchased at the same time as a departure ticket. Tickets purchased three days in advance earn up to two reduced companion ticket (no age restrictions). Check website for web only specials. Passengers accompanying someone with a disability always ride at a reduced rate.

MEGABUS.COM

Roll over Greyhound, there's a new dog in town, and a cheaper one at that! An import from the UK, Megabus.com (us.megabus.com or @megabus) buses travel between most major Midwest cities, including Minneapolis, Detroit, Milwaukee, St. Louis, Cleveland, Indianapolis, and beyond, and a host of smaller destinations across the Midwest.

Fares: Ticket prices are determined by how far in advance you buy your tickets, how popular the route is, and what day of the week you travel on. If your Fairy Godmother is on your side, it is possible that you could take a trip to, say, Kansas City, for as low as $1. Of course, as the service becomes more popular, the fares go up.

Stations: Megabus doesn't have stations, per se. But you'll see the line snaking outside Union Station as you approach. Union Station in downtown Chicago is the arrival and departure stop for all buses out of Chicago. Park yourself at the east side of South Canal Street, between Jackson Blvd and Adams Street, and try to get there early. It's first come, first serve seating.

METRA TRAIN LINES

GENERAL INFORMATION

METRA ADDRESS: **METRA PASSENGER SERVICES, 547 W JACKSON BLVD, CHICAGO, IL 60661**
PHONE: 312-322-6777
WEBSITE: **WWW.METRARAIL.COM**
RTA TRAVEL INFORMATION: 312-836-7000, **WWW.RTACHICAGO.COM**

OVERVIEW

With 11 lines and roughly 495 miles of track, Metra does its best to service Cook, DuPage, Lake, Will, McHenry, and Kane counties with 241 stations scattered throughout the city and 'burbs. The rails, branching out from four major downtown stations, are lifelines for commuters traveling to and from the Loop.

The good news for Metra is that ridership is strong; the sheer multitude of folks who live in the suburbs but work in the city (and hate to deal with rush hour) means that Metra will always have a job. The bad news for riders is that parking at popular stations is difficult, if not impossible, and most people don't live close enough to Metra stations to walk. In an attempt to resolve its parking issues, Metra is purchasing land surrounding many suburban stations and constructing new parking facilities.

LOOP STATIONS

There are four major Metra train stations in the Loop which 11 train lines feed into:

STATION/LINE

Ogilvie Transportation Center: Union Pacific/North Line, Union Pacific/Northwest Line, Union Pacific/West Line

Union Station: Milwaukee District/North Line, Milwaukee District/West Line, North Central Service, BNSF Railway, Heritage Corridor, SouthWest Service

LaSalle Street Station: Rock Island District

Millennium Station: Metra Electric District (Main Line, South Chicago, and Blue Island Branches) and South Shore Line

FARES

Depending on the number of the 12 Metra fare zones you traverse, one-way, full-fare tickets cost between $2.75 and $9.25. Tickets may be purchased through a ticket agent or vending machine at select stations, or on board the train (with a $3 surcharge if the station at which you boarded the train had a ticket agent or ticket vending machine). There is no reserved seating.

The ten-ride ticket provides no discount, but Metra offers a monthly unlimited ride pass which is the economical choice for commuters who use Metra service daily. If your commute includes CTA and/or Pace bus services, consider purchasing a Link-Up Pass ($55) for connecting service on CTA during weekday rush hours (6:30 am–9:30 am and 3:30 pm–7 pm) and on anytime on Pace buses. Metra's Weekend Pass costs $7 and includes unlimited rides on Saturday and Sunday, with the exception of the South Shore route.

BEFORE YOU BOARD

Bicycles are permitted on weekday off-peak hours (inbound before 6:31 am and after 9:30 am and outbound before 3 pm and after 7 pm) and at all times on weekends. Large, bulky items like skis, non-folding carts, water buffaloes, and other large items are not allowed on trains. Pets, with the exception of service animals, are also prohibited aboard trains.

AMTRAK

GENERAL INFORMATION

PHONE: *800-872-7245*
WEBSITE: *WWW.AMTRAK.COM OR @AMTRAK*
UNION STATION: *225 S CANAL ST, CHICAGO, IL 60606*
UNION STATION INFORMATION: *WWW.CHICAGOUNIONSTATION.COM*

OVERVIEW

The best city in America for riding the rails, Chicago hubs Amtrak's 500-station national railroad network, which covers every state but Alaska, Hawaii, South Dakota, and Wyoming. Departing from Union Station, Amtrak trains head west to Los Angeles, San Francisco, Portland and Seattle; east to Washington, DC, New York City and Boston; north to Milwaukee and Minneapolis; and south to New Orleans and San Antonio, Texas.

FARES

Amtrak offers affordable fares for regional travel, with travel times comparable to flying when you factor in today's early airport check-ins. Their prices can't compete with airfares on longer hauls, but just as airlines offer deeply discounted fares, so does Amtrak. Ask sales agents about special fares and search Amtrak's website for the best deals. (Booking in advance does present some savings.) We recommend the website, as callers risk being on hold longer than it takes to ride a train from Chicago to Los Angeles.

Amtrak offers special fares year-round for seniors, veterans, students, children under 16, and groups. The "Hot Deals" page on Amtrak's website lists sale fares. Amtrak has also hooked its cars up with plenty of travel partners to create interesting "Amtrak Vacations" packages, including air-rail deals, whereby you rail it one way and fly back the other—attractive for long-distance travel. The prices listed below are approximate, likely to change and don't include upgrades like sleeper cars. Check with Amtrak for updates.

SERVICE

Someday, high-speed rail may come to the Midwest. Meanwhile, only a lucky few can claim to have arrived on time when traveling the longer routes on Amtrak, so tell whoever is picking you up you'll call them on your cell phone when you get close.

Pack food for your ride, as dining car fare is mediocre and pricey. On the upside, Amtrak's seats are comfortable and roomy; some have electric sockets for computer hookups; bathrooms are in every car; and the train is almost always clean.

And you don't have to travel light. Your ticket lets you carry on two bags and check two for free, each weighing up to 50 pounds. Check an additional two bags and items such as bicycles, golf bags, baby strollers, musical instruments, and skis with handling fees of $5 to $20 each. Amtrak's default liability for checked baggage tops out at $500, so if your designer duds are worth more than that you'll want to ante up for extra coverage. Weapons; large, sharp objects; corrosive or dangerous chemicals; and the like are all prohibited, just like on planes; check for current regs before you pack.

UNION STATION

LOCATION: **225 S CANAL ST AT E ADAMS ST AND E JACKSON BLVD**
AMTRAK: **800-872-7245 OR WWW.AMTRAK.COM**
METRA RAIL: **312-322-6777 OR METRARAIL.COM**
GENERAL INFORMATION: **WWW.CHICAGOUNIONSTATION.COM OR @CHIUNIONSTATION**

An innovation for both design and travel, Chicago's Union Station is the "Grand Dame" of rail service in a city once considered to be the undisputed rail center of the United States. Designed by the architects Graham, Anderson, Probst, and White and built between 1913 and 1925, Union Station is a terminus for six Metra lines and a major hub for Amtrak's long-distance services. In its peak during the 1940s, this local transportation treasure handled as many as 300 trains and 100,000 passengers on a daily basis. While today's volume is just half that, this monumental station stands as the last remaining grand station still in use in the City of Chicago and was given landmark status in 2002. Most commuters don't take the time to gaze skyward when rushing through the Great Hall of Union Station (who really has the time to stop and assess their surroundings beyond that of their intended use?), but by not doing so, they are missing something special. Take the time to look up at the magnificent light-swathed ceiling and maybe then it will become clear why Union Station's ornate Great Hall is considered one of the United States' great interior public spaces. Union Station is also a premiere location for formal functions as it annually plays host to a multitude of private affairs and black-tie gatherings.

Public Transportation: The closest L stop to Union Station is Clinton Street on the Blue Line, which stops two blocks south of the station. The Orange, Brown, and Purple Lines stop three blocks east of the station at the Quincy stop on Wells Street. CTA buses 7, 37, 60, 124, 126, 151, 156, 157 all stop at Union Station. Most commuters heading to work in the Loop enter and exit the station from the Madison Street, Adams Street, and Jackson Boulevard doorways where cabs line up.

RICHARD B. OGILVIE TRANSPORTATION CENTER

LOCATION: **500 W MADISON ST AT S CANAL ST**
LOST & FOUND: **312-496-4751**
METRAMARKET: **WWW.METRAMARKET.COM**

Built in 1911 and known locally as the North Western or Madison Street Station, the Metra's Union Pacific Lines originate from the Richard B. Ogilvie Transportation Center, which serves approximately 40,000 passengers each day. Where Union Station is about form and function, Ogilvie focuses solely on function. Overtly stark and sterile, the tall, smoky-glass-and-green-steel-girder building replaced what was once a classic grand train station similar to the ornate, Beaux Arts-inspired Union Station. Though most of the historic fixtures have been removed, some of the original clocks remain and serve as a reminder of earlier days. The empty space under the tracks is now Metra-Market, which is filling up with thousands

of square feet of shops and restaurants to serve the West Loop/Fulton River District area. MetraMarket also houses Chicago French Market with local vendors offering fresh produce, artisanal cheeses and prepared meals.

Public Transportation: The closest L station is the Clinton Street stop at Lake Street on the Pink and Green Lines, several blocks north of the station. CTA buses 20, 56, and 157 board at Washington and Canal Streets and travel to North Michigan Avenue and the Loop. Coming from the Loop, take the same bus lines west across Madison Street. If you're after a cab, you'll find other like-minded commuters lining up in front of the main entrance on Madison Street between Canal and Clinton Streets.

MILLENNIUM STATION

LOCATION: 151 E RANDOLPH ST AT N MICHIGAN AVE
LOST & FOUND: 312-322-7819
WEBSITE: WWW.MILLENNIUMSTATION.COM

Back when it was just Randolph Street Station, this facility was not much to look at. Now that it sits under one of Chicago's major attractions, it has been spiffed up with new shops and a charming blue-terrazzo floor. The underground station, centrally located in the Loop, serves up to 100,000 commuters daily. This is also the station where the South Shore Line to South Bend, Indiana originates. Schedules for all are somewhat sporadic except during weekday rush hour commutes. (The Van Buren Street Station also serves both the Metra Electric and South Shore Lines and is located at East Jackson Boulevard and Van Buren Street.)

Public Transportation: Millennium Station is served by over a half dozen CTA bus routes, including the 3, 4, 56, 145, 147, 151, and 157. One block west of the train station is the CTA's Randolph/Wabash elevated station, which is served by the Orange, Green, Purple, Pink, and Brown Lines.

LASALLE STREET STATION

LOCATION: 414 S LA SALLE ST AT E CONGRESS PKWY
LOST & FOUND: 312-322-8957

The La Salle Street Station, located underneath the Chicago Stock Exchange, serves the Metra Rock Island District Line's passengers. This former behemoth of a station has been greatly reduced in both size and stature, handling roughly 15,000 commuters daily on the line out toward Joliet.

Public Transportation: The Blue Line's La Salle Street stop at Congress Parkway and the Orange, Purple, and Brown Lines La Salle Street stop at Van Buren Street drop L riders right in front of the train station. CTA buses 7, 36, 126, and 151 stop near the station, as well.

DRIVING

GENERAL INFORMATION

CITY OF CHICAGO DEPARTMENT OF TRANSPORTATION (DOT):
WWW.CITYOFCHICAGO.ORG/TRANSPORTATION OR @CHICAGODOT
ILLINOIS DEPARTMENT OF TRANSPORTATION (IDOT): **WWW.DOT.STATE.**
IL.US OR WWW.GETTINGAROUNDILLINOIS.COM OR @IDOT_ILLINOIS
WBBM-AM 780: *TRAFFIC UPDATES EVERY TEN MINUTES ON THE 8S*

ORIENTATION

Anyone who says baldness is hereditary has never found him/herself in a Chicago traffic jam, pulling out his/her hair to pass the time and calm the nerves. We highly recommend taking public transportation whenever possible, especially since Chicago has such strong bus and rail systems. But if you must drive in the city, Chicago's grid system makes it relatively easy to navigate.

The intersection of State and Madison Streets in the Loop serves as the base line for both Chicago's street and house numbering system. Running north and south is State Street—the city's east/west dividing line. Madison Street runs east and west and divides the city into north and south. Street and building numbers begin at "1" at the State and Madison Streets intersection and numerically increase going north, south, east, and west to the city limits. Street signs will let you know in what direction you're heading. The city is divided into one-mile sections, or eight square blocks, each with a consecutively higher series of "100" numbers. For example, Western Ave, sitting at 2400 W, is further west than Ashland Ave, located at 1600 W. In addition, Chicagoans numerically refer to street locations such as Irving Park Road as "40 hundred north" rather than "four thousand north." An interesting historical tidbit about the city's three primary diagonal streets: Milwaukee, Elston, and Lincoln Avenues all used to be Native American trails.

Buildings with even number addresses are on the north and west sides of streets; odd numbers sit on the south and east sides. Chicago's diagonal streets also follow the grid numbering system, most of which receive north or south addresses. East-west streets north of Madison are named, as in Fullerton or Belmont; south of Madison they are generally numbered, as in 31st or 79th, with several major streets being named.

BRIDGE LIFT SEASON

While bridges spanning the Chicago River contribute to the city's architectural fame, they also serve as a major source of traffic congestion. Boating season demands that bridges lower and rise, so as to allow Chicago's elite access between Lake Michigan and storage yards via the Chicago River. On scheduled days from early April until June the Chicago Department of Transportation raises the movable bridges along the Main and South Branches of the river. Bridges are raised one at a time, in order, and each lift takes about ten minutes. In all, 27 bridges are raised, from the Ashland Avenue Bridge on the South Branch to Lake Shore Drive. The Chicago Department of Transportation announces details in advance, so be sure to check the website for details.

SNOW ROUTES

The Department of Streets and Sanitation manages the ice and snow removal on Chicago's streets. Since failure to efficiently handle city snow removal seals the re-election fate of Chicago's mayors, snow events are a serious business. Thus, Chicago doesn't have mere snow plows—instead the mayor oversees a fleet of nearly 300 "Snow Fighting Trucks." From the city's 911 center, the "Snow Command" utilizes

modern urban surveillance systems to zero in on the (literal) facts on the ground. The Chicago Shovels site (www.chicagoshovels. org) is the go-to for updates and real-time, GPS-enhanced plow information.

Between December 1 and April 1 a Winter Overnight Parking Ban is in place for 107 miles of priority arteries daily from 3 am until 7 am, whether or not snow is present. Parking restrictions will also be in effect for another 500 miles of designated snow routes when snow is piled at least two inches on the pavement. Unfortunately, the two-inch snow routes are a crap-shoot. Tow trucks will enforce these restrictions by their own rules, it seems. On a snow route, you will either find your car gone or buried by a passing plow. Safety dictates you keep your car off of these routes even if only an inch and a half are predicted.

MAJOR EXPRESSWAYS AND TOLLWAYS

While the city's grid system is logical, the interstate highway system feeding into the city is confusing for those who don't travel it often. Chicago has free expressways and tollways which require paying a fee. The expressways are generally referred to by their names, such as "The Kennedy" or "The Eisenhower." When venturing to Indiana, one can experience the Chicago Skyway, a stretch of elevated road that connects I-94 and the Indiana Toll Road that soars 120 feet above the Calumet River. When using the tollways, which includes the Skyway, I-PASS speeds up the process and can be purchased through the Illinois State Toll Highway Authority (800-824-7277 or www.illinoistollway.com).

DMVS

The Illinois Department of Motor Vehicles (DMV) is one of life's unavoidable hassles. But you'd be pleasantly surprised to see how many of your car-related responsibilities (like renewing your driver's license, getting vehicle registrations, etc.) can be completed online (www.cyberdriveillinois. com). While the Secretary of State has made vast improvements to the efficiency of all DMV locations, the facility tucked behind the food court of the James R. Thompson Center truly earns its "express" status.

CAR SHARE

Chicago is blessed with good public transportation, and it's of course possible to get along without a car. That said, there are times—laundry, groceries, beer runs—when a private conveyance becomes temporarily necessary. Thankfully, Chicago has been a pioneer in car sharing. Several companies, including Zip Car (www.zipcar.com), Enterprise Car Share (www.enterprisecarshare. com), and Hertz 24/7 (www.hertz247. com), offer a fleet of vehicles at subscribers' disposal for short errands or all-day rental. Cars are parked at convenient locations throughout the city. Peer-to-peer car share is also an option;. Relay Rides (relayrides. com) and Getaround (www.getaround. com) are two such entities where owners rent out their vehicles. Rates for all services hover around $10 an hour, give or take a buck or two.

GENERAL INFORMATION

OFFICE *OF THE CITY CLERK: CITY HALL, 121 N LA SALLE ST, RM 107, CHICAGO, IL 60602*

PHONE: *312-744-6774*

HOURS: *WEEKDAYS, 8 AM–5 PM*

WEBSITE: *WWW.CHICITYCLERK.COM OR @CHICITYCLERK*

DEPARTMENT *OF FINANCE: PO BOX 6289, CHICAGO IL 60680-6289*

WEBSITE: *WWW.CITYOFCHICAGO.ORG/FINANCE*

PARKING *TICKET ASSISTANCE & "BOOT" INQUIRIES: 312-744-PARK (7275)*

AUTO *POUND HEADQUARTERS (FOR TOWED VEHICLES): 312-744-4444*

OVERVIEW

Parking in Chicago has never been what we would call a joyous experience. Between neighborhood permit-only parking zones, snow routes, and a constant rotation of street fairs, street cleaning, street construction, and parking spot "dibs" in the winter, figuring out where and how to park in the city requires an advanced degree in Asininity. Some areas, like Lincoln Park, Lakeview, and Wicker Park, would test the nerves and the patience of the Dalai Lama. These areas are all easily accessible by public transit, and taxi cabs are plentiful, so unless you want to be part of the problem and not the solution, transport yourself accordingly.

In 2009, former Mayor Daley added to the problem by leasing all of Chicago's parking meters to a private firm (a 75 year lease!), causing fares to increase each year, and allowing for changes like expanded metered parking hours. Maybe the ONE positive side of the meter fiasco is the advent of Pay Boxes. These handy contraptions at least do you the courtesy of allowing you to pay with a credit card—through the nose, or whatever other orifices money shoots. The days of saving your quarters are over; now just start a separate bank account for parking. And for further convenience, the ParkChicago app allows you to pay using your smart phone, so when your meter expires there's no need to hightail it back to your car to replenish.

NEIGHBORHOOD PARKING

Residents of Chicago who own motor vehicles must have an annually renewed city sticker for their cars, which can be purchased from the Office of the City Clerk through the mail (by returning the renewal application you've received in the mail), in person at one of their offices, or online. If you're lucky enough to find a parking spot, zoning in many neighborhoods requires you still need to put a permit on your car. Chicago's Residential Parking Permit program reserves street parking during peak parking hours for neighborhood residents and those who provide a service to the residents. Permits cost $25 annually and are available through the Office of the City Clerk via mail, online, and in person.

PARKING TICKETS

The Department of Revenue (DOR) handles the payment of parking tickets. You can pay parking tickets by mail, online, in person, or at Department of Finance EZ Pay Stations. Scribbling curse words on a ticket, ripping it up, and throwing it at the mailbox does not count as "paying" it, according to the stingy DOR.Three or more unpaid tickets guarantees a metal, yellow surprise fitted to your car tire; yep, say hello to the boot.

AUTO POUNDS

To locate your towed vehicle, use the city's online locator (findyourvehicle. cityofchicago.org) or contact the City of Chicago Auto Pound (312-744-4444). For a standard vehicle, the towing fee is a hefty $150 plus a $20 per day storage fee for the first five days, $35 per day thereafter. Fees can be paid at the pound; they accept cash, cashier's checks, VISA, MasterCard, Discover, American Express, and first-born children. No arms or legs, please.

Important note: "Minor" street repairs and construction are common occurrences on Chicago streets, during which signs should be posted on nearby trees or parking meters stating that parking is temporarily prohibited. If you park there, you will be towed. To retrieve your vehicle, don't bother contacting the city pound. They will have no idea what you're talking about! Save yourself the embarrassment of reporting your car stolen, and call the number posted on the sign where your car was parked. Chances are it was kindly moved to another location so as to allow workers to continue with important road improvements, but it may not have officially been moved by the city of Chicago. Operators should be able to track it down using your license plate number since city code mandates that the kindly moving of a car must be reported within a few hours, whether it be by the city or the other parking powers that be. Otherwise, you can always walk around your neighborhood aimlessly searching for your car, but we don't recommend it. We've only been successful doing that once or twice, and, anyway, it just turned out that we forgot where we parked after a night of heavy drinking.

LANDMARKS

By our minds, the designation of "landmark" can apply to buildings of architectural distinction, or the iconic Morton Salt girl, trailing sodium chloride behind her on the roof of the Elston Avenue Morton Salt facility. It could be internationally recognized Chicago iconography (Buckingham Fountain), or something only the locals are aware of ("Meet me by the Totem Pole"). Landmark status is a historical designation, but local landmarks are how you figure out where the hell you are and where you need to go.

LEGACY ARCHITECTURE

Early skyscrapers such as the **Monadnock Building** can be found in the Loop, alongside other noteworthy structures like Adler and Sullivan's historic **Auditorium Building**. Contrast these with Midwest native **Frank Lloyd Wright's Home and Studio** in the suburb of Oak Park. Jump forward a couple of decades and German Mies van der Rohe arrives on the scene, with his dictum "less is more." Trek over to the **Illinois Institute of Technology (IIT)** in the Bridgeport neighborhood to really immerse yourself in his spare glass and steel structures. Chicago is also home to a triumvirate of quirky Bertrand Goldberg masterpieces—**Marina Towers**, which graces the cover of Wilco's Yankee Hotel Foxtrot, **River City** in the South Loop neighborhood, and the **Raymond Hilliard Apartments**.

HISTORICAL HOUSES

Built in 1836, Prairie Avenue's **Clarke House** claims the title of Chicago's oldest home, never mind that the original building of the northwest side's **Noble-Seymour-Crippen House** dates back to 1833. Although **Robie House** is the most famous, Frank Lloyd Wright's prairie-style homes dot Chicago's landscape, including Sheridan Avenue's **Bach House**.

OUTDOOR SPACES

Chicago's status as a green city got off to a good start, thanks to some forward-thinking chaps. By advocating the lakefront as a place for recreation, Daniel Burnham has left a wonderful legacy. Highlights are **Lincoln Park**, with the free **Lincoln Park Zoo**, to the north and **Jackson Park**, site of the 1893 World's Columbian Exposition, to the south. **Grant Park** is home to the **Buckingham Fountain**, and offers festivals throughout the warmer months. And don't forget the harbors. **Belmont Harbor** is home to the Chicago Yacht Club Sailing School, while **The Point at Diversey** provides a fabulous view of the city from the north. Within the downtown itself, outdoor spaces include **Daley Plaza** (you saw it in the movie The Lake House), which offers free lunchtime cultural events. **Garfield Park Conservatory** is a jewel in the barren West Side landscape.

PUBLIC ARTWORK

Better described as a work of art rather than simply an outdoor space, **Millennium Park** is not to be missed. Legendry architect Frank Gehry has conjured up another of his steel creations with the **Jay Pritzker Pavilion**, an open air venue offering complimentary concerts, while British and Spanish artists have stolen the show with **Cloud Gate** (otherwise known as The Bean) and **Crown Fountain** (a.k.a. kiddies' pool). Another heavy concentration of public artwork is found in the Loop, with the **Miro's Chicago** sculpture and Alexander Calder's **Flamingo** two of the best known pieces. How often do children get the chance to slide down a Picasso?

OVERRATED LANDMARKS

With the nickname "The Windy City" derived from the hot air dispensed by earlier politicians, the city also has its fair share of overrated landmarks. The later iteration of **Soldier Field** fits the bill perfectly: if there were flying saucers in classical civilization, they would look something like this. Also registering on the ugly scale is the **James R. Thompson Center**. Enough said. However, the prize for most over-hyped attraction must go to **Navy Pier** with its wall-to-wall tourists and mediocre eateries. Consider yourself warned.

UNDERRATED LANDMARKS

On the other hand, Chicago has a lot of well-kept secrets worth exploring. Home to a large collection of art glass by Louis Comfort Tiffany, the **Chicago Cultural Center** and **Macy's** (formerly Marshall Field's) on State Street both have spectacular domes. Continuing on the glass theme, the **America Windows** by Marc Chagall are another treat often overshadowed by the heavy-weight impressionist collection at the **Art Institute**. Another find is **The Newberry**, which sits quietly on Washington Square Park, but boasts a hive of activity inside: classes, concerts, and lectures. As for the Hyde Park area, check out the **University of Chicago** and **The Oriental Institute** there. You'll also find the **Nuclear Energy Sculpture** by Henry Moore, which commemorates the first nuclear reaction which took place here. Many of the first silent pictures, starring the likes of Charlie Chaplin and Gloria Swanson (back when they had faces) were filmed at Essenay Studio, before more copacetic weather pushed the film industry out west to a little place called Hollywood.

PRACTICAL INFORMATION

USEFUL CONTACTS

Chicago Board of Elections: 312-269-7900, www.chicagoelections.com or @ChicagoElection

Illinois State Board of Elections: 217-782-4141, www.elections.il.gov

ComEd: 800-334-7661, www.comed.com or @ComEd

People's Gas: 866-556-6001 (Emergencies: 866-556-6002), www.peoplesgasdelivery.com

Office of the Mayor: 311, mayor.cityofchicago.org or @ChicagosMayor

Governor's Office: 312-814-2121 or www.illinois.gov/gov

HELPFUL WEBSITES AND LOCAL BLOGS

www.beachwoodreporter.com or @BeachwoodReport: Analysis of local and national politics.

chicagoist.com or @Chicagoist: Local news/events blog.

chicityclerk.com or @chicityclerk: Office of the Chicago City Clerk; renew your city sticker online!

www.chicagorecycling.org: Where to recycle anything and everything in Chicago.

www.choosechicago.com or @ChooseChicago: Official tourism information about attractions, festivals, events, restaurants, and hotels.

www.cityofchicago.org: Helpful all-purpose guide to city services.

chicago.craigslist.org: Everything from casual jobs to rental encounters.

www.dnainfo.com/chicago or @DNAinfoCHI: Local & breaking news.

chicago.eater.com or @eaterchicago: Go-to site for restaurant/bar news.

www.encyclopedia.chicagohistory.org: An astounding resource, entirely digitized.

forgottenchicago.com or @ForgottenChi: Side streets and byways of the city.

www.gapersblock.com or @gapersblock: A popular Chicago web-publication detailing local news, fun events, and cool places in the city.

chicago.metromix.com or @MetromixCHI: City guide put out by the Trib.

pitchfork.com or @pitchfork: Indie music site and sponsors of the grooviest music fest ever.

www.reddit.com/r/chicago: Reddit Chicago.

www.timeout.com/chicago or @TimeOutChicago: The latest and greatest happenings around town: new restaurants, music listings, you name it.

www.yochicago.com or @YoChicago: Real estate and development news.

TAXI CABS

American United: 773-327-6161

Flash Cab: 773-561-1444

Yellow Cab: 773-907-0020

Sun Taxi: 773-736-3883

CHICAGO TIMELINE

1779: Jean-Baptiste Point du Sable establishes Chicago's first permanent settlement.

1803: U.S. Army constructs Fort Dearborn, which is later destroyed by Native American forces allied with British during War of 1812, and rebuilt in 1816.

1818: Illinois is admitted into the union.

1833: Chicago incorporates as a town of 350 people, bordered by Kinzie, Des Plaines, Madison, and the lakefront.

1837: Chicago incorporates as a city. The population is 4,170. Ogden becomes the city's first mayor.

1851: Northwestern University is founded.

1856: Fort Dearborn is demolished.

PHOTO: KEVIN DOOLEY

1860: Republican Party nominates Abraham Lincoln for president at Chicago's first political convention.

1865: Merry Christmas! Union Stockyards open on Christmas Day.

1869: Water tower is completed.

1871: Great Chicago Fire!

1885: World's first "skyscraper," the 9-story Home Insurance building, goes up on La Salle Street.

1886: Haymarket Riots. Eight Chicago policemen are killed.

1889: Jane Addams opens Hull House.

1892: World's first elevated trains begin operation.

1893: Columbia Exposition celebrates 400th anniversary of Columbus's discovery of America.

1907: Physicist Abraham Michelson is first American to win Nobel

1910: Original Comiskey Park opens.

1914: Wrigley Field opens.

1927: $750,000 donated to honor Clarence Buckingham with fountain.

1929: John G. Shedd presents Shedd Aquarium as gift to city.

1930: Adler Planetarium opens through a gift from Max Adler.

1930: Merchandise Mart built by Marshall Field.

1931: Jane Addams becomes first female to win Nobel Peace Prize.

1931: Al Capone sent to prison for 11 years for evading taxes.

1934: John Dillinger shot by FBI outside Biograph Theater.

1955: O'Hare International Airport opens.

1958: End of the line: Last streetcar in Chicago stops operating.

1968: Democratic National Convention riots.

1971: Chicago Union Stock Yards are closed.

1974: Sears Tower is completed.

1983: Harold Washington elected first black mayor.

1995: A heat wave contributed to the death of over 700 Chicagoans.

1997: City Council absolves Mrs. O'Leary's cow of blame for Great Chicago Fire.

1998: Six-peat! Bulls win sixth championship in eight years.

2003: Four-peat! Richard M. Daley re-elected for historic fourth term!

2004: Millennium Park opens.

2005: White Sox win World Series; Cubs fans weep.

2007: Chicago pitched as US bid for 2016 Olympics.

2008: Gov. Rod Blagojevich arrested on corruption charges.

2011: Mayor Emanuel's election signals the end of the Daley era.

ESSENTIAL CHICAGO MOVIES

Northside 777 (1948)
Man with the Golden Arm (1955)
Raisin in the Sun (1961)
Medium Cool (1969)
The Sting (1973)
Blues Brothers (1980)
Risky Business (1983)
Ferris Bueller's Day Off (1986)
Henry: Portrait of a Serial Killer (1986)
Adventures in Babysitting (1987)

Planes, Trains and Automobiles (1987)
The Untouchables (1987)
When Harry Met Sally (1989)
Backdraft (1991)
Candyman (1992)
Wayne's World (1992)
The Fugitive (1993)
Hoop Dreams (1994)
Mission: Impossible (1996)
My Best Friend's Wedding (1997)
High Fidelity (2000)
Save the Last Dance (2001)
What Women Want (2000)
Barbershop (2002)
Chicago (2002)
Road to Perdition (2002)
The Company (2003)
I Am Trying to Break Your Heart (2003)
Batman Begins (2005)
The Weatherman (2005)
The Lake House (2006)
The Break-Up (2006)
Stranger than Fiction (2006)
The Dark Knight (2008)
Public Enemies (2009)
Transformers 3 (2011)

ESSENTIAL CHICAGO BOOKS

Native Son by Richard Wright; Gripping novel about a young black man on the South Side in the '30s.

Neon Wilderness by Nelson Algren; Short story collection set in Ukrainian Village and Wicker Park.

One More Time by Mike Royko; Collection of Royko's Tribune columns.

The Boss: Richard M. Daley by Mike Royko; Biography of the former Mayor.

The Jungle by Upton Sinclair; Gritty look at life in the meat-packing plants.

Adventures of Augie March by Saul Bellow; More Chicago in the '30s.

V.I. Warshawsky by Sara Paretsky; Mystery series firmly rooted in Chicago landscape.

50 Years at Hull House by Jane Addams; Story of the Near West Side.

Secret Chicago by Sam Weller; Off-the-beaten path guidebook.

Ethnic Chicago by Melvin Holli & Peter D'A. Jones; Insider's guide to Chicago's ethnic neighborhoods.

House on Mango Street by Sandra Cisneros; Short story collection about a Latina childhood in Chicago.

Our America: Life and Death on the South Side of Chicago by Lealan Jones, et al.; Life in the Chicago Projects as told by two schoolchildren.

The Pig and the Skyscraper by Marco D'Eramo; Wandering Italian sociologist comes to Chicago and explores the wide world of capitalism through Chicago's radical history, skyscrapers, and meat-processing plants.

The Devil in The White City by Erik Larson; Account of Chicago serial killer H.H. Holmes and the 1893 Chicago World's Fair.

Chicago Tribune
beyond words

MEDIA

TELEVISION

2 WBBM (CBS) chicago.cbslocal.com

5 WMAQ (NBC) www.nbcchicago.com

7 WLS (ABC) abc7chicago.com

9 WGN (The CW) wgntv.com

11 WTTW (PBS) www.wttw.com

20 WYCC (PBS) www.wycc.org

26 WCIU (the U) www.wciu.com

32 WFLD (Fox) www.myfoxchicago.com

38 WCPX (ION Television) www.iontelevision.com

44 WSNS (Telemundo) www.telemundochicago.com

50 WPWR (MyNetworkTV) www.my50chicago.com

66 WGBO (Univision) chicago.univision.com

PRINT MEDIA

Chicago Defender (312-225-2400, chicagodefender.com or @ChiDefender): Black community newspaper.

Chicago Innerview Magazine (773-904-8903, chicagoinnerview.com or @innerviewmag): Free monthly music mag previewing bands coming to concert in town.

Chicago Magazine (312-222-8999, chicagomag.com or @ChicagoMag): Upscale glossy mag.

Chicago Reader (312-222-6920, www.chicagoreader.com or @Chicago_Reader): Free weekly with listings.

Chicago Reporter (312-427-4830, www.chicagoreporter.com or @ChicagoReporter): Investigative reporting on issues of race, poverty, and social justice.

Chicago Sun-Times (312-321-3000, www.suntimes.com or @Suntimes): One of the big dailies; the White Sox to the Tribune's Cubs.

Chicago Tribune (800-874-2863, www.chicagotribune.com or @chicagotribune): The other big daily; the Cubs to the Sun-Times' White Sox.

Crain's Chicago Business (312-649-5200, www.chicagobusiness.com or @CrainsChicago): Business news.

Daily Herald (847-427-4300, www.dailyherald.com or @dailyherald): Suburban news.

Southtown Star (312-321-2333, southtownstar.com or @SouthtownStar): News for southsiders.

Hyde Park Herald (773-643-8533, hpherald.com or @HydeParkHerald): Local for Hyde Parkers.

N'Digo (312-822-0202, ndigo.com or @NDigoMagapaper): Black community weekly.

Newcity (312-715-8777, newcity.com or @newcity): Alternative free weekly.

The Onion (312-751-0503, www.theonion.com); See local listings in AV Club insert.

Red Eye (312-222-4970, www.redeyechicago.com or @redeyechicago): Commuter-targeted offshoot of the Trib for 20- and 30-somethings.

Today's Chicago Woman (312-951-7600, www.tcwmag.com or @TCWmag): Weekly for working women.

UR Chicago (www.urchicago.com or @urchicago) Free monthly local entertainment mag.

Windy City Times (773-871-7610, windycitytimes.com or @WindyCityTimes1): Gay-targeted news weekly.

AM STATIONS

560 WIND Talk
670 WSCR Sports
720 WGN News/Talk/Sports
780 WBBM News/Traffic
820 WCPT Progressive Talk
850 WAIT Religious
890 WLS News/Talk
1000 WMVP Sports/ESPN Radio
1110 WMBI Religious
1200 WRTO Spanish News/Talk
1220 WKRS ESPN Deportes
1300 WRDZ Radio Disney
1390 WGRB Gospel
1450 WCEV Talk (Ethnic)
1490 WPNA Polish
1500 WAKE Oldies
1510 WWHN Gospel
1570 WBGX Gospel
1590 WCGO Conservative Talk
1690 WVON Talk (African American)

FM STATIONS

88.1 WCRX Columbia College
88.5 WHPK University of Chicago
88.7 WLUW Loyola University
89.3 WNUR Northwestern University
90.1 WMBI Christian
90.9 WDCB Jazz

91.5 WBEZ Chicago Public Radio/NPR
92.3 WPWX Urban
92.5 WCPY Progressive Talk/Dance Music
93.1 WXRT Alternative Rock
93.5 WVIX Spanish-language Urban
93.9 WLIT Adult Contemporary
94.7 WLS Classic Hits
95.5 WNUA Spanish-language
95.9 WREV Classic Hits
96.3 WBBM Top 40
96.7 WSSR Adult Contemporary
97.1 WDRV Classic Rock
97.9 WLUP Rock
98.7 WFMT Classical
99.5 WUSN Country
100.3 WILV Oldies
101.1 WKQX Alternative Rock
101.9 WTMX Adult Contemporary
102.7 WVAZ Urban Contemporary
103.1 WVIV Spanish-language
103.5 WKSC Top 40
103.9 WXRD Classic Rock
104.3 WJMK Classic Hits
105.1 WOJO Spanish-language
105.9 WCFS News
106.7 WPPN Spanish
107.5 WGCI Urban Contemporary

CALENDAR OF EVENTS

JANUARY

Chinese New Year: Chinatown; Sunday after the Chinese New Year (late Jan or mid-Feb).

FEBRUARY

Chicago Auto Show: McCormick Place; The nation's largest auto show, over 100 years old (early Feb, www.chicagoautoshow.com).

MARCH

St Patrick's Day Parade: Columbus Drive; The Chicago River turns green—on purpose (Sat before St Patrick's Day, www.chicagostpatsparade.com).

Chicago Flower & Garden Show: Navy Pier; Escape from winter (mid-March, www.chicagoflower.com).

Black Women's Expo: McCormick Place; Empowering seminars, entertainment, and exhibits geared toward African American women (late March, www.theblackwomensexpo.com).

APRIL

Chicago Latino Film Festival: Various venues; Festival screening the best in local and international Latino film (early Apr, chicago-latinofilmfestival.org).

Chicago Improv Fest: Various venues; Nation's best improv comedy acts descend on Chicago, the genre's birthplace (early Apr, chicagoimprovfestival.org).

MAY

Navy Pier Fireworks: Navy Pier; Fireworks light up the night sky every Wednesday and Saturday (May through Aug, www.navypier.com).

JUNE

Do Division Street Fest & Sidewalk Sale: Division St from Damen to Leavitt; Annual event kicks off Chicago's summer street fest season (first weekend in June, www.do-divisionstreetfest.com).

Ribfest Chicago: Lincoln Ave & Irving Park Rd; Great music, people-watching, and of course 50,000 pounds of finger-lickin' good ribs (second weekend in June, www.ribfest-chicago.com).

Printers Row Lit Fest: Dearborn St, b/w Congress Pkwy & Polk St; Author talks and more at this outdoor street fair (second weekend in June, printersrowlitfest.org).

Andersonville Midsommarfest: Clark St, b/w Foster & Catalpa Aves; Ain't it Swede? (Second weekend in June, www.andersonville.org).

Chicago Pride Fest: Halsted b/w Addison and Grace Sts; Boystown comes to life with plenty of festivities to usher in Gay Pride Parade (weekend before Pride Parade, www.chicagopridecalendar.org).

Gay Pride Parade: Broadway/Halsted Sts b/w Montrose and Belmont; Hundreds of thousands show solidarity (last Sun in June, www.chicagopridecalendar.org).

57th Street Art Fair: 57th St b/w Kenwood and Woodlawn; Oldest juried art fair in the Midwest (First week in June, www.57thstreetartfair.org).

Chicago Blues Festival: Grant Park; As much about the soul food as the music (Second weekend in June, www.chicagobluesfestival.us).

Old Town Art Fair: Old Town Triangle District; Arts and crafts in varied media, entertainment, food and kids activities (mid-June, www.oldtownartfair.org).

Eye on India: Various venues; Experience the best of Indian culture and arts (mid-June, eyeonindia.com).

Grant Park Music Festival: Millennium Park; Free classical music concerts in the out of doors (mid-June through August, www.grantparkmusicfestival.com).

SummerDance: Grant Park; Summer-long series of seemingly every kind of dance style, including lessons, all free (late June to mid-September, chicagosummerdance.org).

Gospel Music Festival: Chicago Cultural Center & Ellis Park; local, national and international gospel performers (late June, www.chicagogospelmusicfestival.us).

Gold Coast Art Fair: Grant Park; Art for sale, entertainment, activities, and food (late June).

Family Fun Festival: Millennium Park; All manner of children's activities all summer long (late June through late Aug, @ MPFamilyFun).

JULY

Independence Day Fireworks: Navy Pier; See the night sky above the lakefront lit up in a spectacular light show (July 4, www.navypier.com).

International Festival of Life: Union Park; Celebrate the food, music, and arts of the African Diaspora on the South Side (July 4th weekend, www.festoflife.biz).

Taste of Chicago: Grant Park; Ginormous four-day food festival (early July, www.tasteofchicago.us).

Chicago Hip-Hop Heritage Month: Various venues; Where "New Beat" culture celebrates its past, present, and future (July 1-31, www.chihiphop.org).

Taste of Lakeview: Lincoln Ave & W Belmont Ave; Live local music and food (second weekend in July).

Pitchfork Music Festival: Union Park; Taste-making three-day music extravaganza (mid-July, pitchforkmusicfestival.com).

Square Roots Festival: Welles Park; Old Town School partners with the Lincoln Square Chamber to showcase world music and craft brews (mid-July, squareroots.org).

Jeff Park Arts & Music Festival: Jefferson Park; Live music, performance, and food & drink (late July, www.jefffest.org).

Taste of River North: Ward Park; Food, music, and shopping along the Chicago River's North Branch (late July, www.tasteofrivernorth.com).

Fiesta Del Sol: Cermak Rd, b/w Throop & Morgan Sts; Largest Latino festival in the Midwest (last weekend in July, fiestadelsol.org).

AUGUST

Lollapalooza: Grant Park; Boffo multi-day, multi-stage music festival (early Aug, www.lollapalooza.com).

Bud Billiken Parade: King Dr/Washington Park; World's biggest African-American parade (second Sat in Aug, www.budbillikenparade.org).

Northalsted Market Days: Halsted St b/w Belmont Ave & Addison St; Ridiculously large street fair with tons of live music and vendors (second weekend in Aug, www.northalsted.com).

Ginza Holiday Festival: Old Town; Annual festival celebrating Japanese culture and art (second weekend in Aug, www.ginzachicago.com).

Chicago Air and Water Show: North Avenue Beach; Superhuge free air show (third weekend in Aug, www.chicagoairandwatershow.us).

Chicago Dancing Festival: Millennium Park; Chicago's and the nation's acclaimed dance troupes strut their stuff (late Aug, www.chicagodancingfestival.com).

Bucktown Arts Fest: Holstein Park; Long-standing art fair showcasing over 200 artists each year (late Aug, bucktownartsfest.com).

North Coast Music Festival: Union Park; Three-day music festival with diverse acts, from rap to indie to electronic to jam bands (late Aug, www.northcoastfestival.com).

SEPTEMBER

Taste of Polonia Festival: Copernicus Center, Jefferson Park; Polish food, music and culture (Labor Day weekend, topchicago.org).

African Festival of the Arts: Washington Park; African dance, music, arts, and exhibits (Labor Day weekend, africanfestivalchicago.com).

German Day Festival: Lincoln Plaza (Western, Lincoln & Leland Aves); Food, music and beer in association with yearly Von Steuben Parade (early Sept, www.germanday.com).

Riot Fest: Humboldt Park; Insane jam-packed roster of top-notch music acts (mid-Sept, riotfest.org).

World Music Festival: Various venues; Music acts from around the world, plus beer (mid-Sept, www.worldmusicfestivalchicago.org).

Children's Book Fair: Nichols Park; Children's authors, readings, and activities (late Sept, www.thechildrensbookfair.org).

OCTOBER

Chicago International Film Festival: Various locations; The best in international cinema. (www.chicagofilmfestival.com).

Open House Chicago: Various venues; Free, behind-the-scenes access to dozens of buildings and public spaces, including many usually closed to the public (mid-Oct, www.openhousechicago.org).

Halsted Halloween Parade: Halsted St b/w Belmont & Addison; Flamboyant Boystown costume extravaganza (www.northalsted.com).

NOVEMBER

Christkindlmarket: Daley Plaza; Monthlong German-themed outdoor winter market (late Nov-late Dec, www.christkindlmarket.com).

HOSPITALS

Chicago hospitals are as varied and interesting as the citizens they serve. Although you don't have to go far to find medical facilities in this city, finding quality medical care is another story.

The Illinois Medical District on the near southwest side is one of the largest healthcare centers in the world. Here you will find **Stroger Hospital** (basically the infamous Cook County Hospital with a facelift), home to the nation's first and oldest trauma unit. It is by far the busiest hospital in the area and serves a large and mostly indigent population. Unless you are in danger of certain demise, avoid Stroger's emergency department since waits of up to 12 hours for a non-life-threatening reason may bore you to death. The medical campus is also home to the **University of Illinois at Chicago**, **Rush University Medical Center**, and several smaller hospitals.

On the north side, your best bet is to go to **Advocate Illinois Masonic Medical Center** for anything serious or **Presence Saint Joseph Hospital** where you might get a room with a view of Lake Michigan. **Northwestern Memorial Hospital** is also a good choice if you are closer to downtown and/or if you have really good insurance. They also house several hospitals in the same campus, and if you break your neck craning to look up at all the pretty skyscrapers in the Streeterville 'hood, they have a first-rate spinal cord unit.

On the south side, the **University of Chicago** hospitals are second to none. A large and imposing set of buildings set in a somewhat dubious neighborhood, the hospital has a first-rate children's emergency department, world-renowned staff, and an excellent reputation.

The Chicago Public Library (www. chipublib.org or @chipublib) rose out of the ashes of the Great Fire of 1871 with an assist from England, whose citizens banded together to donate 8,000 volumes to start a new free library system. The first Chicago Public Library branch opened in 1873 at the corner of LaSalle and Adams Streets in a water tank that survived the fire. Today the system serves Chicago residents with 80 locations across the city and a collection of more than 5 million.

With the **Harold Washington Library** as their anchor, two regional libraries, **Sulzer Regional Library** in Lincoln Square and the Southwest side's **Woodson Library**, serve as backup reference and research collections. It is worth noting that Harold Washington Library has a few stand-out exhibits, including one of the history of the blues in the city and, of course, one on the man himself, Chicago's first African American mayor. Neighborhood branches are geared towards the communities they serve: **Chinatown** has an impressive collection of Asian studies material and literature, the **Rogers Par** branch features a significant Russian-language selection, and Boystown's **John Merlo** collection houses a considerable offering of gay literature and studies.

Many of the smaller branches have a decent selection of juvenile materials as well as career guidance and adult popular literature (and Internet access). Architecturally, some of the more interesting branches include the **Chicago Bee** branch, the former newspaper headquarters that serves as a neighborhood landmark for Bronzeville, and the historic **Pullman** branch, specializing in the history of the Pullman district. Chicago's first library branch, the neo-classical **Blackstone** library in Kenwood, is named after the railroad magnate-philanthropist Timothy Beach Blackstone.

Chicago also has many excellent research libraries and university libraries, one of which is the independent **Newberry Library**, established in 1887. It shelves rare books, manuscripts, and maps, and hosts the raucous annual Bughouse Square debates in late July. Another unique institution, the **Pritzker Military Library**, tells the story of the citizen soldier through an extensive book collection, and exhibits of photographs, medals, uniforms and other artifacts. Chicago's universities and colleges generally welcome the public to their libraries during specified hours, but it's best to call first and check.

LGBT

Chicago's LGBTQ communities are a diverse, politically-influential presence within the city. Just look to the Pride pylons lining North Halsted Street, designating the gay district, or the numerous politicians who vie for a prime spot in the city's enormous annual Pride Parade (which takes place in Boystown on the last Sunday in June). Boystown (a.k.a East Lakeview) and Andersonville comprise the city's two gay friendliest neighborhoods, with Clark Street, Halsted and Broadway being queer corridors of shops, restaurants and nightlife. Those two 'hoods notwithstanding, GLBTQ people and culture can be found throughout the city, from Roger's Park to Midway. Whether your interests are activism or acupuncture, draperies or drag kings, literature, liturgies, or leather bars, or any combination of the above, you will find your niche in Chicago's vibrant and diverse GLBTQ communities.

PUBLICATIONS/MEDIA

Windy City Times (www.windycitymediagroup.com or @WindyCityTimes1): Gay and Lesbian news weekly with good calendar of events.

Chicago Phoenix (chicagophoenix.com or @chicagophoenix): LGBT commentary and news analysis.

Chicago Pride (chicago.gopride.com or @GoPride): News and LGBT happenings across Chicago.

BOI Magazine (www.boimagazinechicago.com): Heavily advertising-based guide to the club scene.

Windy City Queercast (www.windycityqueercast.com): Locally produced Windy City Media Group podcast.

Pink Magazine (www.pinkmag.com or @TweetPINKMag): National magazine headquartered in Chicago; best for its listing of gay friendly businesses and restaurants.

ARTS & CULTURE

Gerber/Hart Library and Archives (6500 N Clark St, 773-381-8030, www.gerberhart.org or @GerberHart): This amazing library houses more than 10,000 books, magazines, newspapers, and videos. Regularly hosts both gay and lesbian book discussion groups, and special events including readings and screenings.

Reeling (reelingfilmfestival.org or @ReelingFilmFest): Annual Chicago Lesbian and Gay International Film Festival each Sept at various venues.

About Face Theatre (773-784-8565, about-facetheatre.com or @aboutfacechi): Roving gay & lesbian theater company.

Artemis Singers (773-764-4465, www.artemissingers.org or @ArtemisSingers): Lesbian-feminist chorus.

Chicago Gay Men's Chorus (773-296-0541, www.cgmc.org or @ChicagoGMC): Chicago's most colorful chorus, mounts fun, campy concerts, including a popular holiday show.

Windy City Gay Chorus (773-6621-0928, www.windycitysings.org or @WindyCitySings): Gay chorus under Windy City Performing Arts umbrella organization.

Lakeside Pride Music Ensembles (773-381-6693, www.lakesidepride.org or @LakesidePride): Umbrella organization for various LGBT ensembles, including the Freedom Marching Band.

Homolatte (www.homolatte.com): Bi-weekly queer spoken word and music series with writers and musicians, curated and hosted by Scott Free.

SPORTS & RECREATION

Chi-Town Squares (773-425-7584, chitownsquares.org): Gay and lesbian square dancing.

Chicago Metropolitan Sports Association (www.chicagomsa.com): Organizes all varieties of gay and lesbian competitive athletics: bowling, softball, etc.

Chicago Smelts (www.chicagosmelts.org):
Gay & lesbian swim club.

Frontrunners/Frontwalkers Chicago
(www.frfwchicago.org): Weekly LGBT
running and walking club.

SOCIAL GROUPS/ORGANIZATIONS

Chicago Area Gay and Lesbian Chamber of
Commerce (773-303-0167,
www.glchamber.org or @chiglchamber)
Charged with developing gay and lesbian
businesses, the chamber also hosts events for
gay and lesbian professionals.

Oak Park Area Lesbian and Gay Association
(opalga.org): LGBT-focused events and
activitives for the Oak Park area.

Affinity Community Services (773-324-0377,
www.affinity95.org): Social justice organization working on behalf of black LGBT
communities.

Association of Latinos/as Motivating Action
(ALMA) (773-234-5591,
www.almachicago.org or @almachicago):
Advocating on behalf of the Latino LGBT
community.

Asians & Friends Chicago (312-409-1573,
www.afchicago.org or @afchicago_org):
Supporting gay Asian community, with fun
events.

Chicago Gender Society
(www.chicagogender.com): Providing
education, support, social opportunities, and
outreach to the transgender and transsexual
community.

POLITICAL GROUPS/ACTIVISM

Equality Illinois (773-477-7173,
www.equalityillinois.us or @EqualityILL).

Human Rights Campaign Chicago (800-777-
4723, www.hrcchicago.org).

RELIGIOUS SERVICES

Archdiocesan Gay and Lesbian Outreach
(AGLO) (773-525-3872,
www.aglochicago.org): Catholic.

Broadway United Methodist Church
(3338 N Broadway, 773-348-2679,
www.broadwaychurchchicago.com or
@ChicagoBUMC): Reconciling United
Methodist.

Congregation Or Chadash (5959 N Sheridan
Rd, 773-271-2148, www.orchadash.org):
LBGT synagogue.

Dignity Chicago (312-458-9438,
www.dignity-chicago.org): LBGT Catholic.

Lake Street Church of Evanston
(607 Lake St, Evanston, 847-864-2181,
www.lakestreet.org): InsideOut LGBT group.

Pilgrim Congregational Church
(460 Lake St, Oak Park, 708-848-5860,
www.pilgrimoakpark.com): Actively
inclusive.

St. Paul's United Church of Christ (2336 N
Orchard St, 773-348-3829, www.spucc.org).

New Spirit Community Church (542 S
Scoville, Oak Park, 708-848-5460, www.
newspiritoakpark.org).

HEALTH CENTER & SUPPORT ORGANIZATIONS

Haymarket Center (932 W Washington St,
312-226-7984, www.hcenter.org): Addiction
programs.

Center on Halsted (3656 N Halsted St,
773-472-6469, www.centeronhalsted.org or
@CenteronHalsted): The Midwest's largest
lesbian, gay, bisexual, and transgendered
social service agency. Since opening its
doors to the public in 2007, The Center on
Halsted, Chicago's GLBTQ community center
and cultural hub, has been the meeting spot
for numerous community social groups
and organizations, from gay senior groups
to youth programs. The facility houses a
full-sized gymnasium, a theater, a huge
outdoor deck with a vista over Halsted
Street, and computer center, and shares an
entry with the adjacent Whole Foods grocery
store. Theatrical events, affirming liturgies,
movies, recovery and support groups, co-ed
volleyball and yoga for seniors are all part of
the program.

Illinois State HIV/AIDS/STD Hotline:
800-243-2437.

Howard Brown Health Center (4025 N
Sheridan Rd, 773-388-1600,
www.howardbrown.org or @hbhcinfo):
General counseling as well as anonymous,
free AIDS testing and GLBT Domestic Violence Counseling and Prevention Program.
Also provides general practitioner care for
men and women, on a sliding fee scale.

New Town Alano Club (909 W Belmont Ave,
2nd Fl, 773-529-0321,
www.newtownalanoclub.org or @NTAClub):
Gay and lesbian AA, CA, OA, ACOA, Coda, etc.

Chicago House (1925 N Clybourn Ave,
773-248-5200, www.chicagohouse.org or
@ChicagoHouse85): Homeless shelter for
people living with HIV/AIDS.

Serving the nation's busiest convention center, most Chicago hotels are designed for business travelers, complete with expense-account prices. Even a modest downtown room can be outrageously steep. Airbnb.com is definitely worth worth a scan when booking during tourist-heavy summer events like Lollpalooza.

Livin' Large: For a special urban splurge, book a suite at one of Chicago's palace hotels, such as the *Ritz-Carlton*, *Four Seasons*, *Peninsula*, or *Waldorf Astoria*.

Classic: *The Drake* is the classic Chicago hotel, and a landmark for drivers heading downtown from the northside via Lake Shore Drive. The *Allerton Hotel* is an architecturally significant Chicago landmark circa 1934, restored to its former glory after years of decline. In the Loop, the *Palmer House Hilton*'s lobby is all divans and chandeliers. More notoriously historic, the *Hilton Chicago* was the site of the 1968 Democratic National Convention.

Modern: Hip travelers will want to stay at one of downtown's two W hotels, either the *W Chicago Lakeshore* or *W Chicago City Center* Hotels, the *Sofitel*, *Hotel 71*, or the *Hard Rock Hotel*, located in the vintage Union Carbide building on Michigan Avenue. *Hotel Sax*, located next to the corn cob Marina Towers, boasts folk-art decorated rooms and a Sunday gospel brunch.

Boutique: Located in a historic landmark, the *Hotel Burnham* is a lovely boutique hotel near the heart of Chicago's theater district. Burnham and its Kimpton Hotel Group sisters, *Hotel Allegro* and *Hotel Monaco*, also in the theater district, feature free wine receptions every evening for hotel guests. *Hotel Blake* on Printer's Row offers boutique-type amenities with handsome rooms, although the views can leave a bit to the imagination.

Cheap: Steer budget-conscious out-of-town guests toward the *Travelodge Downtown*. It's not eye candy, but the location (just off Michigan Avenue, between Millennium Park and the Museum Campus) makes it quite a deal. Around the corner at the *Congress Plaza Hotel*, the site of a decade-long strike by cleaning and maintenance workers, believed to have been the longest hotel strike of all time.

Good values can also be had away from downtown. *City Suites*, and its "Neighborhood Inns of Chicago" partners, the *Majestic*, and *Willows*, in Chicago's Lakeview and Lincoln Park neighborhoods, offer small hotel charm at reasonable rates. If those are still above your station, *Heart o' Chicago Motel* is skipping distance from the Edgewater White Castle and a short walk from the vivacious Andersonville strip. *Sheffield House*, once a transient hotel, offers spare, cheap

rooms, appealing to backpacking European travelers and frugal Cubs fans—it's a pop fly's distance from Wrigley Field.

B&Bs: Compared to cities of similar expanse, Chicago doesn't offer much by way of B&B's. *The Wheeler Mansion*, near McCormick Place, is luxurious and antique-filled, with fireplaces, custom baths and bedding, and ridiculously high ceilings. The more modest *Wicker Park B&B* dishes up a good breakfast—the owners also own the nearby Alliance bakery, where morning sweets are baked fresh daily. *Flemish House* is on a quiet, tree-lined lane, a calm refuge from the Rush Street and Oak Street Beach hullabaloo. The *Old Town Bed and Breakfast*, run by the friendly and eccentric Serritella family, features stylish bedrooms and a common area with a grand piano, formal dining room, and deluxe gourmet kitchen available for guests to use—it's where a John Cheever character would bunk. On the Southside, the quaint *Benedictine Bed & Breakfast* is run by monks from the adjacent Monastery of the Holy Cross.

Real Cheap: There are also three youth hostels in Chicago open to the public with rates under $50 a night for card-carrying International Youth Hostel members. For deals, Hot Rooms is a Chicago-based reservation service offering low-rates on undersold rooms: www.hotrooms.com.

Flop House: Before the construction of I-90/94, Lincoln Avenue was the main access point to the city from all points north. In the 20s-40s, a bunch of motels sprouted up on north Lincoln to serve truckers and other travelers entering the city. For a while these vintage motels were popular cheap spots for touring indie bands on a budget; eventually most of them become too seedy for even traveling indie bands on a budget. Many of the motels have fallen prey to the wrecking ball; a few, including the local landmark, the *Diplomat Motel* and the *Apache Motel* remain, frequented, we assume, by people having affairs.

As a general rule, if a Chicago hotel price seems too good to be true, it is. Chicago is chock-a-block with run-down SROs providing semi-temporary housing to the down-on-their-luck, and extremely short-term housing to the occasional unwitting and unfortunate foreign traveler, cheapskate, or hapless student.

RESTAURANTS

OVERVIEW

Chicago is widely regarded as a world-class food destination, and rightly so, we say. It's a goldmine for anyone searching for flavors, romantic dining or simply a place to clog arteries. Whether you're looking for a $2 hot dog at one of the city's hot dog stands, a $200 20-course marathon at one the city's foodie destinations or a meal at one of the myriad mom-and-pop neighborhood spots where you can't understand the costs because you don't speak the owner's language, you'll find it here.

In the past decade, Chicago's adventuresome appetite has come to life with a whole new school of Chicago restaurants coming to the fore. Once fueled by students of the masters: Bayless, Trotter, Gordon Sinclair, and so on, the Chicago dining renaissance is already in its second or third generation, and now the students of the students, those who honed their skills at places like Trio and Tru, are taking the reins as they charge into Chicago's culinary future. Terms like "farm-to-table," "locally sourced," and "nose to tail" have settled into the culinary community's lexicon and whatever dish or ingredient is currently nourishing foodies' every gastronomic desire.

Chicago's culinary, um, chops continue to grow with venerable mainstays and new trend-centric spots popping up weekly (poutine tacos, anyone?). And with underground supper clubs and tickets-only restaurants quickly granting access via social media, the web has become your palatable guide. What follows is a breakdown of some of our favorite spots, old and new. Of course, with every restaurant opening, there is likely another one closing. Check in with **Yelp** or **eater.com** for up-to-the-(yes)-minute local restaurant news.

CHICAGO STAPLES

Some restaurants are more than just places to eat and drink; they're defining institutions of the city where politicians scheme and drunk baseball fans pass out. The original **Billy Goat Tavern** is known to baby boomers as the birthplace of John Belushi's "cheezeboiga" skit, but Chicagoans appreciate it as the dank watering hole where reporters from the *Tribune* and *Sun-Times* would once gather after work to talk shop. Today, it's mostly frequented by wide-eyed tourists who play at slumming it. "The original Chicago-style pizza" is a title claimed by nearly every pizza shack in town. Of the lot, **Pizzeria Uno's** claim seems the most legit—their cheese-filled recipe dates back to 1943. Other Chicago pizza institutions include **Lou Malnati's** and **Gino's East**. Equally important is the Chicago Dog—that is, a hot dog on a steamed bun "dragged through the garden" with a virtual salad on top—onions, relish, tomatoes, pickle spears, sport peppers, mustard (no ketchup, thank you very much), and a dash of celery salt. Post-pub dogs at **Wiener's**

Circle are a Lincoln Park rite-of-passage–the servers are infamous for their saucy attitudes. Chicago is more than hot dogs, though. It's hamburgers and heavy metal at **Kuma's Corner** where tatted servers dish up patties named after Pantera, Slayer and other bands with guitar gods. While there are plenty of Chicago institutions that put the city on the international culinary radar, Rick Bayless' pack of restaurants, **Frontera Grill**, **Topolobambo** and **XOCO**, stands out with creative and upscale Mexican fare for every wallet.

THE NEW KIDS ON THE BLOCK

Recent openings have seen a burgeoning trend in multi-purpose eateries. Head down to Pilsen's historic Thalia Hall to dine at **Dusek's**, drink at Punch House and enjoy local music. Mammoth international emporium **Eataly** caters to diners looking for high-end five course Italian, a quick panini or a place to hand-select every ingredient to make it on your own; where you'll really want to make a stop is at the Nutella bar. Separately, amidst the flash of downtown spots like wine-centric **Boarding House** and seafood-heavy **Nico Osteria**, neighborhood spots are becoming destinations in their own rite. Beat the crowds by lining up early outside Logan Square's **Fat Rice** for an inimitable taste of Portugal and Macau.

CHICAGO'S BEST DINING BETS
FOR THE DINER WITH DOLLARS TO BURN

So you have a lot of money? Well, congratulations. There's no better way to get rid of your cash than to go on a dining tour of Chicago's high-end dining destinations. **Girl and the Goat** arrived on the scene and wasted no time taking money from hungry guests. **Alinea** welcomes you with scientific culinary creations and sends you home with a bill that will leave your wallet limping toward the door. Diners are increasingly willing to put some work into landing a coveted table. At **Next**, diners can shell out an insane amount of cash before they even eat with highly sought after tickets to experience the restaurant's frequently changing thematic menus. **Schwa** patrons enter the kitchen staff's good graces by offering up a bottle of whiskey upon arrival, and **42 Grams** supplies diners a list of wines to purchase prior to their fixed price dining extravaganza. Looking for less maintenance and more beef? Head to Chicago steakhouse classics like **David Burke's Primehouse**, **Gene & Georgetti** or sleek chophouse **Chicago Cut**.

FOR THE DINER HOLDING A SIGN BEGGING FOR DOLLARS

So you're broke? Do not fret, dear friend. Cheap taquerias, hot dog stands, and corner grills abound. For a romantic dinner without the added weight of a bar tab, try **Los Nopales**. This super delicious and BYOB Mexican spot offers authentic south-of-the-border flavors with south-of-the-border prices. Basically, order anything and go swimming in the Mole sauce. Costa Rican BYOB **Irazu's** award-winning veggie burrito guarantees leftovers for days. Head to **Taqueria el Milagro** for platillos of pollo and salsa that's like a drug (we've heard).

PIZZA PIZZA PIZZA

Crust, cheese and more cheese. Chicago is a pizza city, and classic spots such as **Pizzeria Uno**, Lou Malnati's and **Gino's East** attract tourists and suburbanites in droves. Locals head to Lincoln Park's **Pequod's** for signature deep dish with a caramelized crust. **Art of Pizza** has won numerous awards and acclaim for its scrumptious deep disher. If you're not into three inches of mozzarella, you're in luck: this city offers thin crust 'za, too. **Piece** serves up New Haven-style pies with a selection of microbrews crafted in-house. Farther north, **Spacca Napoli** gives the wood-fired pizza a Neapolitan twist.

CHICAGO FOR HERBIVORES

Yes, people love gulping down a succulent steak here, but many Windy City restaurants are introducing more veggie items than the token pasta or risotto. Additionally, more vegetarian-only restaurants been appearing on our beefy shores to let Midwestern cattle breathe a sigh of relief. **Chicago Diner** and **Heartland Cafe** (which does serve some meat) are the crunchy, old-school standard bearers. Raw foodies flock to **Karyn's** in Lincoln Park, which attracted such a following for its raw food menu that Karyn opened **Karyn's Cooked** in River North. For upscale vegetarian, try the **Green Ze-**

bra, or **Mana** in Wicker Park. In Logan Square, down-to-earth scenester spot **Lula** is known for being particularly vegetarian friendly, and the redesigned interior makes this great for casual dates. For a very special and seriously spendy night, choose the fixed-price vegetarian tasting menus at **Arun's**. Finally, vegetarians and non-vegetarians alike line up for breakfasts served by followers of Sri Chimnoy at Roscoe Village's popular **Victory's Banner**. Call first: the followers close twice each year for a spiritual retreat.

POOR MAN'S STEAK AND OTHER MEATY MATTERS

In the past few years, **Kuma's Corner** has emerged as the popular and critical favorite for best burger in the city, although Northside loyalists still swear by **Moody's**. Even the fast food burger has stepped up its game. Trendy spots **Owen & Engine** and **Au Cheval** regularly vie for the title of the city's best burger. If, on the other hand, you like your meat served on the bone with tangy sauce, head to street-festival mainstay **Robinson's**, and **Honey 1**. Fried chicken is also making its way beyond the fast food set with **Honey Butter Fried Chicken** and **Leghorn Chicken**. As for encased meats, Chicago has no lack of options–just follow the Vienna Beef signs.

SOUTHERN COOKING

For Cajun food, try Chicago breakfast staple **Wishbone**. The legion of trendy but good regional spots continues to grow with **Big Jones** and **Carriage House**.

DRINK MORE, SPEND LESS

Nothing says romance like a bottle (or box) of wine, and Chicago's restaurant scene makes it easy to keep your beverage total low with an array of BYOB spots. If you're looking to savor South American flavors while sipping your own bottle of red, head to **Tango Sur** for massive cuts of Argentine steak. Forget travel restrictions and bar tabs when you head to **90 Miles Cuban Cafe** where you'll find a more casual dining experience and more meat. Sushi also tastes better when you're not paying for cocktails, so head to **Coast** for slow service that lets you drink more. For non-seaweed options, **Cozy Noodles 'N Rice** serves up noodle dishes close to the endless line of bars in Wrigleyville. Grab a bottle of tequila for house made margaritas at **Chilapan** with authentic Mexican far beyond the average taco.

PASSPORT TO GOOD EATING

Culinarily, you can travel the world and never leave Chicago. While some of Chicago's dining emporiums fly high on the local radar, we have a soft spot for the ramshackle storefronts where the home cooking's happening. Pilsen is the destination neighborhood for Mexican muy authentico. **Nuevo Leon** has been serving revelatory Mexican home cooking for ages, and **Birreria Reyes de Ocatlan** is a favorite of celebrity chef Rick Bayless. The city's best Vietnamese can be found in the New Saigon section of Argyle Street, right under the L stop, and Albany Park is the place to go for Middle Eastern and Korean fare. The greater northwest side is bountiful with Eastern European restaurants and supper clubs. Devon Avenue on the far north side is the place to got for the best Indian food in the city. You'll find plenty of great African and Caribbean food behind no-frills storefronts in Rogers Park. As for **Good to Go Jamaican Jerk and Juice Bar**, the name says it all. We shouldn't have to tell you to head to Chinatown for dim sum or Greek Town for flaming cheese or Little Italy for a sampling of Sicily. Perhaps one of the most surreal ethnic dining experiences in Chicago is the Thursday night-only all-you-can-eat Korean vegan buffet at **Dragon Lady Lounge**, the ultimate dive bar.

BREAKFAST

There is one crucial ingredient for the morning after an extended evening of exploring Chicago's magnificent miles of bars: breakfast. Well, more like brunch. From egg scramble creations at **John's Place** to syrupy-soaked goodness at **Waffles** to a brick of a breakfast burrito at **Kitsch'n**, you and your hangover can travel anywhere in the city and find some solace with a fork, a plate and perhaps a Bloody Mary.

DINERS

Chicago has plenty of other greasy spoon breakfast options, including **Salt and Pepper Diner**, **Nookies**, **Salonica**, **Lou Mitchell's**, and **The Golden Apple**.

SWEET HOME CHICAGO

Amidst the overwhelming array of options for dinner, pastry chefs are giving us more reasons to forgo dinner for dessert. Try Mindy's Hot Chocolate for velvety cocoa and house made marshmallows, or indulge in the recent donut craze at **Glazed and Infused**. For frozen concoctions, don't miss **Black Dog Gelato**, **Margie's Candies** and the **Original Rainbow Cone**. For a superior slice of chocolate pecan? **Bang Bang Pie Shop**.

FLAVORS ON THE GO

A rapidly developing food trend in Chicago is unfortunately one that we can't place on a map: the food truck craze. From macaroni and cheese to falafel to cupcakes, Chicagoans have fallen in love with flavors served from the back of a truck. The location of these mobile businesses varies from day to day, and many residents follow their favorite four-wheeled chefs on social media to be the first in line at whatever corner they're calling home for the day.

FOODIES ON THE WEB

NEED A RECOMMENDATION?

Both professional food critics and the vox populi weigh in on the popular restaurant sites of the **Chicago Reader** (www.chicagoreader.com), the Chicago Tribune's **Metromix** (chicago.metromix.com) and **Time Out Chicago** (www.timeout.com/chicago). Both offer search categories, so you can find places by location, price, type of cuisine, etc. If you're going somewhere off-the-beaten path, however, be sure to phone first.

Professional chefs and passionate eaters chat about both the latest hot spots and hidden neighborhood gems on the **LTH Forum** (www.lthforum.com). The foodie debates, all in the spirit of fun, can get raucous, and sometimes even local celebrity chefs enter the fore to throw down. A warning: Regular posting on the LTH Forum is a tell-tale sign of your descent down the slippery slope of food geekdom.

GET IT DELIVERED

Finally, if the sun scares you from leaving the comfort of your home, **Grub Hub** and **Seamless** are your hook-ups for delivery that isn't pizza. Well, there's pizza, too, but you can also choose from a massive array of culinary hotspots where you might not be able to get a table.

Chicago is a city of neighborhoods, and as such, we are a city of great little neighborhood taverns. These are the places where the beer you drink is on tap, the bartender throws a basket of pretzels in front of you when you grab your stool, and you can find the men and women who fill the pages of Studs Terkel's beloved *Working*, stealing precious time between the bossman and the kids. And then there's the jukebox. The best ones feature all your favorite bar songs, from Hank Williams to The Cars, Blondie to Sly and the Family Stone, and "My Way" sung in Polish or Korean just for the hell of it.

Although you'll find a low-key feel at many bars, Chicago has built a strong reputation as a nightlife capital. With bass-pumping dance clubs, warm weather rooftop bars and VIP lounges, the city keeps the rapt attention of every club crazy scenester.

No matter your interest, there's always something going on in the city. To help you keep on top of it all, check out listings in *The Reader*, *Time Out Chicago*, and *New City*. Websites like **Gapers Block** (www.gapersblock.com) list events and specials.

DIVE BARS

Rub shoulders with the characters from a Nelson Algren story at any of the following joints: In Old Town, the **Old Town Ale House** was once voted best dive bar in the country by someone-mumblemumble-we-for-get-who. In Edgewater, **Ollie's Lounge** has long drawn a friendly crowd of boozy locals. Other dives such as **Ola's Liquor** can be identified by the mere presence of the "Old Style" bar sign out front.

ARTY CROWD

Young urban arty types have carved out their kitsch-embracing niches at Ukrainian Village and Wicker Park spots such as **Club Foot**, The **Gold Star Bar**, **Inner Town Pub**, **Rainbo Club**, and **Small Bar**, while their Logan Square brethren drink their PBR at **Marble**, respectively. On the north side, get drunk with happy hipsters and local punters at **Village Tap**, **The Long Room**, and **Edgewater Lounge**.

LIVE MUSIC

Some of Chicago's best live music venues are also neighborhood spots. The legendary **Checkerboard Lounge** is making a comeback in Hyde Park. **Katerina's**, on an unassuming stretch of Irving Park in North Center, features regular live gypsy music along with local acts. In West Town, the **Empty Bottle** is the place to catch touring indie bands. Catch live jazz any night of the week at Uptown's **Green Mill**. If you want to put some twang in your thang, alt-country acts from the Bloodshot Records label regularly perform at Bucktown's **Hideout**. See indie bands and comics without the cover at **Cole's**. Be seen amongst the indie crowd at **Thalia Hall**.

SHAKE A TAILFEATHER

In Chicago, even the best place to get your groove on is often the one right around the corner. Despite the concentration of huge, dazzling and super expensive high-concept nightclubs in River North and River West, (which are typically the domains of tourists and suburbanites), many local folk prefer smaller, friendlier, and cheaper local options to catch Saturday (or Monday, or Thursday) night fever. In Lincoln Park, **Neo** attracts children of the Eighties and their wannabes with retro dance tunes ranging from goth to new wave. Legendary gay bar **Berlin**, in

Lakeview, draws a pansexual crowd for their ever-rotating array of theme nights. **Smart Bar**, in the basement of the rock club **Metro**, spins dance music with an edge. **Funky Buddha** draws a diverse crowd united by a desire to get funky, and **Danny's** hosts the late night dance party so your living room doesn't have to.

WHAT'S YOUR POISON?

Whether you are a wino, a beer swiller, a whiskey sipper or a tequila shooter, have we got a bar for you.

BEER

Craft brews are quickly finding their way into the taps every new bar in town, but at **Map Room**, **Fountainhead** and **Sheffield's** be prepared to read full-on booklets listing all their brews before you order. At **Quenchers** you can drink your way around the world. If it's Belgians you crave, try getting a seat at Andersonville's **Hopleaf**.

In the last couple of years, the cocktail has become king in Chicago, with many noted mixologists shaking up fresh ingredients to make some of the best stuff you've ever tasted. Celebrity chef Grant Achatz's **The Aviary** has upped the game in the cocktail scene the way his Alinea redefined the culinary world. **The Violet Hour** is designed as a speakeasy (look for the yellow light outside) with some of the best mixes in the city. For those who

appreciate a good cocktail but are on a budget, check out **The Whistler**, whose short list of classic cocktails won't sap your wallet.

STRAIGHT UP

If it's something stronger that you crave, **Delilah's** serves a world-class collection of whiskey to an amiable crowd of aging hipsters and once-were punks. **Marty's** is a fine place to be shaken and not stirred. Gin drinkers will find an extensive collection at **Scofflaw**. The tropical rum concoctions at downtown tiki bar **Three Dots and a Dash** are so strong that after a few you'll swear you can hear the waves crashing along the coast.

IRISH PUBS

Yes, Chicago is full of Irish–and "Irish"–pubs. Some are pretty damn authentic though, so if you're on the north side and it's a good Shepherd's Pie or football match you're craving along with your pint, seek out **The Irish Oak**, **Chief O'Neill's**, or **The Globe Pub**. On the South Side, well, you can't even contemplate Irish drinking culture in the city without a tip o' the hat to the strip of Western Avenue in Beverly that is home to the annual South Side St. Patrick's Day Parade.

ON-SITE SIPPING

A recent crop of breweries and distilleries are giving boozers a chance to taste test right at the source. Local craft favorites **Revolution** and **Half Acre** offer tours of their facilities, and sampling is encouraged. **City Winery** sources grapes from all over the world to produce wines you can sip throughout their bar, restaurant and concert facilities. And as whiskey continues its hold on the local hipster population, **Koval Distillery** offers classes, tours and plenty of bottled varieties to take home.

SMOKER-FRIENDLY

Since the smoking ban hit, it's harder than ever to enjoy two vices at once. However, some places are more enjoyable than others, including the stoop at **Club Foot**, the beer garden at **Happy Village**, the back porch at **Simon's**, and **Fizz Bar & Grill** that's tented during the winter.

MAG MILE AND OAK STREET:

BRING YOUR BARS OF GOLD

The Mag Mile has long replaced State Street as downtown Chicago's premier (and tourist-friendly) shopping strip. This stretch of prime real estate, spanning from the Chicago River to Oak Street features Chicago outposts of many destination shopping spots, including **Niketown**, **The Apple Store**, Needless-Mark-up (a.k.a. **Neiman-Marcus**), and the high-end boutiques and department stores, (think **Tiffany**, **Gucci**, and **Hermes** connected to **Water Tower Place** and the **900 North Michigan Mall**.

Around the corner on Oak Street lay tonier boutiques. While Mag Mall attracts goggle-eyed Midwestern families, who'll likely stop for lunch at the Cheesecake Factory or Bubba Gump, Oak Street appeals more to the Gold Coast and North Shore set: **Prada**, **Barney's** and **BCBG MAXAZRIA** are all located on this tiny strip.

Not far away on Rush Street, **Ikram** is a favorite of FLOTUS Michelle Obama.

BOUTIQUE SHOPPING

You don't have to go down to Oak Street to find funky designer boutiques selling everything from original fashions by local designers to housewares and hostess gifts. Lincoln Park and Wicker Park in particular are heavy on cool women's fashion boutiques. In Lincoln Park, check out Armitage, Clark, and Halsted for shops such as **Lori's Designer Shoes** and **Kaveri**. In Wicker Park, the highest concentration of cool little shops, like the fashion boutique **Penelope's**, line Division street, but if you love to shop, you'll want to work the whole Bermuda triangle of Division, Milwaukee, and North Avenue. Southport Avenue in Wrigleyville boasts a string of women's boutiques, including **Krista K** and **Leahey & LaDue Consignment**.

HOME DESIGN AND DECOR

Forget River North, Clark Street in Andersonville has emerged as a mini designer's row. Shops like **Scout** and **Cassona** have designers flocking from all over the city. **Architectural Artifacts** and **Salvage One** are treasure islands for vintage rehabbers. **Community Home Supply** is one of the city's best (and priciest) kitchen and bath boutiques.

For modern housewares and furniture, **Crate & Barrel Outlet** serves as a wallet-friendly step up from IKEA. Green up your home (or someone else's) with nurseries **Sprout Home**, **Gethsemane Garden Center** and **Asrai Garden**—all of which sell a wide range of housewares and gifts.

BEST OF THE 'HOODS

In many cases, Chicago's neighborhood shopping destinations say something unique about the character of the 'hood. Funky little punk-rock indie shops in Logan Square for example, or gay-friendly places like **GayMart** and **Unabridged Bookstore** in Boystown. Lincoln Square caters to the NPR-lovin', micro-brew swillers that call that 'hood home, and Andersonville has something for everyone: feminist books (**Women & Children First**), chic home furnishings, men's and women's fashions, Swedish souvenirs, and, count them, two clean, friendly, and non-oogly-feeling sex-toy stores (**Early to Bed** and **Tulip**).

Ethnic enclaves also make for great shopping. Try gifts and cookware in Chinatown, gorgeous saris and Bollywood flicks on West Devon, hookahs and Moroccan teas sets on north Kedzie in Albany Park, and Irish arts and crafts in Beverly.

ONE MAN'S TRASH...

Is another man's treasure. Whether your wants are driven by the desire to save the planet or just to save a buck, Chicago offers a plentitude of places to buy other people's old crap. Vintage wear boutiques thrive in arty 'hoods like Wicker Park, East Lakeview, and Pilsen. Some faves: **Una Mae's**, **Silver Moon**, **Knee Deep** and the **Hollywood Mirror**. **Ragstock**, a used-and-off-sale clothing chain, has two Chicago outposts: one near Clark and Belmont, the other on Milwaukee Avenue.

For one-stop antique shopping, check out one of Chicago's many antique malls—huge enclosed spaces that lease space to small dealers. Not to be missed are the **Broadway Antique Market** and the **Edgewater Antique Mall**.

In terms of thrift stores, there's either a **Salvation Army**, a **Unique Thrift** or a **Village Discount** in nearly every neighborhood in the city. Meanwhile, **The Brown Elephant** thrift store benefits Howard Brown Health Center's HIV research.

AUDIOPHILIA

Tower Records and Virgin are both long gone, but Chicago loves its independent record stores. Among our faves, **Reckless Records** serves the indie rock crowd and **Borderline** spins Euro dance hits. **Gramaphone** is where Chicago's DJs pick-up the hottest wax. **Hyde Park Records** supplies Hyde Parkers with all its old-school vinyl needs. **Laurie's Planet of Sound**, in Lincoln Square, offers an eclectic array of mostly-indie music without the attitude that is often associated with indie record store clerks.

For stereo equipment and electronics, DJs shop at **Midwest Pro Sound**. **DeciBel** serves the Wicker Park and Bucktown crew. **Saturday Audio Exchange**, only open on Thursdays, Saturdays, and Sundays, sells high-end stereo brands for cheap, (well, relatively cheap, anyways) as well as used and refurbished woofers, tweeters, receivers, and all that other audio-geek stuff.

GET FOODIE

The gourmet and specialty food trade has exploded in the past few years, as have the high-end houseware stores that are supplying upscale home cooks with their Le Creuset pans and Wüstof knives. Today, if you find yourself hard-up for locally-produced caviar, lavender extract, stinky artisanal cheese, curry leaves, or whatever other weird ingredient they don't stock at the Jewel, all you have to do is follow your nose. Of Chicago's many, many gourmet or specialty food shops, there are a few that are particularly dear to our hearts. **Pastoral Artisan**, a specialty cheese and wine shop, is a great stop on your way to a dinner party to pick up cheese, wine, olives, or other tasty treats. We also love **Goddess and the Grocer**, **Provenance Food and Wine**, and, perhaps, the best-smelling shop in town, Old Town's **The Spice House**. In Logan Square, **The Dill Pickle Food Co-op** is the place to pick up locally sourced and organic food goodness. Ethnic markets are great places to track down hard-to-find ingredients. **Middle East Bakery** in Andersonville sells amazing homemade hummus and falafel, as well as olive oil, pine nuts, and dried fruit at prices significantly lower than Whole Paycheck.

MALL RATS

Normally we'd scoff, but look, it's Chicago, and it gets damn cold. So, if occasionally you want to do your shopping without having to venture too far into the great outdoors, we're not going to point any fingers.

Block 37 is an entire city block of mall greatest hits, and it's in the Loop. On the Mag Mile, **Water Tower Place** offers pretty typical mall fare–there's a Sephora, Godiva, and Victoria's Secret–but their food court

has more in common with a Las Vegas buffet than anywhere you'd be able to grab an Orange Julius or a Mrs. Fields cookie. A block north, the shops at **900 N Michigan**, offer higher-end fare, (no surprise, as it's attached to the super-luxe Four Seasons hotel). Shops here include Coach, Diesel, MaxMara, and Williams-Sonoma. In East Lakeview, the **Century Shopping Centre** is kept in business by its fine art house cinema and LA Fitness s outpost, certainly not by the mundane shops contained within .

ODDITIES

At **Uncle Fun** you can find all the coolest vintage and wind-up toys, as well as oodles of strange and playful things for under $5, making it the gag gift headquarters of Chi-town. Recent acquisitions: a bacon-scented air-freshener, a week's worth of fake mustaches, and a "Mr. T in Your Pocket" keychain. Legendary actress and Chicago native Joan Cusack's cheeky gift shop **Judy Maxwell** boasts all the necessities: You know, like rubber gloves that double as hand puppets and toilet bowl-shaped pool floats.

To cast a curse or to break one, stop by **Athenian Candle Company**, where, in addition to 12-foot, gold-detailed, church-quality candles, you can also pick up a bottle of "Law Be Gone" floor wash or "Love Come Back" air spray. Prefer high-end designer beach wear with your candles? Stop by **Calypso Christiane Celle** for sunny beaded tunics and sweet-smelling French candles. Looking for a one-stop shop for all potions, powders and balms? Founded as a corner drugstore in 1875, **Merz Apothecary** has become a destination for natural bath and body care products.

TO MARKET, TO MARKET

With retail district rent continuing to skyrocket, many designers and artisans are finding pop-up shops and festivals an ideal place to reach consumers without the brick and mortar expenses. Randolph Street Market, Vintage Garage, Dose Market and Vintage Bazaar all play host on a monthly or seasonal basis. Since locations may vary based on weather, check respective websites for details.

STATE STREET: STUDENT MECCA

The student population in the Loop has soared, thanks to new student housing for Columbia and School of the Art Institute students. State Street has made a comeback by filling up with cheap, hip, chic shops catering to this crowd. **H&M**, **Urban Outfitters**, **Blick Art Materials**, and **Central Camera** cater to the art student within all of us.

ART INSTITUTE OF CHICAGO

GENERAL INFORMATION

NFT MAP: *6*

ADDRESS: *111 S MICHIGAN AVE, CHICAGO, IL 60603*

PHONE: *312–443–3600*

WEBSITE: ***WWW.ARTIC.EDU OR @ARTINSTITUTECHI***

HOURS: *DAILY 10:30 AM–5 PM, THURSDAY UNTIL 8 PM; CLOSED THANKSGIVING, CHRISTMAS, & NEW YEAR'S DAYS*

ADMISSION: *$23 FOR ADULTS ($20 FOR ILLINOIS RESIDENTS, $18 FOR CHICAGO RESIDENTS), $17 FOR STUDENTS/SENIORS ($14 FOR ILLINOIS STUDENTES/SENIORS, $12 FOR CHICAGO STUDENTS/SENIORS), FREE FOR CHILDREN UNDER 14, FREE FOR ILLINOIS RESIDENTS ON THURSDAY EVENINGS 5–8PM*

OVERVIEW

Built in 1892, the Classical Revival-style Allerton Wing of the Art Institute of Chicago began life as the World's Congress Auxiliary Building for the World's Fair . Today the Art Institute is one of the preeminent art museums in the country, housing the largest collection of 19th–Century French art outside of Paris. There are also impressive exhibitions such as the Japanese wood block prints and the Touch Gallery designed specifically for the visually impaired. Everyone comes here for an up–close and personal look at such celebrated paintings as Caillebotte's *Paris Street; Rainy Day*, Seurat's *Grand Jatte*, Grant Wood's *American Gothic*, and Hopper's *Nighthawks*, along with the museum's impressive collection of Monets, Manets, Van Goghs, and Picassos.

The completion of Renzo Piano's Modern Wing in 2009 made the Art Institute the nation's second largest art museum which includes a first floor gallery of film and electronic media, and an impressive exhibition of the museum's Surrealist collection, with many pieces new, reframed, or on display for the first time. A pedestrian bridge connected the new wing's third floor to Millennium Park, across the street.

RESTAURANTS AND SERVICES

The Museum Café, on the lower level of McKinlock Court, offers self–service dining,

Chef Tony Mantuano's Terzo Piano on the third level of the Modern Wing brings a fine dining experience to the museum, and Caffè Moderno overlooks the Modern Wing's Griffin Court.

While postcards, books, and magnets may be purchased at kiosks throughout the museum, the Museum Shop and the Modern Wing Shop supply all your art needs.

SCHOOL OF THE ART INSTITUTE OF CHICAGO

Boasting such illustrious alumni as Georgia O'Keefe, Claes Oldenburg, Laurie Anderson, and David Sedaris, the School of the Art Institute of Chicago (www.saic.edu or @saic_news) offers a fine art higher education for tomorrow's budding Renoirs.

GENE SISKEL FILM CENTER

The film branch of the Art Institute, Gene Siskel Film Center (164 N State St, 312–846–2800 www.siskelfilmcenter.org or @filmcenter) offers art house, foreign films, and revivals, with frequent lectures by academics and industry professionals and annual events like the European Union Film Festival.

HOW TO GET THERE

By Bus: Numerous lines serve this strip of Michigan Avenue. Important buses include (from the south) the 3 King Drive, the 4 Cottage Grove, and the 6 Jackson Park Express, (from the west) the 126 Jackson and 20 Madison, and (from the north) the 151 Sheridan and the 146 Inner Drive/Michigan Express.

By L: From the Red and Blue lines, exit at Monroe. Brown, Orange, Purple, Pink and Green exit at Adams and Wabash.

BOOKSTORES

INDEPENDENT BOOKSTORES

Printer's Row, a section of Dearborn Street in the South Loop, was once the epicenter of Chicago's print and publishing trade. While most of that industry has shuttered or moved on, the remaining stalwart indie bookstore **Sandmeyer's** is worth a visit for bibliophiles.

For general, all-purpose bookshops, **Barbara's** is a Chicago institution, as is **Unabridged Bookstore** with its specialties in literary fiction, kids' books, travel, cookbooks, and gay and lesbian titles. Down by the University of Chicago campus, **57th Street Books** and **Seminary Co-op Bookstore** both appeal to the brainiac set. Up north, **Book Cellar** is a super-friendly Lincoln Square indie with a cute wine bar.

SPECIALTY BOOKSTORES

Specialty stores abound in the city. We think **Women & Children First** may have the largest selection of feminist and woman–focused books in the country, and their children's section is also top-notch. The **Occult Bookstore** on Milwaukee Avenue offers everything a budding witch or warlock could desire. **Quimby's** in Wicker Park specializes in esoteric small-press books and 'zines with a marked counter-culture feel.

USED BOOKSTORES

Shuffle through the used stacks at **Bookworks** on North Clark or **Myopic** in Wicker Park. **Selected Works** on Michigan sells used books and sheet music. **Ravenswood Used Books** is as chaotically crammed with books as a used bookshop should be.

COMICS

Chicago Comics is such a pleasant store that it's easy to forget about any comic-nerd stigma (but don't fool yourself—you're still a nerd). **Dark Tower** and **Variety Comics** serves Lincoln Square fanboys. In Wicker Park they head to **Brainstorm** while in Lincoln Park, **Graham Crackers** is full of Marvels...

READING SERIES AND LITERARY HAPPENINGS

Several Chicago bookstores are known for their active reading series, including **Seminary Co-op Bookstore**, **Women & Children First**, **Myopic**, and **Book Cellar**.

The **Harold Washington Library** is another great place to catch free author readings and literary events. Furthermore, Chicago is host to a plethora of fun and dynamic literary series that occur on a regular basis at bars and cafes all around town. Of them, we recommend the Sunday night Uptown Poetry Slam at the **Green Mill**, Reading Under the Influence at **Sheffield's**, 2nd Story at **Webster's Wine Bar**, Danny's Reading Series at **Danny's Tavern** Homolatte at **Big Chicks**, and Sappho's Salon at **Women & Children First**.

In late July, the Newberry Book Fair is a used book lover and value hunters dream, and the Printers Row Lit Fest in early June will satisfy all devotees to the written word.

MUSEUMS

ART MUSEUMS

Although the Art Institute of Chicago's collection is undeniably impressive, Chicago's true art lovers know to look past the lions to some of Chicago's less-celebrated treasures. Columbia College's **Museum of Contemporary Photography** is one of two accredited photography museums in the nation. Other campus-linked art museums include University of Chicago's **Smart Museum**, where the collection spans some 5,000 years. Catch the Lunch at **Loyola University Museum of Art** series for a quick bite with artists and experts on exhibits. One of the country's largest collections of art post-1945 is housed at the always eye-opening **Museum of Contemporary Art**.

HISTORY

The **Chicago History Museum** is a tremendous archive of the city's past and present. African American history is celebrated at the nation's oldest museum focusing on the black experience, the **DuSable Museum of African American History**. **The Oriental Institute** specializes in artifacts from the ancient Near East, including Persia, Mesopotamia, and Egypt. Nobel Prize-winning sociologist Jane Addams's **Hull-House** examines Chicago's history of immigration, ethnic relations, and social work. Finally, the **Museum of Broadcast Communications** is one of only three broadcast museums in the country, and is home to the only Radio Hall of Fame in the nation.

SCIENCE AND TECHNOLOGY

As if the aforementioned **Adler Planetarium**, **Shedd Aquarium**, and **Field Museum** and the **Museum of Science and Industry** weren't enough to satisfy your inner nerd, Chicago is also home to a handful of quirky, smaller science museums. The **International Museum of Surgical Science** offers a window to the world of questionable surgical practices of yore. Conservation and the environment are the focus of the **Peggy Notebaert Nature Museum**, which also features a butterfly haven, delighting the child in us all.

ARCHITECTURE

The city itself is perhaps one of the best architecture museums in the world. Examine it by embarking on one of the tours offered by the **Chicago Architecture Foundation**. Frank Lloyd Wright's influence on Chicago architecture can be examined at the **Robie House** in Hyde Park and the **Frank Lloyd Wright Home and Studio** in Oak Park. Chicago's Prairie Avenue District offers an architectural glimpse of Chicago's Victorian Golden Age. Joint tours of the oldest house in Chicago, the **Clarke House** (c. 1836), and the neighboring **Glessner House** offer the curious an interesting inside peek.

ETHNIC MUSEUMS

Immigration made Chicago into the "City of Neighborhoods." The **Swedish American Museum**, the **Chinese American Museum of Chicago**, the **National Hellenic Museum National Museum of Mexican Art** and the **Spertus Institute of Jewish Studies** celebrate ethnic culture through art and culture.

MOVIE THEATERS

The impeccably restored **Music Box Theatre**, built in 1929, features fantastic Moorish architecture, floating clouds on the ceilings, and live organ music at many weekend screenings. Specialties include the latest art house and international releases, as well as restored classics and weekend matinee double features that follow monthly themes. Holiday season sing-alongs of White Christmas are huge hits that sell out in advance. The Music Box is also the major screening ground for International Film Festival and Gay and Lesbian Film Festival releases.

Other worthy art-house screening rooms include the **Landmark Century Centre Cinema** at the Century Mall. For even more refined or esoteric options, pick up schedules for the **Gene Siskel Film Center** of the Art Institute, **Facets Multimedia** in the DePaul neighborhood, **Chicago Filmmakers** in Andersonville.

The latest action features should be seen at the **Webster Place 11**, **ShowPlace ICON** and Streeterville's **AMC River East**, which offer ample theaters and show times. Cheap seats on relatively new releases can be had at Lincoln Square's **Davis Theater** and Rogers Park's **New 400 Theaters**, while second-run films can be found at a discount price in the renovated (thank god) **Logan Theatre** in Logan Square. The legendary **University of Chicago Doc Films** in Hyde Park has the perfect balance of historical, contemporary and international films. This student-run film society boasts cheap shows and seduces the intellectual crowd.

One of Chicago's most notorious places to catch a flick is "Brew and View" (www.brewview.com) at **The Vic** where the bar stays wide, wide open during screenings of sometimes lovably bad movies. What could possibly go wrong?